FROM THE BARREN LANDS

FROM THE BARREN LANDS

Fur Trade, First Nations and
a Life in Northern Canada

A MEMOIR BY **LEONARD G. FLETT**

GREAT PLAINS
PUBLICATIONS

Great Plains Publications
1173 Wolseley Avenue
Winnipeg, MB R3G 1H1
www.greatplains.mb.ca

Great Plains Publications gratefully acknowledges the financial support provided for its
publishing program by the Government of Canada through the Canada Book Fund; the
Canada Council for the Arts; the Province of Manitoba through the Book Publishing Tax
Credit and the Book Publisher Marketing Assistance Program; and the Manitoba Arts Council.

Design & Typography by Relish New Brand Experience

Printed in Canada by Friesens
Third printing 2018

LIBRARY AND ARCHIVES CANADA CATALOGUING IN PUBLICATION

Flett, Leonard, author
    From the barren lands : fur trade, First Nations and a
life in Northern Canada / Leonard Flett.

ISBN 978-1-927855-33-1 (paperback)

    1. Flett, Leonard. 2. Hudson's Bay Company--Employees--
Biography. 3. Cree Indians--Canada--Biography. 4. Fur trade--
Canada, Northern--History. 5. Canada, Northern--History.
I. Title.

FC3963.1.F64A3 2015   971.9'03092   C2015-903706-9

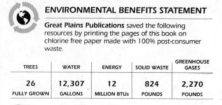

This book is dedicated to my wife, Marguerite, who lost me for the year and one-half that I spent penning and editing my story.

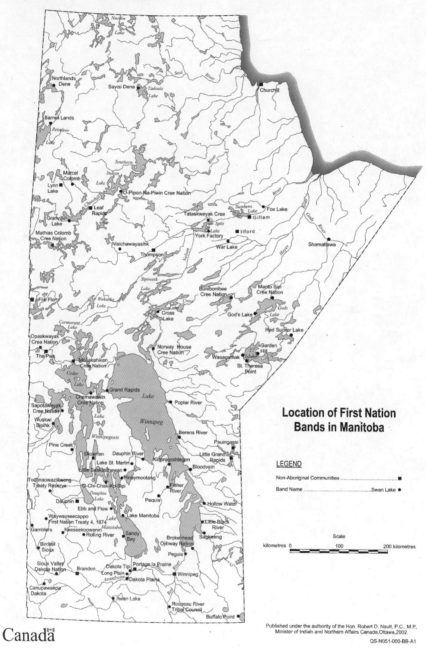

Indian and Northern
Affairs Canada

Affaires indiennes
et du Nord Canada

Nueltin Lake

Northlands Dene

Sayisi Dene

Tadoule Lake

Seal River

Churchill

Barren Lands

Reindeer Lake

Southern Indian Lake

Marcel Colomb

Lynn Lake

O-Pipon-Na-Piwin Cree Nation

Churchill River

Stephens Lake

Fox Lake

Leaf Rapids

Tataskweyak Cree

Gillam

Granville Lake

Split Lake

Ilford

Mathias Colomb Cree Nation

York Factory

War Lake

Shamattawa

Nisichawayasihk

Thompson

Nelson River

Hayes River

Gods River

Sipiwesk Lake

Bunibonibee Cree Nation

Manto Sipi Cree Nation

Flin Flon

Wekusko Lake

Cross Lake

Cross Lake

God's Lake

Gods Lake

Red Sucker Lake

Cormorant Lake

Opaskwayak Cree Nation

The Pas

Norway House Cree Nation

Garden Hill

Mosakahiken Cree Nation

Wasagamack

Island Lake

St. Theresa Point

Cedar Lake

Grand Rapids

Lake Winnipeg

Poplar River

Chemawawin Cree Nation

Sapotaweyak Cree Nation

Wuskwi Sipihk

Lake Winnipegosis

Berens River

Pauingassi

Pine Creek

Skownan

Dauphin River

Kinonjeoshtegon

Little Grand Rapids

Lake St. Martin

Bloodvein

Little Saskatchewan

Tootinaowaziibeeng Treaty Reserve

Pinaymootang

Fisher River

O-Chi-Chak-Ko-Sipi

Dauphin Lake

Pequis

Hollow Water

Dauphin

Ebb and Flow

Lake Manitoba

Little Black River

Waywayseecappo First Nation Treaty 4, 1874

Lake Manitoba

Sagkeeng

Gamblers

Kinosao

Kleeseekoowenin

Rolling River

Sandy Bay

Brokenhead Ojibway Nation

Birdtail Sioux

Peguis

Sioux Valley Dakota Nation

Brandon

Dakota Tipi

Portage la Prairie

Long Plain

Assiniboine River

Dakota Plains

Winnipeg

Canupawakpa Dakota

Swan Lake

Rosseau River Tribal Council

Red River

Buffalo Point

Location of First Nation Bands in Manitoba

LEGEND

Non-Aboriginal Communities .... ■

Band Name .... Swan Lake ●

Scale

kilometres 0   100   200 kilometres

Published under the authority of the Hon. Robert D. Nault, P.C., M.P.,
Minister of Indian and Northern Affairs Canada, Ottawa, 2002.

QS-N051-000-BB-A1

Canada

Acknowledgements

I have many people to thank—people who have made the writing of my book possible—including the Hisops and Perrins who tend our property and other matters when we are away.

I want to thank Jay Struth of the *Killarney Guide* for the beautiful job of restoring an old family picture which has become the cover for my book.

I am deeply indebted to my journalist friend, Kim Langen, also of the *Killarney Guide*, who was of valuable assistance in sub-editing the first few chapters of my book, providing critical comments and advising how best to lay out my stories.

I want to acknowledge an old friend, journalist and author Doug Cuthand, whose book *Askiwina* influenced my own work in describing Sweat Ceremonies.

I am also grateful for the critical feedback received from good friends on portions of my book, including Fred Petrie, Bill Shead, David Horbas, and Mary Simon.

My family, including my wife Marguerite, brother Harold, and daughters Geraldine, Harmony, and Lynda-Gale, were my biggest fans in encouraging my initial attempts at writing this book.

Finally, I owe the end product to editor and publisher, Gregg Shilliday, of Great Plains Publications. Thank you.

1

BORN ON
THE BARRENS

It was in northern Manitoba, next to the remote banks of God's River where the beautifully named Echoing River joins as a tributary, that I was born into this world.

The year was 1942. And it was cold and frigid, as only a February can be, when one's family lives not far from the crystalline beauty of the Arctic, and just a few miles from the great waters of Hudson Bay.

My birthplace was Shamattawa, a First Nations village that has long been home to Cree trappers and their families. These are a people who have eked out an existence trading furs to the Hudson's Bay Company for more than 250 years. The village itself consisted of a handful of buildings: a combined store and residence; a warehouse; a church; and the church residence, which housed the local minister.

When I was young, most Indigenous people of the area lived "out on the land" on their traditional hunting and trapping grounds. But each spring they migrated to gather together in Shamattawa, transforming what had simply been an open field into a village of tents. Here they settled in for the summer.

Around us, the northern air was fresh and crisp. And it combined deliciously with the pleasant smell of wood smoke that curled lazily

upward from every tent. It wafted amongst all the residents, temporary and otherwise, of the village on the river.

One of the few permanent structures in Shamattawa in those days
was an important one-and-a-half-storey building. The front half of its
main floor housed the Hudson's Bay Company store, while the rear
part, along with the upstairs, was our family home.

And it was there, with the assistance of Cree midwives on that cold
February morning, that I was born—literally and figuratively—into
the life of the Hudson's Bay Company, and the fur trade.

My mother was only 16 when I was born. And I was not the first-
born. Abigail had given birth to my brother, Glen Clarence, on August
17, 1940, just nine days before her 15th birthday. Abigail was 14 when
she married my father, Horace, who at the time was 32 years old. In
today's world he would have been imprisoned for corrupting a minor.
However, such were the days, and Abigail's father, the venerable Chief
Samson Beardy, had given Horace and Abigail his blessings.

Abigail, at 5 feet 9, was an inch taller than Horace and strong from
a life of wilderness travel to and from hunting and trapping grounds
with her father. Horace was not a large man at 5 feet 8, but he was
wiry strong and very experienced in the northern outdoors life. They
were in love and they enjoyed each other's company very much.

Every spring they would paddle out to the muskrat marshes where
Abigail would use her skill in calling the little animals. The muskrats
would respond to her whistling calls, giving Horace the opportunity
to shoot large numbers over the course of the spring season. Abigail
was expert in cleaning and stretching the skins onto the wood forms
that Horace had made.

Camping out in the marshes for several days at a time, they lived
on the muskrats they shot. Muskrats are delicious in spite of the name.
Once skinned and cleaned, they can be skewered on willow sticks and
roasted over an open fire. They can also be boiled, and if potatoes,
onions, and other vegetables are available, so much the better.

Abigail, raised in the wilds of northern Ontario, was a natural in
the bush. She twittered for birds, whistled for muskrat and beaver,

quacked for ducks, honked for geese, and could imitate the plaintive cry of a loon on a lonely lake. However, she had never been allowed by her father to call moose as this was the realm of her brothers, Enos and Eleazer. But she could set snares and small traps and was expert in bringing in rabbits.

My younger brother, James, was born on July 9, 1943. Abigail was now 17, with two toddlers and a baby. Our tiny bedroom in the upstairs of the Hudson's Bay Company building had two beds set closely side by side. One bed was for our parents and the other for Glen and me. Baby James slept in a traditional hammock strung over the parents' bed. Whenever the baby fussed, one of the parents reached up and pushed the hammock, setting it into a swinging motion. The gentle rocking motion quickly lulled the baby back to sleep.

Dad was always the first up in the mornings as he had to fire the wood stove to take the chill out of the morning air. We stayed in bed until the house was cosily warm. Dad also put a tin basin of water on the stove to heat for washing. Glen and I were never allowed to make any noise in the mornings when either of our parents or the baby was still asleep. We would whisper to each other under the blankets and occasionally peek out to see if our mother was yet awake. She often pretended to be still asleep and as we inquisitively looked at her, suddenly she would open one eye and look at us with a smile.

This always brought squeals of delight from Glen and me, and we would scramble up and jump onto her bed to roughhouse our young mother. Soon she would be up, hopping up and down on the bed in her nightgown, and jumping from bed to bed, screaming with laughter along with Glen and me. Mom always said that she literally grew up with her boys.

Mom would then help dress us and once we were fully clothed, she would send us downstairs to Dad. Dad would wash, and then feed us our bannock and porridge while Mom tended to the baby. I clearly remember this division of responsibility between my parents and invariably, when asked how they managed to raise their eventual 14 children, they always mentioned their teamwork.

Spring breakup in Shamattawa is a natural event that is indelibly imprinted in my memory. One would have to be in the far north or close to the mouth of a major river draining into Hudson Bay to fully appreciate power of nature. Spring breakup would begin far to the south on our river and the swollen river carrying the melt would slowly start to back up as the waters reached the still hard frozen ice of the far north.

The tremendous water pressure exerted on the ice by the swollen river would finally cause the ice to buckle, break, literally explode with crashes and thunderous booms, pushing and piling large slabs of river ice onto the shore. At that particular time of year, Glen and I were not allowed near the shore of the river as the ice slabs often piled or leaned precariously on top of each other. The ice floes would often crash down from haphazard piles as they slowly melted in the heat of the sun.

With the breakup of the river ice and the warm air turning spring into summer, Glen and I would anxiously await the arrival of the York boats hauling Dad's annual trading supplies from York Factory. When we would finally espy the boats in the distance, we would run as fast as our little legs could carry us to meet the freighters. The men manning the boats knew we were the children of the Hudson's Bay Company manager because we were both so easily recognizable: Glen with his fair skin and sandy hair and I so dark with black, unruly hair.

Three or four boats would be travelling together and one would pull to shore where an oarsman would jump out, pick and lift us up into the boat. We would then be placed in the bow of the York boat so that we would be the first to greet our father and the small crowd now standing in anticipation at the dock. Dad always made a big production of greeting us as if we were returning from an epic journey into the wilderness. We excitedly shook hands with all the people on the dock.

On one of these boat rides, an oarsman lunching on a piece of moose meat offered to share his meal. He held the piece of meat with one hand and put the other end of the chunk into his mouth, clamping the meat with his teeth. He then proceeded to saw off generous pieces with a knife held in his free hand. The oarsman then offered the morsels from his mouth to Glen and me which we eagerly accepted and hungrily devoured. Somehow, I do not think our mother would have approved.

The arrival of the York boats in Shamattawa created a day of excitement and anticipation as the people greeted those boatmen that they knew and met those who were on their first trips. Once the boatmen offloaded all the goods onto the dock, the people from the community who were gathered on the dock and surrounding banks of the river assisted in carrying the goods to Dad's warehouse. Men, women and children each picked up a box, crate or bag and in single file carried the goods up the embankment to the front area of the warehouse where Dad directed what should go where.

Dad checked goods to a bill of lading presented by the head boatsman and once everything was accounted for, he had his assistants carefully pile the goods for storage in his warehouse. Dad would then break out a crate of sweet biscuits and pass out the treats to all the people who had assisted in carrying the goods up from the river.

The boatsmen always spent the night so, after all the freighting matters had been attended, they busied themselves making camp. A feast in the community was organized and already several fires burned in a clearing surrounded by the village tents. A number of women were busy with kettles of fresh fish, moose, ducks and geese. Others prepared bannock over the open fires. That evening after the feast, the people brought out their drums, sang, and danced.

Before the York boats departed for their return trip to York Factory the next morning, Dad loaded his bales of furs that he had successfully traded for during the past winter and spring trapping season. The bales contained the pelts of beaver, otter, mink, muskrat, marten, weasel, squirrel, fox, lynx, wolf, and wolverine. With a wave of their hands and the splash of their oars, the men and their York boats departed downstream.

One childhood memory I hold of Shamattawa stands above all others and haunts me still. In the late fall of 1944, I was almost three years old and Glen had just turned four a few months before. It was November 8 and fresh snow had fallen. It was still too early in the season for the river to freeze over completely. Ice was just starting to form along the shorelines.

Glen and I had gone walking, towing a sled behind us. Momentarily we had forgotten the warnings issued by our parents to stay away from the river and we found ourselves near the steep banks that enticingly promised us an exciting sled ride. As Glen was older, there was no argument that he would be the first to try the sled ride. There was an ominous, damp mist rising into the frigid air from the river just beyond the few yards of ice that had formed along the shore. Glen reassured me that he would be able to stop the sled before it reached the river.

Burned into my memory is the horrifying picture of Glen careening down the steep riverbank. The sled had wooden sides which prevented him from getting out before the sled hit the ice and spun into the icy water with a splash. The sled bobbed upside down in the water. Glen was nowhere to be seen. Dad heard my screams and came running. I was in the water desperately trying to get onto the ice when Dad reached me. He grabbed me and ran with me to shore where he was able to launch a canoe that had been stored upside down on the bank. It was too late. To this day when I recall that event, a hollow ache, darkened with anguish, fills my heart. One never totally recovers from the loss of a loved one, not even after 70 years.

We left the area after my father was transferred by HBC to Caribou Post at Little Duck Lake in 1946. Nevertheless, I often wonder about Shamattawa because that is where my brother is buried. The news that has been emanating in recent years from my birthplace has not been good. The community has been beset with self-destructive behavior triggered and aggravated by alcohol, drugs, and solvents abuse.

Little wonder that Shamattawa and similar isolated communities face such monumental dysfunctional issues. There are more than 1,500 First Nations people registered to this reserve. Five hundred have already left the community, while 1,000 remain in an area that can safely and comfortably sustain probably no more than 50 people. Hunting, trapping, fishing, guiding make up the only viable source of an economy that is sustaining, albeit only for a small number of people. An economy to support larger numbers would have to include something like a mine in the area.

The lack of resources and infrastructure and the general overcrowding make this a difficult place in which to try to raise healthy families.

The present community of 1,000 includes police, teachers, social workers, nurses, municipal administration, in total probably numbering no more than 50 viable jobs. The sheer isolation of this lone community located in the northeast corner of our key-shaped province adds tremendously to the already prohibitive cost of living. The future for this community is bleak and grim. Gainful employment and sustainable livelihoods are life-giving sources of self-esteem, pride and dignity, qualities that our people possessed before disastrous government policies confined our people to reserves.

One wonders how a community like present-day Shamattawa survives. It shouldn't. Normally, this community would never have been allowed to grow to its present size. It should have become a ghost town long ago, or more realistically, it should have remained at a size that was sustainable with no more than 25 to 50 people. Today's reality is that Shamattawa does exist, with the majority of its 1,000 people barely sustained by government programs overarched by welfare. Do the people want to remain here? Ask the more than 100 youth that have attempted suicide in the past few years. Ask our governments that sleep easily at night knowing communities like Shamattawa, overcrowded and poverty-stricken are so far off our radar that no one really cares. Out of sight—out of mind.

One does have to wonder about whether our people weren't better off in the supposedly bad old days of the fur trade era.

2

HISTORICAL BACKGROUND

CREATION OF THE HUDSON'S BAY COMPANY

The foundation of the Hudson's Bay Company was laid down in the mid-1600s by two rascally French adventurers: Pierre-Esprit Radisson and his older brother-in-law, Médard Chouart des Groseilliers.

Radisson and Groseilliers cut their teeth hunting, trapping and exploring the areas of New France opened by explorer Samuel de Champlain. They also learned the ways of the First Nations people, siding and trading with the Huron as Champlain had done earlier, and battling with the Iroquois, who had become lifelong enemies of the French. In pursuit of the riches to be obtained from furs, Radisson and Groseilliers had, by 1659, pushed their way to the forests that edged the northern shores of Lake Superior.

As a result, these two men were the first Europeans to make contact with my people, the Cree, who told them that to the north of Lake Superior there lay even greater riches in furs. Radisson and Groseilliers absorbed this compelling news before returning to New France (present day Quebec) with their canoes already heavily laden with a mass of northern furs.

The following year the pair were fired up with desire to explore the northern regions described by the Cree. But they were denied permission by the French governor, who wanted to keep the focus of the fur trade within the boundaries of New France. The governor believed life would be easier if the First Nations people simply travelled themselves to New France in order to trade their furs with the French.

Radisson and Groseilliers did not agree with the policy and decided to strike out on their own without the governor's permission. In doing so, they discovered the rich fur country in James Bay, and by 1663 they returned to New France with canoes richly loaded with furs, the likes of which had never been seen before. However, the governor of New France confiscated their treasure of furs, as punishment for trading against his orders.

Understandably peeved, the duo left New France, and travelled instead to London, England, in search of financial backing from British investors for another trading foray into James Bay. And it was this very meeting with the English that would later trigger major world events: the formation of the Hudson's Bay Company, and, 100 years later, the conquest of New France by Britain.

In 1668, Radisson and Groseilliers did indeed find financial backing in England, a group that included Prince Rupert, a cousin to the king. The group of English investors provided the French brothers-in-law with two ships, the *Nonsuch* and *Eaglet*, which promptly set sail for the new land that same year.

Unfortunately, the *Eaglet* ran into storms, and the ship returned to London, along with Radisson. But the *Nonsuch*, with Groseilliers and his crew aboard, endured the journey and successfully sailed into James Bay. After safely landing, they commenced building a trading fort at the mouth of the Rupert's River.

The following year, they triumphantly returned to London with a cargo of furs that wildly exceeded the expectations of the English investors. Over the course of that winter, the investors organized themselves into a company. Their next move was to lobby the King for a charter, which would grant them a monopoly over the fur trade in the New World.

And on May 2, 1670, King Charles II granted a Royal Charter to Prince Rupert and the group of investors, who now called themselves "The Governor and Company of Adventurers of England Trading into Hudson's Bay." This powerful charter granted the company exclusive trade and the rights to all the lands drained by the waters flowing into Hudson's Bay.

As it was later to be realized, this landmass so generously bestowed upon the company included all of the present day province of Manitoba, most of Saskatchewan, the southern half of Alberta, the eastern part of Nunavut, the western part of Labrador and all of the northern parts of Ontario and Quebec. This area, comprising a mass of over 3.9 million square kilometers, came to be called Rupert's Land, and was named after Prince Rupert, the first governor of the Hudson's Bay Company.

Here the question arises: How did a foreign king come to have the right to so generously bestow the land of our First Nations' forefathers to Prince Rupert and his business cronies?

Throughout the course of history it appears that it was the powerful that made the rules. And there was no one more powerful at the time then the Pope in Rome.

As the leader of Christianity, the Pope and his Vatican council issued a Papal Bull in 1445 and another in 1493, after Christopher Columbus had landed in America the previous year. (Bull is named for the waxed seal, Latin name *Bulla*, which was attached to the document).

The first document, the Papal Bull of 1445, legitimized the enslavement of non-Christian blacks captured during raids on West African countries by Spain and Portugal.

The second, the Papal Bull of 1493, gave authority to explorers to take possession of lands in the names of their countries—so long as those newly-found lands were "not already possessed by any other Christian Prince." The Catholic Church further rationalized the issuance of these Bulls by requiring the colonizing country to "civilize" any and all "savages" who lived within them.

What followed was the conquering of nations, the legitimacy of enslavement, and the mass murder of Indigenous people all over the world—all in the name of Christianity.

In Canada's case, the Indigenous people were fortuitously not enslaved or massacred; they were simply dispossessed of their lands over a period of time. Instead, it was European diseases, against which the First Nations and Inuit had no immunity, which devastated their populations. And the deliberate and uncontrolled slaughter of buffalo (bison), which began as a planned war tactic of the United States Army, destroyed the First Nations' source of food on both sides of the border. The demands of the fur trade for buffalo pemmican also speeded the demise of the great herds.

All this allowed the rapid encroachment of white settlers onto Indigenous lands. The end result was made possible by *Terra Nullius* (Latin for "empty or unoccupied lands"), on which the Doctrine of Discovery heavily relies. These were, and continue to remain, principles of international law used to rationalize the subjugation of Indigenous peoples around the globe. The entire concept was— and to this day remains—ludicrous.

Even more absurd is the fact that Pope Alexander Vl, (head of the infamous Borgia family), who authorized the Papal Bull of 1493, was a corrupt, worldly rake who amassed a personal fortune and fathered a number of children. A corrupt, evil Pope legitimizes the theft of Indigenous lands?

As absurd as those documents may seem today, the Papal Bulls have never been reversed by the Roman Catholic Church, in spite of all the political activism carried on by Indigenous organizations around the world.

We ask, "Why not simply repeal these abominable documents?" We are told that after centuries of law-making atop these principles, they have become part of the building blocks of the British judicial system, which we adopted. An attempt to pull them out would, of course, cause the possible collapse of the entire system. Our laws are so interwoven it would be a Herculean task to attempt reform by reaching so far back into history.

This is a tenuous explanation. A formal judicial review initiated by our government, as suggested by the Royal Commission On Aboriginal People, would certainly be appropriate.

On the social and spiritual side of this issue, the church—at the very least—could acknowledge and extend an apology for the damage done to Indigenous people worldwide.

The Orkney and Shetland Islands

My father, and his father before him, were also born of the fur trade. Our mothers were either Métis or First Nations women. I consider myself a First Nations person and hold a Treaty Card. But our Scottish heritage came to us through an adventurous islander called James B. Flett, my great-grandfather. It is said that the blood of the Vikings course through the veins of the Orkney and Shetland Islanders. It was likely this sense of the Viking wanderlust that drew James to answer the call of the New World.

Mixing and intermarrying with the First Nations people was often a matter of survival for the early explorers and traders, and men like my Gaelic ancestor were no fools. Canny Scots from the northerly Orkney and Shetland Islands readily intermarried with the women of the First Nations.

These men knew they needed the New World expertise to cope with the harsh winters of the land. They had to learn to make and use new modes of transport, build adequate shelters, wear the proper clothing, and hunt, fish, gather and preserve foods.

Intermarriage also offered safety and security, provided by the allegiance of First Nations family clans, something a Scotsman fully understood. Scotland, and especially the northern remote areas of the Orkney and Shetland Islands, were the favoured recruiting areas to find hardy men to staff the Hudson's Bay Company in the New World.

The similarities of conditions in the new lands, across the seas to the west, made it likely that the Orcadians and Shetlanders would fulfill the usual minimum five year terms of their contracts as servants of the Company. Such was the case with James B. Flett's father,

James Sr. He was employed by the Hudson's Bay Company for a five period at Moose Factory, from 1815 to 1820, before returning home to Birsay Parish, Orkney.

Many men like my great-grandfather, James B. Flett, never returned to their ancestral homes. Instead, they made the Hudson's Bay Company their life career. My grandfather Alexander Flett, my father Horace Flett, and I myself all followed in James' footsteps in making the company our life careers.

Our four generations together have a combined continuance of service to the company of 184 years. I had the least amount of service at 41 years, and James had the most at 52. My father Horace had 48 years and Alexander 43.

James B. Flett

James B. Flett, born in 1828 in Birsay Parish, Orkney, Scotland joined the Hudson's Bay Company as a young man in 1846. He was just 18.

His joining took place a mere 25 years after the Company itself had merged with The North West Company, an event that finally concluded years of bitter, and sometime violent, competition. And it would be 21 more years before the creation of Canada, under Confederation, took place.

At this point, most of Canada was still being claimed as a property of the Hudson's Bay Company under the Royal Charter of 1670 granted by King Charles II of England. Sir George Simpson was still the Governor, and continuing to participate in epic journeys, which involved repeatedly crisscrossing the vast wilderness.

And still to come during my great-grandfather's HBC career was the Red River Rebellion and the creation of the Province of Manitoba. These historic events would soon be followed by the building and development of the railways.

The same period would eventually see the total extinction of the passenger pigeons that once darkened the skies, and the last sightings of the great buffalo herds that thundered across the prairies.

The final dark change in James' time would be the signing of the numbered Treaties with First Nations and the displacement of these people from their traditional lands. They would eventually be relocated onto tiny reserves, many of them isolated and most of them situated on lands of a quality not conducive to development.

The total area of all the reserves today make up less than one percent of the total landmass of the country. This removal of the First Nations from their lands and onto restricted reserves, helped open up the remainder of the West to European settlement.

But all this still lay ahead for my Scottish ancestor. My great-grandfather, James, first stepped up onto a Company ship, which was to sail westwards from the Orkney port of Stromness to the New World, back in 1846.

It was to be a gruelling six-week journey, which involved crossing the frigid Atlantic Ocean and an iceberg-laden Hudson Strait, with sights set for the company's York Factory. Most likely the ship he sailed in was the 303-ton *Prince Albert,* purpose-built in England for the Hudson's Bay Company in 1841. It was 103 feet long, 25 feet 6 inches wide, and 17 feet 6 inches deep.

But when the ship arrived sometime in July or early August, the vessel was too large to traverse the shallow Hayes River. Instead, the crew anchored her at the river mouth, at the aptly named Five- Fathom Hole in Hudson Bay.

This was an expected challenge, however, for the company's seasoned crew. From this anchorage point, passengers and supplies were offloaded into a schooner, built and manned by Company servants for this very purpose. People and goods were soon moving again along the water, for this last seven miles up the river. At long last, they disembarked at their final destination, York Factory.

York Factory

York Factory, North American headquarters for the Hudson's Bay Company, was a bustling depot at this time of year, receiving mail, supplies and trade goods from England.

The trade goods had to be unloaded and unbundled, and then re-packed into smaller bundles for redistribution by York boat and ca-noes to the Company's many trading posts located in the interior of the country.

It was here in York Factory, for many years the headquarters of the Hudson's Bay Company, that James Flett first set foot in the New World in 1846.

Brigades of York boats and canoes, laden with furs from the trading posts, also began arriving at York Factory, as soon as breakup made river travel possible in the spring. And every item of trade good and piece of fur was meticulously accounted for and recorded by the servants of the company.

Young James would have been amazed by the military-like effi-ciency of this factory, with its several large square-beamed and shiplap wood-clad buildings and its smaller sheds and workshops.

The larger buildings included the Governor's home itself, with quarters for the domestic servants including cooks, cleaning staff, and waiters. Next door was the dwelling-house for the officers, along with a communal dining area, commonly referred to as "The Mess."

Several other buildings comprised the common quarters for the company's servants, which included clerks, interpreters, carpenters, sawyers, boat builders, chandlers (candle makers), coopers (wooden barrel makers), an armourer and blacksmiths.

Muskets were the firearm of the day. They were also an important trade item, because over time the First Nations hunters and trappers had lost the use and skill of bows and arrows and had become dependent upon firearms. Without a musket they would be unable to hunt or trap.

The keg built by coopers was an important container for the fur trade. It had to be leak proof, light enough to be carried over portages, and yet strong enough to withstand repeated manhandling over hundreds of miles of journey. There was, however, a shameful period of the fur trade, during the late 1700s to the mid-1800s, when these coopers became most essential for the business for another purpose entirely.

The Hudson's Bay Company and the The North West Company, along with American free traders, all became involved in freely dispensing alcohol to the First Nations as part of the fur trade. And these handcrafted kegs were required for the secure transport of liquor into the fur trading areas.

The Honourable Company's stock in trade was rum, easily accessed from Britain's colonies in the West Indies. The North West Company, based in Montreal and influenced by the French, traded cheap brandy.

However, after their amalgamation in 1821, the Honourable Company continued its trade in liquor for about another 20 years. It was finally prohibited, for the sake of long-term company profits, by its governor, Sir George Simpson, in 1843.

But before that cessation, the Americans were the most shameful of the lot, allowing whiskey to flow as freely as water. Not only were the First Nations debauched by the liquor trade, but the traders greatly maximized their profits by watering down their liquor.

First Nations people that caught onto this practice then began testing the quality of the liquor before exchanging any furs. This was done by spitting a mouthful of the liquor into the campfire. If the liquor fizzled in the flames, it was unacceptable. If the liquor flared in the flames, then it was deemed acceptable. And this is the origin of the name "firewater."

This black chapter in Canadian history finally closed shut in 1874, with the forced closing of the notorious "Fort Whoop-up," a wild, forted settlement in southern Alberta. The shutdown was carried out by the newly formed North West Mounted Police.

Country Wives

Smaller buildings and tents dotted around the perimeter of York Factory housed the boatmen, guides, hunters, fishermen, gardeners and woodcutters, most of whom were aboriginal Cree or Métis.

There were also a number of First Nations women, mostly Cree and some Dene, in addition to a number of Métis women. Some were employed as domestics, but most were either married, or living as "country wives" to the contracted employees of the Company.

A country wife was a common term for a First Nations or Métis woman, married through common-law to a white fur trader. It was a union of convenience, as the extended family of the country wife usually expressed their loyalty to the fur trader by bringing all their furs to him.

The wives, in turn, were skilled in sewing, especially in the making of winter moosehide coats and moccasins, and in the making of snowshoes and in repairing birch bark canoes.

Around the tents, which encircled the factory, women tended to blackened pots and kettles hanging over campfires. Children playfully ran about, screaming and laughing in moccasined feet. With the snow gone, tethered dogs no longer required for the pulling of sleds barked howled and snarled at each other.

On his arrival at the factory, and while gazing at the wondrous scene before him and slapping at the endless buzz of mosquitoes and blackflies around his head, my great-grandfather James began to get a sense of the new life that was in store for him.

York Boats

After a period of rest, James was prepared for the next leg of his trek to Norway House, where he would catch a brigade of boats departing for the far northwest. The first leg of his trip, which would take him to Norway House by York boat, would be a memorable one. As he was a strapping young man, he was immediately put to work as a tripman, manning one of the six oars used to propel this craft.

Orkney boat builders first built the York boat, based on an Orkney boat design which was a descendant of the Viking longship, in the mid-1700s. The river craft to which James was introduced was the smallest model, at a little over 30 feet in length and capable of carrying up to five thousand pounds of freight. The York boats that plied the waters of Lake Winnipeg were larger craft, stretching up to 45 feet in length and carrying up to 12,000 pounds of goods. They were propelled by up to eight oarsmen, guided by a steersman manning a long oar at the stern much like a rudder and assisted by a square sail when wind conditions were favourable. At night the sail served as the crew's tent.

As waters flow down and empty into Hudson Bay, traversing the Hayes River to Norway House meant battling the currents every inch of the way. The approach to waterfalls and rapids was especially daunting and often meant some of the men would have to disembark the boat to take up a stout line and manually drag the boat upstream. Others in the boat used their oars or poles to keep the craft away from the shore while at the same time pushing and poling for headway.

My father, who had experience with this mode of transportation early in his career as a fur trader, used the word "tracking" to describe this laborious action which could continue for miles along muddy and slippery shoreline. When faced by a waterfall or a set of rapids too swift, wild and dangerous to continue tracking the boat, a "portage" to circumvent the obstacle would become necessary.

The York boat would be put to shore and emptied of its load. The tripmen would carry the load manually on their backs around the waterfall or rapids, a distance which could stretch from a few yards to a half mile or more. The York boat itself, too heavy to carry, would be dragged over the portage, most often aided by rolling over logs cut and laid for this purpose.

The Cree Indians of the area and other First Nations who regularly traversed these waterways had the portages marked and cut to enable the carrying of their light birch bark canoes around the waterfalls and rapids. Even today, canoers travelling these waterways need only look for the openings in the forests which identify the portages used for millennia by the original inhabitants of this land.

First Nations families often travelled together and to this day in some of the more remote First Nations communities you will see the odd *tikinagan* still being used. The tikinagan is a cradleboard upon which a bag, originally of deer or moosehide but later of a substantial cloth, would be fastened to hold a baby. The woman would sling the tikinagan and baby onto her back and adjust the carrying strap onto her shoulders to evenly distribute the weight. The women took great pride in the appearance of their tikinagans and they would be beautifully decorated with dyed porcupine quills and later with glass beads sewn in intricate designs.

The bag would be filled with sphagnum moss which, being very absorbent, made it ideal for swaddling babies. Whether stowed in canoes or propped up against a tree while the parents portaged canoe and goods, the tikinagans were ideal conveyances for babies.

As the babies were laced tightly in their tikinagan bags, they could not use their arms and hands to ward off the insects. Instead, they wore bonnets with leather fringes which hung down over their faces to protect them from the mosquitoes and blackflies of the land. With a flick of their heads the fringes would brush off any offending insects.

My mother often reminded me that this was also very much a part of my early life, as not only baby girls but also baby boys were topped with bonnets festooned with deer hide fringes. As mosquito netting was introduced, a curved whittled stick was added to the top front of the cradleboard so that the entire board could be covered by the netting and yet leave plenty of breathing room for the baby. Before the advent of disposable diapers, moss hanging in trees and shrubs to dry and be later used in tikinagans was a common sight.

With the first portage blessedly completed, as the work was arduously backbreaking and tedious, James was gladly back in the York boat with oar in hand. I doubt he knew that he had about 30 more portages to endure before the end of his two-and-one-half to three-week trip to Norway House. Before day's end and as the sun was gradually descending, the tripmen rowed the boat into a suitable camping spot for the night. The boat and its cargo would be secured, tents pitched, fires built, firewood cut and stacked, and the evening meal prepared.

Pemmican

The tripmen carried sufficient pemmican to last them the entire trip to Norway House. However, pemmican was a preserved food and therefore used only when necessary, as game along the route was bountiful. They shot whatever presented itself on the banks, and if no moose or deer was available then they hunted the plentiful ducks and geese that filled the marshes alongside the river. Whenever they felt the need for a change or variation in their diet they would often shoot a fat beaver sunning on the banks.

Pemmican drove the fur trade. Métis and Indian hunters, expert horsemen on the plains, brought down buffalo not only to feed and clothe themselves and their families, but also to produce pemmican for sale to the Hudson's Bay Company.

Pemmican was made by cutting buffalo meat into strips and then hanging on racks of poles to dry in the sun. Lazy smoky fires under the racks kept the flies away from the drying meat and often imparted a not unpleasant smoky taste to the dried meat. After several days of hanging and curing in the sun and smoke, the dried meat would then be pounded by the women using hammers fashioned by lacing heavy rounded stones onto wooden handles.

Fat rendered from the buffalo, (the main source would be from the marrow contained in the bones), would then be mixed with the dried pounded meat. Anyone who has savoured the rich, high caloric taste of marrow from the bone of a roast of beef would appreciate the flavour added to the dried pounded meat. Often saskatoon berries, cranberries or blueberries would be added, and the mixture was then stored in buffalo-hide bags expertly prepared and sewn by the women.

It is estimated that a single serving of a half to three-quarter pounds of pemmican contained approximately 6,000 calories, which the tripmen expended during their 14- to 18-hour stints on the oars. The recommended caloric intake for the average man today is about 2,400.

Preparing the pemmican for meals was fast and simple. It was put into a pot of water, brought to a boil, then flour or rolled oats and quite often both were added, and then it was seasoned with salt before serving. This culinary dish of the voyageurs was referred to as "rubiboo." Even to this day First Nations people in some of the more remote communities laughingly call their traditional dish of boiled duck with flour and rolled oats "rubiboo."

The Birch Bark North Canoe

James' mode of transport from Norway House to Fort Simpson now changed to the sleeker and swifter birch bark canoe.

The difference between the plodding York boat and the stream-lined North Canoe was like jumping into a sports car after riding in a two-ton truck. The North Canoe was about 22 feet long, and weighing less than 300 pounds, it was light enough to be carried by two men. The craft was paddled by a crew of six men.

The front man was called the Bowsman, and it was his responsibility to keep a watchful eye out for reefs and shallows. He was also responsible for charting out the safest course through fast water when the decision was made to "shoot the rapids." This was the most exhilarating, but also the most dangerous part of canoe travel. A misreading of the currents could result in an overturned canoe, or a gaping gash cut into the flimsy birch bark by an unseen rock.

The rear man was called the Sternsman, and his main responsibility was steering the craft and keeping it upright. The middle paddlers were appropriately called the Middlemen.

Equipped with longer paddles, the Bowsman and the Sternsman stood at their positions when traversing dangerous waters and shouted instructions to each other and to the Middlemen. The resulting co-ordinated effort by all the voyageurs working together could swiftly turn and safely guide the craft through the roughest waters.

James would be called on to serve as a Bowsman in the wild and dangerous Mackenzie River District from 1852 to 1854. It is noted in Hudson's Bay Company journals that the most common cause of death for many of its servants was from drowning, and that the highest number of drowning deaths were recorded in this District. But all that James knew about where he was headed was gleaned from the stories passed on by his fellowmen in York Factory and Norway House.

Norway House

After the evening meal, and with the pail of tea warming over the campfire, the men would fill their pipes with tobacco, and then lounge about telling stories of past excursions into the wilderness. It was a time of peaceful rest, with the sun gradually setting in the late summer evening.

The encampment chosen would be on a rise, a location as open as possible to let whatever breeze was available keep the mosquitoes and blackflies in check. If the bugs still became nasty, then some green leafy branches would be thrown onto the fire to produce a "smudge," as the resulting heavy smoke was called. With nightfall, the men would wrap themselves in their blankets and sleep away the weariness in their bones.

James would be awakened from his sleep by calls from the chief guide, just as the dark night sky was being tinged a pale pink hue, which gradually brightened with the dawning sun. He had quit the tedious task of shaving long ago. If his thick beard started to become too unruly and interfering he would simply use his sharpened knife to trim it to a manageable shape.

His day began with a quick refreshing wash in the ice-cold river water. Then it was a matter of breaking camp as quickly as possible, loading the boat, and pushing off for about three hours of rowing and portaging. The men then took time to break for a rest and enjoy their first meal of the day.

As the days drudgingly wore on, James became more accustomed to the work, and muscle-hardened from the toil of rowing, tracking, portaging, and making and breaking camp. After two weeks the rowing was becoming less strenuous, as the river began to widen and the flow of water eased. In another day or so the York boat was able to ease its bow onto Little Playgreen Lake, and before nightfall the voyageurs were able to locate the Jack River and their destination of Norway House.

James' arrival and brief stay in Norway House was much the same as his experience upon first arriving at York Factory. The officers and servants, many of them from the Orkneys, were pleased to hear of any news from home, and they in turn had great fun in striking awe and fear into young James with their hair-raising stories of this strange new land.

After a few days stay in Norway House, James would bid goodbye to his newfound friends, and be bound for Fort Simpson, in what is now known as the North West Territories.

Fort Simpson was named for the ruling governor of the Company, Sir George Simpson, who was still criss-crossing the northwest wilderness in epic journeys: by canoe in summer, and on snowshoes in winter.

James could not know that upon fulfilling the terms of his initial five-year contract in the Mackenzie River District, he would renew his contract. He also could not know that the company would return him to Norway House in the fall of 1854.

North Canoe to Methye Portage

James soon learned that the Mackenzie River District was the source of the richest fur in the country. He heard that the territory abounded with man-eating grizzly bears and man-hunting savages.

James was at once terror-stricken and also wild with excitement about his coming adventure. He would find that while the stories about the bears were factual, his friends had stretched the truth somewhat when it came to the so-called savages.

He was already learning in the short time he was in this New World. And it would be confirmed, once he found himself in the Mackenzie area, that his survival would ultimately depend on the assistance of the First Nations and Métis people, and the valuable skills they would impart onto him.

James' journey from Norway House took him around the vast northern end of Lake Winnipeg and to the spectacular rapids appropriately called Grand Rapids, near where the Saskatchewan River empties into the lake. James had by now become accustomed to the plodding pace and back-breaking work involved in manhandling a York boat over portages. He was therefore pleasantly surprised at the speed and the relative ease with which they were able to portage their birch bark North Canoe.

Their route then took them through Cedar Lake to The Pas, and up river to the Company establishment in Cumberland House, which served as an important pemmican depot for the Company's canoe brigades.

Here they would stock up on enough pemmican to carry them through the remainder of the journey to Fort Simpson. James could not have known that one day some of his descendants, including myself, would eventually call this place "home."

From Cumberland House they plied the water systems through Pelican Narrows and Lac La Ronge where they entered the Churchill River and then travelled through Pinehouse to Ile-à-la-Crosse, up to Buffalo Narrows and finally to the Great Methye Portage at Portage La Loche.

Methye Portage is a 19-kilometer overland trek, and midway to it is Rendezvous Lake, where the southbound canoe brigades from the Athabasca and Mackenzie River Districts would meet the northbound brigades from Fort Garry and York Factory.

Here, the Athabaska and Mackenzie brigades would exchange their cargo of furs for the trade goods transported by the Fort Garry and York Factory brigades. The canoe brigades would then turn around and head back to their respective homes before the onset of cold weather.

At Methye Portage, James assisted with the 180-pound loads that each man lugged overland for the 19-kilometer stretch. Once the canoe brigades were set to resume their journeys, James bade goodbye to the men that had brought him this far. He joined the Mackenzie brigade for the final leg of his travel.

Down River to the Mackenzie

It was early September and the brigade still had over a month of paddling ahead. The weather was cool but the mosquitos and blackflies that had dogged them for so long were now gone.

The leaves were changing from their blanket of green to one of yellow and gold. Young waterfowl of all types were exercising their wings preparing for their mass migration south. Beaver and muskrat were busy laying in their winter supply of food. Majestic bull moose, bellowing and threshing their antlers in search of females, were becoming common sights. The paddlers instinctively picked up their pace. They knew that the back end of their journey would be a tight race with the coming freezing weather.

Methye Portage was the Great Divide in their trek. From there the waters flowed not to Hudson Bay, but west and north, winding their way to the Arctic Ocean. For the first time James found himself canoeing down river. Now, instead of portaging, the travellers had the option of shooting rapids. James would find this experience both exhilarating and breathtaking.

The brigade made their way from Methye Portage on the Clearwater River to the Athabaska River. This river would take them to the lake of the same name on which they arrived at Fort Chipewyan. After dropping off the post's annual supply of trade goods and a brief rest, they continued down the Slave River to Great Slave Lake. They stopped briefly at Forts Resolution and Providence to deliver their trade goods. At Fort Providence, James finally cast his eyes upon the mighty Mackenzie River, or Deh Cho, as it was known by the Dene.

The Mackenzie River / Deh Cho

The travellers were now on their homestretch and the mornings were cold, damp and foggy. Ice crystals were forming along the shorelines.

The deciduous trees stood bare. Vees of migrating geese pointed southward as they wended their way across the grey sky, driven by the north winds. When Fort Simpson, sitting at the confluence of the Laird and Mackenzie Rivers, finally came into sight, James and the weary paddlers whooped with relief and joy.

The Mackenzie River, the Amazon of the North at 1,738 kilometers, is the largest and longest river system in what is now Canada. Including its tributaries, it is one of the longest in the world. The Mackenzie River is named for Alexander Mackenzie, a fur trader for the North West Company who, upon receiving information and direction from the local Dene travellers, followed the Deh-Cho to its end in 1789. He had hoped it would lead to the Pacific Ocean, but instead found himself at the Arctic Ocean.

The river he followed is broad, clogged with numerous islands and sandbars, and lined with many side channels. The Mackenzie Mountains to the west picturesquely run parallel. The river is rather placid and slow moving, except for several rapid stretches, the most spectacular being immediately south of Fort Good Hope. Here, just 50 miles short of the Arctic Circle, the river narrows to less than one half kilometer, and swiftly flows through a murderous 130-foot deep canyon called "The Ramparts." This five-mile stretch walled by towering white limestone cliffs can be especially dangerous in the spring when the mighty river is swollen by its feed of spring thaw mountain run-off water.

Running out of the Mackenzie Mountains, the Nahanni River empties into the Mackenzie River about 110 kilometers north of Fort Simpson. This river provides the most spectacular hair-raising river travel anywhere in North America— and the entire world, for that matter. Four canyons aptly named the First, Second, Third and Fourth Canyons line this wild white-water river and includes the thunderous Virginia Falls, or Nailicho in Dene, that, along with Sluice Box Rapids, falls more than twice the height of Niagara Falls.

Downstream from this killer falls are many more notable rapids including Figure Eight, George's Riffle and Lafferty's Riffle. Home to grizzly bears, mountain sheep and caribou, this untamed backcountry with ominous sounding names like Deadman Valley, Headless Creek and Funeral Range bore testimony to the territory to which James would call home for the next few years.

James was based in Fort Simpson, North West Territories, for the first six years of his career from 1848 to 1854. His work history shows he spent the first four years of his career with the Hudson's Bay Company as a labourer, assisting the carpenters, sawyers, blacksmith, and others who were his senior. Archival documents reveal a contract signed in Fort Simpson in the year 1854. This would have been James' renewal contract, signing on for an additional five years. Dr. John Rae, his superior, who would become one of early Canada's great explorers, had accepted the signed contract on behalf of the Hudson's Bay Company.

James Flett at Norway House

James arrived in Norway House from Simpson in 1854 and worked as a labourer for the next three years before advancing to the position of Storesman in 1857. He had also fallen in love, and with this promotion that more than doubled his salary to 100 pounds annually, he was now in a position to wed. James, at the age of 29, married Mary Peebles, then aged 15. Marriage by men to much younger women was very common at the time.

Mary was the daughter of James Peebles and Elizabeth (Betsy) Morrison, a Métis from the Red River Settlement. James and Mary would go on to have 18 children: three, including my grandfather, in Norway House; four in Nelson River, Manitoba; nine in Berens River, Manitoba and two in the Red River District around the vicinity of Selkirk.

Most of the Hudson's Bay Company staff houses were of a standard size, the most common being two bedrooms. It is difficult picturing a family of 18 children being raised in a company house; however, we have to assume as soon as the children reached the age of majority, they had to move on to make room for their siblings. (See Appendix for list of James' and Mary's 18 children).

James remained in the position of storesman, working in the store and warehouses until his transfer to Nelson River, where he served as clerk from 1861 to 1869. James then transferred back to Norway House as Clerk from 1869 to 1870, and then as Clerk at Rossville, a short distance away, from 1870 to 1871.

The Treaties of Canada

In 1870, James Flett was transferred from Norway House to Rossville, which is only two or three miles away. The main difference was that the move put James directly into the First Nations community.

Shortly thereafter, on July 15th, 1870, the Hudson's Bay Company's Deed Of Surrender came into effect ending the Company's 200 years of monopolistic control of the fur trade in Rupert's Land. Once the Deed of Surrender came into effect it made possible the emergence of Manitoba as a province the same day.

It was akin to someone firing a starter pistol signalling the onslaught of a land rush. The First Nations people of the plains envisioned the coming of large numbers of settlers to their lands, the end of the great herds of buffalo, and the end of their roaming ways on the prairies. The dearth of buffalo induced starvation conditions. Debilitating diseases ravaged the population. They needed to adapt once again to a changing way of life.

In 1870, when the First Nations were informed of the sale of Rupert's Land by the Hudson's Bay Company to the newly formed Dominion of Canada, they were flabbergasted. In two hundred years of relations with the Hudson's Bay Company no one had ever discussed ownership of lands. The Company never attempted overtly to assert sovereignty. Its Royal Charter was treated simply as a business arrangement whereby in return for furs the company provided much needed trade goods.

The Company's movement inland from the shores of Hudson Bay and James Bay was welcomed by the First Nations as this greatly reduced travel times to conduct trade. At no time were they or any other First Nations aware of any land dealings with the company, and of course, no one within the company attempted to explain the Royal Charter to the First Nations.

With the Manitoba Act establishing the territory as the fifth province of the Dominion of Canada, the government sent surveyors to map out townships and the track of the future railway. Other workers began stringing telegraph lines to bring instant communication to the west. The First Nations understandably became agitated and began initiating strong resistance, threatening violence and demanding to meet with representatives of the crown before allowing any settlers to move onto their traditional lands. To secure peace in the region, the government sent Treaty Commissioners headed by Alexander Morris as chief negotiator.

On August 3, 1871, Treaty 1 was entered into at Lower Fort Garry by the Chiefs of seven First Nations including Brokenhead, Fort Alexander (Sagkeeng), Long Plain, Peguis, Rouseau River Anishinabe, Sandy Bay and Swan Lake. This would be the first of a string of 11 numbered Treaties that Canada would enter into with the First Nations.

Treaties One and Two were amended April 30, 1875 because the First Nations complained that the actual treaty documents, once completed, were inaccurate and did not contain all the promises as discussed at the negotiations. Essentially those Treaties were amended to increase the annual payments from three dollars to five dollars per person.

It is difficult to understand how such a fundamental point could be misinterpreted or misunderstood by the Treaty Commissioners. It seemed to be simply a case of the Canadian government attempting "to pull a fast one" on the First Nations.

The issue of promises discussed and agreed to but subsequently ignored on the documents are prevalent throughout all the numbered Treaties. In the final analysis, the Treaties were an effective means of separating the First Nations from their lands, clearing the way for settlement.

Of particular personal interest are the Adhesions to Treaty 5 in the northern part of Manitoba. The Adhesion signed at Berens River on the 20th day of September, 1875, is signed by nine witnesses to the Treaty including my great-grandfather, James Flett, who was the manager of the Hudson's Bay Company trading post in Berens River.

The Adhesion to Treaty 5 signed at Nelson House on the 30th day of July, 1908 is signed by 11 witnesses to the Treaty, including my grandfather, Alexander Flett, who at the time was the manager of the Hudson's Bay trading post at Split Lake.

In 1873, James Flett was transferred from Rossville to Berens River, Manitoba where he was to spend the next 12 years of his career managing the trading post. As already mentioned, in 1875 he was a party to Adhesion Treaty 5 as a witness to the participation of the Berens River First Nations.

I think James would have been proud when he set his signature to the Treaty, given the peaceful nature of the process. He well remembered the angst of the Red River Rebellion five years prior. Across the border in 1862, President Lincoln had authorized the single largest mass execution in US history, with the hanging of 38 out of the total of 303 Sioux warriors who had been condemned to death by the courts of Minnesota for their part in the "Indian wars." Throughout North and South Dakota and Montana, the United States Army was still actively waging war with the Lakota, Dakota, Nakota (collectively the Sioux), Cheyenne and Arapahoe nations.

The strife culminated a year later, in 1876, with the battle of Little Big Horn wherein General Custer and his Seventh Calvary were wiped out. Chief Sitting Bull subsequently brought his people into Canada seeking refuge, which Canada provided for a time. To this day there are Sioux Reserves in Manitoba and Saskatchewan which fall under the responsibility of Indian Affairs in spite of the fact no treaties exist between the Sioux and Canada.

From 1885 to the date of his retirement in 1898, James worked in the southern part of Manitoba in what was called the Red River and Lake Winnipeg Districts. He would have spent some time in Fort Alexander, presently Sagkeeng. James B. Flett retired in the community of Selkirk where he died on December 31, 1906.

3

OUR STORIES MERGE

ALEXANDER FLETT

I first met my paternal grandfather when he was 80 years old. He was an elderly man, but alert, and still imposing in size and presence.

Grandfather Alexander was tall, lean and powerful, with large hands and a raw-boned but handsome appearance. He was fair complexioned and his hair, dark when he was younger, had now turned white with age. Alexander still had a commanding presence. He had the pensive eyes of a widower, remembering better times past. The eyes were blue-grey in colour, a trait inherited from his father, James.

Grandfather was a Métis man who was very comfortable in his dual cultural role. His father hailed directly from the Orkney Islands in Scotland and his mother was a staunch Métis woman from the Red River Settlement. He spoke both Cree and Ojibway, languages acquired from the communities in which he had worked. It is difficult to remember him without one of his several pipes in mouth.

My grandfather was born in Norway House on August 21, 1870. One of 18 children, he grew up in Berens River but spent a part of his time in Red River obtaining his education. He entered the service of the Hudson's Bay Company on June 1, 1888 as Apprentice Clerk at Fort Alexander, presently Sagkeeng, located near Pine Falls, Manitoba, at the mouth of the Winnipeg River. Interestingly, he would retire on the Winnipeg River only a few miles upriver from Fort Alexander. He is buried in the Anglican cemetery at Pine Falls.

Alexander spent four years in training at Fort Alexander until his promotion in 1902 to Post Manager of the Hudson's Bay Company in Split Lake, Manitoba. Upon his promotion he promptly married Edith McLeod of Norway House. They were married at Cross Lake on August 15, 1902, by Reverend Edward Paupanekis.

Alexander and Edith would have nine children, all born in Split Lake, Manitoba. Three of the children died within days of being born. Infant mortality rates in the isolation of the north were atrociously high as no medical services or facilities were within reach. It must have been heartrendingly sad for parents to stand by helplessly with an ailing child.

The first born was Alice Grace born June 29, 1903. I remember her as Aunt Grace. She was born the same year as the first successful aircraft flight engineered by the Wright brothers. Aunt Grace never married. She was a kindly woman, tall, big-boned and rather plain looking. Some would call her homely. I don't recall where she lived but I do remember her occasional visits to Powerview, where I lived with my Uncle Archie and Auntie Annie. Every Christmas was made that much more special because she never forgot to send gifts for each of us.

Islay Elisabeth was born January 13, 1906. Although she was six years older, she reminded me of a miniature Aunt Greta. She was a widow living with grandfather Alexander with three of her younger children: Tom, Lorna and Andy.

My father, Horace George, was born December 30, 1907. I tell his story in later chapters of this book. Alexander Archibald was born January 14, 1910. He married Annette Armondine Lavallee, my auntie Annie, a Métis woman from Fannystelle, Manitoba, in 1934.

Marjory Greta was born February 24, 1912. Aunt Greta, when I first met her, was a single mother living with grandfather Alexander.

I remember her being tall, thin and graceful. She was always well dressed with her hair carefully coiffed. Aunt Greta was fairly attractive with a thin pinched face, and she possessed somewhat of a take-charge personality. She was rather dismissive of me and I suspect she was not proud of her Métis background.

Henry Charles Otter was the surviving baby of the family, born on June 14, 1914. I never met Uncle Henry, although I am told by cousin Edie that he was a kindly, gentle person. As a young man he had moved to Toronto where he took up a trade as a roofer. In his later years he had an accident, fell off a roof, and then spent the remainder of his working life on disability.

In 1917, Alexander was transferred to Big Trout Lake in Ontario. The Big Trout Lake trading post was a busy centre with a number of camp trades spread out within a 200-mile radius for which he was also responsible. Camp trades were small trading posts usually run by local First Nations or Métis employees or junior Scottish clerks learning the ins and outs of the fur trade. Here he, my paternal grandfather, would have first come face to face with the imposing Chief Samson Beardy, my maternal grandfather. Alexander spent just two years here before being transferred to York Factory.

York Factory was no longer the seat of control of the Hudson's Bay Company in 1919, but it was still a busy port and an important trading post. Alexander spent six years in this location managing the huge main depot, along with a fairly large number of buildings still standing at that time, albeit many of them empty. At the fort's height in 1873, as the headquarters of the Hudson's Bay Company in North America, the trading centre had a total of approximately 50 buildings. Dad and his siblings growing up here must have had the greatest games of Hide and Seek! Today, only the central main depot building still stands as a National Historic Site.

In the spring of 1920 at York Factory, Alexander's wife Edith, after a period of illness, died on April 25th at the relatively young age of 40. Her eldest child, Grace, was 17 years old, dad Horace was 13 and the youngest, Henry, was only six years old. Most of the children, the exception being Henry, were attending school either in Selkirk or in The Pas. Alexander had 17 siblings who would readily take in their nephews and nieces as boarders. Alexander was a successful manager earning well and paying well to ensure his children were looked after and educated.

In 1925, he was again transferred to Big Trout Lake, but before leaving York Factory he used his influence as an important man in the field to have his son Horace taken on by the Company as an apprentice clerk.

Unlike York Factory, Big Trout Lake was a growing business, and the fur trade, especially in foxes, was booming just prior to the Wall Street economic crash of 1929. Alexander was reaping a rich harvest of furs from his northern Ontario location and with this harvest he was being well paid. In addition to his central post at Big Trout Lake, he had fur traders located at his outposts in Muskrat Dam, Kasabonika, Wunnummin Lake, Big Beaver House, Bearskin Lake, Kingfisher Lake, Sachigo Lake, Weagamow and Webequie. These outposts combined contributed to his success as one of the great fur traders of his day.

In 1926 his daughter Islay married an HBC man, Andrew McClymont Sloan Allison, who was the Post Manager at Fort Severn.

In 1929 Horace was transferred to Big Trout Lake, where he worked for his father for a short period of time. He was sent to Bearskin Lake as an outpost manager and as this camp trade location was little more than a log-walled tent, he along with First Nations assistants constructed a more permanent building of logs. By this time Alexander was 59 years old, had a significant sum of money safely put away and was planning retirement.

The same year, 1929, Alexander was transferred to Fort Hope, Ontario, a semi-retirement location for him as Fort Hope was not as hectic as Big Trout Lake. However, it was still a fairly busy location as a distribution centre. In summer, York boat and canoe shipments of trade goods would come up the river from Fort Albany to Fort Hope. Alexander would receive the goods and then repack into smaller canoe shipment loads for transport to Lansdowne House and Big Trout Lake.

The French Company

Alexander, then a widower, had two daughters, Grace and Greta, with him in Fort Hope. Islay was already married and living in Fort Severn. Henry was 15 years old and likely still living with his Aunties while going to school in Selkirk. Horace was outpost manager at Bearskin Lake. Archie at this time being 19 years old was also involved in the fur trade but employed by the opposing company of Revillon Frères Fur Trading Company Ltd., which was headquartered in Montreal.

Revillon Frères, then known as La Maison Givelet, was an old established fur and luxury goods company founded in 1723 and based in Paris. In 1839, the company was purchased by Louis Victor Revillon and he developed it into the largest fur company in France.

By 1900, Revillon Frères had stores in Paris, London, New York, and Montreal. In 1908, the French company rapidly expanded into the fur trading business and by 1912 had 125 trading posts in Canada and some in Siberia. In Canada they became established in northern Alberta around the Athabaska region, had posts in northern Saskatchewan and Manitoba, and around James Bay in Ontario. They firmly established themselves in the Eastern Arctic region servicing their trading posts with their own fleet of ships.

In 1926, the Hudson's Bay Company purchased 54 percent of the Revillon Frères Fur Trading Company and by 1936 the French company was completely owned by HBC. The elders of the First Nations, Inuit and Métis communities that were actively involved in the fur trade remember and refer to Revillon Frères as "the French company."

The rapid growth of Revillon Frères in Canada and especially into the Eastern Arctic might have gone unchecked if not for an enterprising Fur Commissioner, Ralph Parsons, "the King of Baffin Land." Anticipating the demand for arctic fox, Parsons pushed the Hudson's Bay Company into the Arctic and strengthened their position in Labrador and Arctic Quebec.

Plummeting demand and collapsing prices for fur followed the stock market crash of 1929. Revillon Frères found themselves overextended with debt they could no longer service. The Hudson's Bay Company reorganized their resources, and blessed with deeper pockets, were able to absorb the French company.

The Hudson's Bay Company, once again a hundred years later, as before with the North West Company in 1821, rose to dominate a formidable opposition.

Flett's Point

Alexander retired from the Hudson's Bay Company on May 31, 1931. Both Archie and Horace had been let go by their respective companies after the crash of 1929 as part of the reorganization that was necessary for survival.

They spent the following year working with a carpenter in constructing Alexander's retirement home in an idyllic location on the shores of the Winnipeg River just a few miles upriver from Pine Falls. Alexander had also invested in a fox farm so he appreciated the assistance young Horace and Archie were able to provide. The fox farm closed as the demand for furs continued to drop.

Archie remained in the Pine Falls area, finding employment as a pulp cutter for the paper mill and later as a truck driver during the construction of the power dam just outside Powerview.

My father, Horace, was rehired by the Hudson's Bay Company in 1933 and posted to Big Trout Lake, Ontario.

I was in Powerview living with my Uncle Archie and Auntie Annie along with their children. My parents sent me there for school in 1949. I was a black-haired, brown-eyed, dark-complexioned urchin no different from a typical First Nations child you see on any reserve. My grandfather lived out in the country, at Flett's Point which bears his name, about three or four kilometers from the village of Powerview and five from Pine Falls, on the Winnipeg River in Manitoba. His house was located on a beautiful piece of waterfront property. The shoreline was a combination of Pre-Cambrian shield rock and dark pine forest mixed with oak tree stands.

I loved going to visit Grandpa as I felt he had a quiet affinity for me. His memory has influenced my life in a positive way. I was in awe of his home and property and I tucked away in the back of my mind that when I retired I would also have a home by a lake or river. The affluence of his home was in stark contrast to the borderline impoverished home where we lived in Powerview.

Every long weekend or special holiday, Grandpa sent for me. I always found him in one of two places at his house. He would either be sitting in his kitchen at the table next to the hall doorway and gazing out the window, or I would find him outside. He had an oversized outdoor swing lounge that comfortably fit his large frame. He would lie stretched out or propped up on several cushions. He usually had one leg dangling so he could push and set the swing into motion if he felt so inclined.

Grandpa always wore a white shirt with dark dress wool pants. He smelled pleasantly of tobacco and Sunlight soap. He would greet me with a hug and a few soft gentle words, then he would let me go, swat me gently on the behind with his ever-present cane, and tell me, "Okay, be off now, you little beggar!"

Every morning he was always the first one up. He would get the fire going in his kitchen range and put on a pot of porridge and a percolator of coffee. When you smelled the coffee, it was time to get up. As I, and maybe a cousin or two, walked into the kitchen, grandpa would be sitting on his chair by the doorway, both hands propped up on his cane in front of him. If you neglected to greet him with a "Good morning, Grandpa," he would swat your behind with his cane. His porridge was always made thinly, a watery gruel. Occasionally Aunt Islay would make the porridge when grandfather had to be off to tend to his fish net first thing in the morning. Aunt Islay's porridge would always be a treat because it was thicker than Grandpa's.

The riverbank was on a steep incline from the house. There was no running water, but out his backdoor on a deck was a large wooden wheel with a crank handle. Around the wheel was wound a wire running down to the river. At the river, and set into the riverbed, was another smaller pulley wheel, and the entire setup resembled a pullied clothesline. Grandpa would hook his bucket to the line, spin his wheel so that the bucket glided down and into the water. He would then crank up his bucket of fresh water.

At the river's edge he had a slipway cut into the riverbank, like a small canal, lined with posts driven into the riverbed. He could then bring his rowboat safely in from the river current and into the slipway. He would then step out of the boat onto a set of stairs (three small steps up) which made it very easy for an elderly man to get in and out of his boat. I remember his slipway very vividly because I fell headfirst into it. It was my first experience underwater. I can recall looking about in panicky fascination as I struggled to upright myself.

In the river, fairly close to his boat slipway, he kept a large wire cage into which he would throw freshly caught fish taken out of his fish net. He would check his net every morning. The fish he threw into the cage were those that he knew would survive the gill netting. Thus he always had a fresh supply of pickerel and catfish on hand.

Grandfather had a large three-bedroom, one-and-a-half-storey home with a full-size verandah attached at one end. The verandah made the house look much larger than it actually was. The house had three bedrooms joined by a dark hallway. The far bedroom was Grandpa's. I would sneak into his bedroom (by Auntie Islay's orders, his bedroom was out of bounds for me and my cousins) and gaze in wonderment at the crossed snowshoes and dogsled whip displayed prominently on his bedroom wall. On a side table was a canister of tobacco and next to the canister a selection of four or five pipes including a Meerschaum, one with a curved stem like the kind you would see hanging out of Sherlock Holmes's mouth.

Opposite grandfather's bedroom, a hallway door opened up to a set of stairs leading up to a large open room which served as a guestroom. Another door opened onto a bathroom which contained a toilet, washstand and a bathtub sitting on four curved short legs. The toilet sat in a corner, covered, with a small black pipe running from it, the pipe disappearing into the ceiling. Inside the covered toilet was a bucket which had to emptied every morning. It was used only by my Auntie Islay and cousin Lorna. Grandpa, Tom, Andy and I and any male visitors had to trek to the outside toilet discreetly located behind the house.

The same hallway at the end opposite the bedrooms led into the dining room and parlour or living room as we would call it today. The dining room held a dark massive dining table with matching chairs and a matching sideboard topped by a large silver platter. The platter was somewhat skewed and had long scratches running along the underside.

The silver platter, large enough to hold a big turkey or a small boy, had been presented to grandfather on his wedding day by the Hudson's Bay Company. One fine winter day when dad and his brother Archie were young boys, they spirited the platter out for a day of sliding. The platter was of the ideal shape and size for the purpose they had in mind. Grandfather proudly displayed the platter on his sideboard and, with a chuckle, always took the opportunity to tell the story about his boys and the tanning he subsequently gave them.

The parlour had an overstuffed green chesterfield and matching chair. A set of exquisite china table lamps trimmed with hanging crystal sat on little tables on each side of the chesterfield. Cousin Andy and I were roughhousing one day and accidentally knocked one of the lamps to the floor. As we watched horrified, the china lampshade shattered into several pieces on one side.

Andy and I were able to glue the pieces back enough that the lamp looked almost as good as new, as long as the side that had been broken was kept out of direct view. We discreetly ensured the glued section always faced the wall.

The floors were of hardwood and a massive fieldstone open fireplace almost filled one wall. The fireplace had a mantle upon which sat a large wooden encased clock that sounded with a lonely "dong" on the hour. Next to the clock sat a heavy set of brass binoculars. The binoculars were an endless source of fascination for me.

Stories were told of the grand times people would have whenever Grandfather hosted a square dance at his house. The dining room table and any movable piece of furniture would be moved onto the verandah. The chairs and chesterfield would be pushed and lined up against the walls. A corner would be set up for the fiddler and guitarist. The dance stories are embedded firmly in my memory because someone painted a picture in my mind of Auntie Annie standing on a chair, clapping her hands and calling the square dances.

A parlour door opened onto a spacious screened verandah. The highlight of the verandah was a wooden white restaurant booth trimmed in red paint and finished with matching red leather seats. On warm summer mornings it was a joy to have breakfast there. Outside on the lawn grandfather had a canopied swinging lounge. Here he would spend several hours every day, usually after his walks, resting, reading, lazing and dozing in the warm summer air.

At the time I started school, my Aunt Greta, a single mother, and her daughter Marilyn Donna Flett lived with grandfather. Alexander at the time of his retirement kept a cow for a supply of fresh milk, cream and butter. In a shed he kept a cream separator into which he poured his milk. The separator had two spouts: one for milk and one for cream. There was also a butter churn in a corner of the shed.

By 1950 he had rid himself of the cow and pigs. He converted the small barn into a house and rented it out for extra income. A young family with two children were renting the house, and in the early spring they asked Marilyn if she could babysit their children. She agreed. She had her friend from next door come babysit with her.

As they were leaving the house Marilyn laughingly said to Grandpa and her mother that they were going to sleep with "Bossy." That was the name grandfather had given his cow. Marilyn and her friend, along with the children, perished in a tragic fire on March 30, 1950. This had a horrific effect on Grandpa as Marilyn had been his constant companion since she was born. Aunt Greta moved to Toronto shortly thereafter.

At about the same time, Auntie Islay lost her husband Andrew to a hunting accident. Widowed with several children still in her care, she moved in with grandfather. There was cousin Tom who was about 14, Lorna about 12, and Andy who was my age, eight. Aunt Islay also had adult children, Stanley, Little Grace and Eileen, who were already out and making their way in the world.

Aunt Islay supported herself and her children as a seamstress who specialized in wedding gowns. She used the dining room as her work area, the large table ideal for a cutting. She had a treadle sewing machine which would hum when she applied her heel and toe motion to the treadle. An adjustable mannequin completed the equipment of her trade.

I said before that grandfather was very proud of his Cree heritage. Every New Year's Day it was his custom to proudly don his moosehide coat and fur hat, summon a taxi, and go to town for his annual visit with old friends.

Grandfather died in the Pine Falls Hospital on March 13, 1957. He had been out for his daily walk and slipped on ice and broke his hip. He never recovered and died at the age of 87. Aunt Greta came back to assist Islay with all the decisions necessary after a death. They disposed of Grandfather's personal belongings, burning his letters, documents and mementos of anything referencing his First Nations background. They clipped the brass buttons stamped with the HBC logo on them from his moosehide jacket and mailed the buttons to my father. The jacket was then either thrown out or burned. Dad was absolutely furious with his sisters for being ashamed of their heritage. I do not think he ever forgave them.

To this day there is a question about Grandmother Edith's background. Some have said that she was adopted as a baby by the McLeods in Norway House and that she was actually a Robinson from Cross Lake. The implication is that she was actually a First Nations person and not Métis. This may also have had something to do with the fact that Alexander and Edith were married in Cross Lake and not in Norway House.

Grandpa is buried in the Anglican cemetery in Pine Falls. I make it a point to visit his grave at least every few years. He lived through two World Wars and saw the cruelty of man at his worst. Alexander died the same year and just a few months before the former Soviet Union successfully launched Sputnik, the first satellite in space.

From York boats to the first air flight at Kitty Hawk in 1903, the development of automobiles, radios and television, through two World Wars, the atomic bomb, and start of the space age, Grandfather lived in a period of rapid, breathtaking development.

Len's grandfather, Alexander Flett, dressed in his Métis finest

4

THE CREE SIDE OF THE FAMILY

CHIEF SAMSON BEARDY

No knew how old Samson was. He was born sometime around 1880 and somewhere on the traditional lands of his family.

The people of Kitchenuhmaykoosib Inninuwug, the Cree name for Big Trout Lake, shared the territory of northwest Ontario but each clan had the responsibility for the care of a certain area. The families within the clans were further responsible for the care of their family hunting and gathering lands. This was their traditional responsibility, for without the land and the bounty the land provided they were nothing. The land and the people were as one.

The family clans of the tribe had to spread out over the wide area of their territory in order to remain sustainable. Every few years at least, the family groups would move to a new location so that the land they left could regenerate and replenish itself. Some families moved more often. They had learned over millenia not to put any unnecessary strain on the limited resources of their land, the land that gave them life.

This was the environment in which my First Nations grandfather, Samson Beardy, was raised. Not much is known or remembered about our ancestors before Samson. My cousin, Frank Beardy, before he died recently, was able to provide me with the name of our great-grandfather, Wasakanootchie, and our great-great-grandfather, Paquetna. In those days the people were known only by the one name. There were no surnames. The surname "Beardy" began with Samson.

We are not aware of the origin of the name Beardy. I searched the Hudson's Bay Company archives; however, there were no Beardys ever employed. The name appears to originate from southern England, so I surmise a Beardy may have been a minister of the Church of England. Samson himself later became a minister of the church so he may have adopted the name or was possibly given the name at his baptism. Anglicanism remains the dominant religion in the land of my First Nations grandfathers.

It is certain he was not given the name by an Indian agent, as was so often the case when the First Nations people were being registered under the Indian Act. Samson Beardy already bore the name when he signed the Adhesion Treaty of 1929.

Frank also passed on to me that Paquetna had mutiple wives, two, for sure, that he had in his lodge at the same time. We also know that both Wasakanootchie and Paquetna were Chiefs as it is recorded that Samson was the last of a long line of hereditary chiefs. And we know Samson was a spiritual person, a trait probably inherited from his father and grandfather.

Here are their stories. However, as we know so little about Wasakanootchie and Paquetna, I have generalized and taken liberties as I fitted them into the historical context of early First Nations life. I explain how Paquetna possibly came to have two wives in a bigamous relationship from what we know about early Indigenous custom. I also attempt to explain how they passed a deep sense of spirituality to Samson by explaining First Nations common spiritual beliefs and practices.

Chief Paquetna

Chief Paquetna, even in old age, was an imposing man: tall, lean, his face weathered by age and by the open wind. His hair was long, still dark but streaked with enough white to give his hair an overall gunmetal-grey appearance. It was kept out of his face and dark piercing eyes by a headband of deer hide. His thick hair was kept shiny by the bear grease regularly applied.

Samson Beardy's father was Wasakanoochie but, as the firstborn grandchild, in keeping with the tradition of his people, he was raised by his grandparents. As an adult, Samson would be expected to care for his grandparents in their old age. That was the way of the people. In the tradition of their people, Samson was also groomed for the position of Chief by his grandfather, Paquetna.

Paquetna could still walk and paddle long distances in his birch bark canoe, but not so far that he could not be back in the comfort and safety of his lodge by nightfall. He always took Samson with him on his hunting and fishing trips.

Paquetna no longer hunted big game nor would he shoot any big game he came upon unless he knew Wasakanoochie was home. The task of cleaning big game and hauling it back to the lodges was now too much for him and Samson was still a skinny young boy not yet to be relied on for heavy work. Wasakanoochie hunted and trapped much further afield and hauled back moose, deer and bear as and when required.

The teaching of Samson never ceased. There were so many different plants and roots and trees with different barks and bark linings, all with unique medicinal purposes. The roots of different trees had varied textures which, when pounded, separated into strands. The strands could then be braided into string, the string braided into cord, and the cord into rope.

String, rope, and snare wire were now available from fur traders; however, Paquetna felt it was still an essential skill for his grandson to learn to make his own snares and rope in the wild. He learned to make snowshoes, whittling and bending the wood to the proper shape. He learned to make "babiche," dried rawhide used to string the snowshoes. Samson could now build his own canoe of birch bark and make it leak-proof with spruce gum.

Paquetna taught Samson to identify the footprints of animals in the snow. He was taught to track and call moose, although he was not yet allowed to shoot them. He was taught never to shoot cow moose with calf. He could find and build shelter in the wild and, in short, Samson was taught all there was to know for survival in the wild.

Paquetna hunted small game, shot ducks, geese and partridges, and snared rabbits. In season he trapped beaver, muskrat, mink, marten, fox and lynx, all within a day's trek by foot or canoe from the home lodges. Samson was always in tow and he observed closely and learned quickly. Paquetna constantly tested him with questions and requested Samson correctly demonstrate his newly acquired skills.

Nothing that Paquetna or Wasakanoochie hunted or trapped was wasted. The two home lodges of strong poles, birch bark, moss, and spruce boughs, one for Wasakanoochie and his family and the other that of Paquetna and his two wives, were warm, snug and well stocked.

The lodges were built teepee style and located in the treestand for protection from the winter winds, but still close enough to the lake where cold pure water was easily available. The tops of the lodges were open for the smoke to escape and light to enter and brighten the cosy homes. A heavy bear rug hung in the doorway.

Behind the lodges stood a majestic tree with the front leg-bones of several bears tied to the trunk at a height that was out of reach of their camp dogs. Every fall, a bear, at its fattest stage just before hibernation, would be hunted and killed and its fat rendered and stored for the winter. Its forelegs, now bared of all flesh, were displayed on the tree, tied by leather thongs. Bears mark their territory by reaching up to their full height and scratching the trunk of the largest tree in its area with their sharp claws. This was a warning to any other bears wandering by that they had better be able to match the size of the resident bear before deciding upon a challenge. The hunters thus paid homage to the spirit of this regal animal. In the branches of the tree was a platform built of saplings upon which they laid the bones of the beaver they ate—another act of humble respect.

Nearby, the domed frame of a sweat lodge constructed of saplings tied with root strands sat in the woods next to the lake. When it was time for a ceremony, the frame would be covered with hides that were presently stored in the lodges away from gnawing animals. Inside, a small circular pit was dug for the sacred fire. A small pile of "Grandfather" rocks, those to be used for ceremony, was next to a pile of wood.

The term "Grandfather" was often used as a reference to the Great Spirit. It was the general belief of the people that the spirit of God was imbued in all things created by him. Each tree in the forest, all plants, all living creatures including humans, insects, animals, fish or birds, the waters flowing in the brook, stream or river, all contain within the Spirit of God the Creator. This was at the heart of the spiritual beliefs of First Nations people across the land and it manifested itself in the respect of all living things and all else that represented Mother Earth.

Fellow human beings are considered no different from other living creatures of the world. We are a link in the chain of life that comprises the environment, a part of the world lifecycle that demands no special treatment. All living things of this world must be treated with equal respect because, in the end, we are dependent upon one another.

Samson had been taught to recognize the type of rock required for sweat lodge ceremonies and where they could be found. He could not collect the rock strewn on the shores of the lake that were so easily and readily available because they still contained enough moisture to crack, split, and mildly explode. This often occurred in the hot preparatory fire outside the sweat lodge, but occasionally it would happen inside the lodge when water was thrown on the red hot rocks.

Paquetna knew that his responsibility to Samson went beyond Samson's physical well-being. He knew that, besides hunting and survival skills, if Samson were to develop into a leader of his people, he had to instill in Samson a deep sense of spiritual presence and awareness.

The sweat lodge would be used on a number of different occasions and oft times for different reasons. Ceremonies were held to mark the changing seasons and to give thanks for life. Ceremonies were held to give thanks for the bounty of the land after successful hunts. At times the ceremonies were for the men only. Sometimes for the women only. Most times the ceremonies were communal, including both men and women.

The sweat ceremony was a time for the cleansing of the body, mind and spirit. The participants often prepared for the ceremony by braiding their hair. The three plaits that made the braid are representative of the body, mind, and spirit. They prayed as they braided, similar to prayers aided by the use rosary beads. It was a time for contemplation, meditation, the giving of thanks and acknowledgement of the Great Spirit.

Depending upon the occasion, Samson would often be included. However, most times, Samson acted as the "Fire Keeper," ensuring the fire outside the sweat lodge was kept aflame and fed with dried and split wood, and also attending to the needs of the ceremony participants.

From the seashell that Paquetna carried, wafted gentle curls of smoke from the smoldering sacred spiritual medicines of the people: tobacco, sage, cedar and sweetgrass. As he walked around the outside of the sweat lodge, he wafted the smoke with his eagle feather toward the structure, all the while silently offering a prayer of thanks and acknowledgment to the Great Spirit.

This ceremony is simply referred to as "smudging." He walked around the fire and wafted more smoke from his offering, which blended with the smoke from the fire. Paquetna then stood in front of Samson and, with both hands cupped together, Samson ceremoniously pulled some of the smoldering smoke to his chest, continued the motion to his face, and then over his head in a symbolic cleansing of his body, mind and spirit.

Paquetna then offered the smoldering spiritual medicines to the ceremony participants. Paquetna and his family thus communicated with the Great Spirit, the smoke symbolically carrying the prayers upward to Him.

A bald eagle, the white of its head and tail feathers glistening in the sunlight, wheeled in wide circles overhead. It rode the air currents, gliding with ease, majestically moving its wings only occasionally to steer itself through the heavens.

Paquetna and his family regarded the presence of the bald eagle as acknowledgement by the Great Spirit of the homage being paid to Him. The bald eagle, because of its ability to fly and soar to great heights, is regarded as the living creature being physically closest to the Great Spirit. It is the messenger of God.

The men then stripped down to their loincloths. Paquetna, who would lead the ceremony, would be first in. He would sit to the immediate right of the doorway. Once inside, he would be handed his drum and medicine bundle which contained his ceremonial pipe, several eagle feathers, the claws of a grizzly bear which represented his clan and his role as a protector of women, and various roots and herbs. Finally, a birch bark container of water would be handed to him.

The women, wrapped in blankets or robes, would crawl on hands and knees into the lodge, and in the darkness of the lodge remove their covering. Samson then passed the red-hot stones into the lodge with a set of deer antlers when Paquetna called for them.

Paquetna lit his pipe and then acknowledged the Four Directions which were responsible for the four life-giving seasons of the year. This was and is not worship of the directions, sun, or winds. It was and is simply an acknowledgment of the omnipresence of God the Great Spirit, God the Creator.

The Hollywood stereotyping of the pipe ceremony pervades movies and literature. It belies the solemn use of the pipe as an instrument of worship. It is often shared with friends and guests. First Nations people are honoured when invited to share and participate in a pipe ceremony.

The pipe is often lightly referred to by white people as a "peace pipe," the name probably originating from early settler days when

First Nations were battling white settlers who were encroaching on their lands. When a white man was invited to participate in a pipe ceremony, all he knew was that he would not be harmed in the process—hence the name "peace pipe."

Paquetna pointed his pipe first toward the entrance of the lodge which faced East. The East, Wapunuk, keeps the sun and sends it across the sky on its daily journey. The East is represented by the colour red, often the colour of early morning. Wapun, in Cree, is the dawn of a new day. Paquetna silently gave thanks.

Paquetna then pointed his pipe to the South, Sawinuk, the warm healing wind. Sawin is represented by the colour yellow, the colour of the sun. He again silently offered a prayer of acknowledgment.

Paquetna turned his pipe to the West, Nepawanuk, that receives the sun at the end of each day. Nepawan means the place where the sun goes down to sleep. It is represented by the colour black, evoking darkness. Paquetna again silently gave thanks.

In the final act of the pipe ritual, Paquetna offered his pipe to the North, Keewatinuk. Keewatin is the cold wind that brings us winter. It is represented by the colour white, as of snow. Paquetna gave thanks and acknowledgment.

The pipe was then passed to all the participants in the sweat lodge who offered prayers of thanks and acknowledgment. Outside the lodge stood a tall thin pole of sapling, and at the top of the pole were tied four pieces of coloured cloth: red, yellow, black and white. The colours represent the four directions, the four seasons, and more recently the four major races of man.

When ready, Paquetna signaled, "ahow," and Samson lowered the hide-cover, sealing the entrance from any light. Samson could hear the hiss of the steam as the cold water was thrown onto the red hot rocks and the "ahhhs" of the sweat lodge participants as the hot clouds of steam rolled over them.

Samson had with him birch bark containers of tobacco, sage, cedar and sweetgrass, the sacred medicines of the First Nations people, obtained as gifts or through trade with other tribes. These he would throw into the fire as offerings when the participants requested. The throbbing of the drum and the chanting of the worshippers within the small lodge reverberated in the darkness of the woods, and a calming peace settled over the lake.

Paquetna, the eldest of his family, had lost his younger brother to the Severn River. On the way to the great bay in the east, where he would find the fur trading posts of the Hudson's Bay Company, Paquetna's brother came to a familiar but formidable set of rapids. He decided to shoot the rapids as he had done many times before. Unexpectedly, his canoe struck a "deadhead," a sunken log jammed amidst underwater rocks and out of sight. It ripped a three-foot gash into the flimsy birch bark canoe, quickly filling the craft with water and overturning it. He was swept away in the white foaming water, bobbing up and down, being sucked under by swiftly, swirling whirlpools.

After two weeks Paquetna began to worry. His brother should have returned by now. He found Wasakanoochie and conveyed his concern. They packed supplies into Wasakanoochie's canoe and began paddling the river in search.

At the bottom end of a set of rapids, they found the damaged canoe, partially submerged in a pool of quiet water. A search of the immediate area turned up a blanket roll caught in branches along the shoreline. The blanket was familiar, one his brother always travelled with. They searched the shorelines below the rapids, looking for signs that Paquetna's brother had pulled himself out of the water. The search was futile. They returned to their lodges with the sorrowful news. Paquetna cut his long hair as an expression of grief.

As was the custom, Paquetna took his late brother's wife as one of his own. For who else was there to care for her in the wilderness? The family moved some rabbit skin robes, baskets, and all her personal possessions to Paquetna's lodge. They took her tools for cutting and sewing and her needles and thread.

She would not forget her combs carved from bone and antler for her hair. She would not forget the bright red ribbon that her late husband had brought back for her on a previous trip from Hudson's Bay. These gifts she treasured.

Paquetna then set fire to his brother's lodge that contained what remained of his possessions. He had great love for his brother. Paquetna's heart, it felt to him, was gripped tightly by an unseen fist, so tightly he could barely breathe. His body convulsed as quiet sobs broke forth from his chest. The tears slowly welled in his eyes and then streamed uncontrollably down his face.

Paquetna struggled to regain his dignity. He choked back his tears and, taking up his drum, gently started a rhythmic beat, and in torn anguish, began a chant of lament.

He, Wasakanoochie, Samson and the wives then offered tobacco to the flames and quietly, tearfully, prayed to the Great Spirit to care for he who was recently departed.

Samson enjoyed the attention from his grandmothers. He and Paquetna had the nicest moosehide moccasins and coats and the finest pants and shirts of soft deerskin. With both wives sewing they found they had the time for intricate decorating. They skillfully and artfully worked beautiful patterns with beads and dyed porcupine quills.

Samson was kept busy hauling water in the watertight birch bark baskets the women had made. The baskets were fairly simple to make. Strips of birch bark were cut from the trees, the size and shape depending upon what was to be made. An awl made of bone or antler was then used to punch holes along the edges to be joined together. The birch bark pieces were then strung together with cord, pounded from the correct root used for this purpose. If the container needed to be water-tight, the holes were punched closely together for a tight seal. Heated spruce gum completed the waterproofing seal.

He was also responsible for going out into the woods and hauling back dry firewood. The women cooked over an open fire in a blackened copper pot acquired from the fur traders. Sometimes they cooked in the old traditional way of dropping red-hot stones into birch bark containers filled with water. The water quickly boiled and imparted onto whatever was being cooked a unique flavour that Paquetna and Samson savoured.

The women changed the spruce boughs used as flooring every three or four days so the lodge always smelled of fresh pine. The spruce boughs were changed regularly and frequently to prevent them drying out and becoming a fire hazard. The lodge was heated by an open fire in the centre of the lodge. Sparks often flew when a log popped, releasing the steam which had gathered in a pocket of the wood.

The heavy bearskin rugs which covered the spruce boughs and the woven rabbit skin robes used as blankets were regularly taken outside and hung on a pole strapped between two posts. The rugs and robes were then beaten with a stick to dislodge the inevitable dust and ashes which would fall from the indoor open fire. There was nothing more comforting to young Samson than to snuggle under the freshly aired robes with his grandfather and two grandmothers.

Wapoose (rabbit) were plentiful in this area and the people were expert in weaving rabbit skin. The white fur of the winter skin was the only one used. The brown summer fur was rarely used as the pelt of the rabbit was too thin and papery at that time of year. The fur was cut in long quarter-inch strips and then tightly woven. The women made fine undershirts for the men, and when cut in broader strips and woven more loosely, the pelts made warm and comfortable coats for children.

As chief of his people, Paquetna was available for counsel when the tribe would meet and gather at Kitchenuhmaykoosib Inninuwug in the early spring. At other times, if his counsel was urgently required, emissaries would make the necessary trip to his hunting and trapping grounds. The annual spring gathering took place once the great flocks of ducks and geese had completed their migration and the pickerel (walleye) had completed their spawning. The gatherings were always festive and food was plentiful. Night after night the evening air resonated with the booming sound of drumming. The people danced.

The days were filled with visits to and from relatives and friends. The chief and elders sat in all-day meetings, many speeches were made, questions asked, and decisions made. No one could stand and speak with as much eloquence and authority as Paquetna, with the possible exception of Wasakanoochie, who would one day accept the mantle of chief on his father's passing.

Chief Wasakanoochie

Wasakanoochie inherited the tall muscular stature of his father and grandfather. His hair was jet black, thick and unruly. He rubbed bear grease into his hair, usually after a sweat lodge ceremony. Like his father Paquetna, Wasakanoochie was an imposing figure. Amidst the crowd of the spring gathering it was easy to pick out the two as the leaders. The older man was stately and dignified. The younger, towering and commanding. Wasakanoochie had great respect for his father and listened carefully to the words of Paquetna whenever the old chief addressed his people.

Wasakanoochie travelled easily and frequently. His territory yielded much game and furs, and he had the skills of a great hunter and trapper. When his larder was full, and with enough furs drying on racks to trade for all his necessities, he took the time to trek out on snowshoes or in his canoe, depending on the season, to visit his people. He was not yet chief; however the people also sought his counsel.

On a visit to Kitchenuhmaykoosib Inninuwug late one summer he met a minister preaching to a group of his people. The man of black cloth had travelled by canoe inland from the big bay in the east. He spoke to the people through an interpreter who had accompanied him.

The strange white man held a black book in one hand and in the other what he would later learn to be a crucifix, which every so often he would wave over his head while speaking. He spoke of Jesus, whose words were written in his black book. The young man listened for several hours, the entire time the missionary spoke, because the message this man was delivering to the people had to be important enough for him to make this difficult and distant journey.

Once home, he spoke to his father about the messages he heard from the minister about the white man's God and God's son, Jesus. Paquetna listened with interest, but he was set in his ways. Paquetna's faith in the Great Spirit and His embodiment in everything He created was unshakable.

Wasakanoochie, however, was affected by the white man's messages and henceforth carried with him both the beliefs of his father and that of the missionary. Wasakanoochie passed on to his son Samson the messages of Christianity, and Samson was also deeply affected. Later in his life Samson would seek the ministry of the white man, and become a powerful spokesman for the bible.

Crucifixes and Sweetgrass

Family oral history was passed to me through another cousin, Charles Fox, who related that there were many medicine men who practised a darker version of spirituality, and who instilled fear amongst our people. This might explain in part the seemingly wholesale shift by our people to Christianity that promised a more enlightened belief.

In the final analysis, the "enlightened" belief of Christianity is no different from other organized religions in that Christianity is also rife with extremists and extremism, anti-feminism, anti-homosexuality, contradictory teachings, superstitions, and corrupt leadership.

There are also many good people with kindly intentions who do charitable work and who are involved with Christianity and its churches. It is a shame that they are tainted by so many who choose to work within its institutions, motivated by greed and self-gratification. It is a shame that sexual predators gravitate toward this and similar institutions that provide them easy access to the innocent.

Our people have not been served well by the Christian churches.

There are eleven other so-called major religions of the world besides Christianity, including Buddhism, Confucianism, Hinduism, Islam, Judaism, Shinto, and Sikhism, and many other lesser religions that have sprung from the above. Christianity does not have a monopoly on faith and purported truth.

Indigenous ethnic religions including that practised by my grand-fathers Paquetna and Wasakanoochie have been, to a great extent, trivialized by the so-called "great" religions of this world, led by Christianity. Church leaders, under contracts to the federal govern-ment, led the assault on native spirituality through the educational system of residential schools.

While residential schools have their roots in the Indian Industrial Schools begun in the 1830s, it was after the Indian Act was passed in 1876 that the schools began to flourish in numbers, with the as-sistance of the churches. From the 1870s until the last school was closed in 1996, 142 Indian Residential Schools operated at one time or another across Canada under a government policy of "Aggressive Assimilation."

The purpose of the schools was to assimilate the First Nations through the children. Remove the children from the influences of their families so that they can no longer practise their culture or be "Indian"—the policy was often referred to as "killing the Indian in the child." Make them vulnerable, cut their hair, dress them in standard white man's clothing, teach them to speak English, whip them if they try to speak their own language, denigrate their spiritual beliefs, and finally, Christianize them.

The government hoped these children would then pass their new lifestyle and Christian belief onto their own children. In time, the tra-ditions, languages, culture and customs of the First Nations people would be forgotten—the Indians now civilized.

The generational damage this policy wreaked upon our people is unfathomable. Imagine seven generations of First Nations children that had been raised without parents, thereby deprived of learning and passing on parenting skills. Imagine the child upon leaving the school: confused, lonely, self-loathing, angry from the many years of assorted abuses. Some call this cultural genocide.

As history has borne out, residential school abuses, perpetrated by many so-called Christian leaders, went far beyond emotional abuse to include physical and sexual abuse. The Truth and Reconciliation

Commission will issue its final report in October of 2015; however, in addition to the abuses, it has revealed that at least 4,000 First Nations children died in these schools—mostly by disease and neglect.

Just as sad, and absolutely outrageous, is the fact that the churches and the federal government, in many instances, did not even bother to communicate many of these deaths to the parents. A number of families are still in search of their "missing" offspring—many to be found in often-unmarked graveyards around the schools.

I do not support one religious or spiritual belief over another; however, I lean toward Native Spirituality, the beliefs of our forefathers, mainly out of a matter of personal principle. I will not have missionaries or evangelists dictating my spiritual beliefs.

I no longer practise or follow any organized religious order. Many people in my circle, including those in my family, hold a Christian belief and allegiance to a church in which they find solace, community, guidance and morality. I respect and cannot deny them that belief and source of comfort.

Other friends and some relatives still attend Aboriginal ceremonies. I am proud that they realize their own beliefs and values, passed down by our forefathers, are just as good, if not superior, in the purest sense, to Christianity. There is no grasping for money or evangelism driven by the arrogant belief that its religion is the only worthwhile one. The deep respect found in Native Spirituality goes beyond that accorded the Great Spirit and extends to everything the Great Spirit has created; the rivers, lakes, trees, mountains and all living creatures. That is where I find the simplicity and beauty of a spiritual belief.

My personal belief does not include concepts of heaven, a better life after death, of reunion with loved ones after death. If these concepts were not so zealously espoused by organized religion, people would better appreciate the here and now. A much higher value on life would be realized; there likely would be less propensity toward violence, war and suicide.

I look ahead to my own imminent death with the knowledge that I have led the best life I could, and that I have descendants, most of them now firmly established in their own lives. Life is not perfect. We all have some regrets, where we could have made a stronger effort or taken a different path. However, on the whole, there comes a time when one must forgive oneself, and conclude that we did our best with what we had.

My personal opinions on spiritualism and religion have been developed over a period of many years, most it on my own journey to heal my self-esteem. The elementary school I attended in Powerview, Manitoba was run by Roman Catholic nuns. Most of the students were white, either English or French, along with a fair number of Métis kids. A very few First Nation students were bussed in from Sagkeeng for their high school program. My sense of worth was damaged and weakened by the zealousness of religious nuns, priests, and ministers within the educational system, and by the ignorance and outright maliciousness of racism. I agree with my daughter Harmony's sentiments, that there will come a day when indoctrination in any form, religious or otherwise, will be considered a form of child abuse.

During my formative years in school I was emotionally traumatized by a weeping nun teaching us about the capture of Jesuit priest, Jean de Brebeuf, by Iroquois who tortured and put him to death. He was later canonized and declared a saint. I assume that was why the teacher was so emotional. I don't recall the teacher explaining that Brebeuf was a war casualty, caught in the ongoing Iroquois battle with the Hurons. The Iroquois were always less tolerant of foreign missionaries set on destroying Indigenous spirituality and imposing their own religious beliefs.

I was the only native person in that classroom and I was very aware that I was an Indian. I was made to feel that I was personally at fault for Brebeuf's death, and that, somehow, I was morally or innately evil.

Man and technology have progressed tremendously in the past few centuries, and especially so in just the past few decades. The invention of the microscope in the late 1500s and the telescope in the late 1600s opened the world to whole new dimensions.

Someone said, "Faith in God diminishes with the progress of science." Science and technology have been the keys to unravelling and answering many questions and unknowns in the past; the same questions previously explained by blind faith in religion.

An anonymous quote, "I used to be a Christian, but then I thought about it," set me on a path of questioning and examining the concepts of god and religion a number of years ago.

It took many years to free my thoughts from the deep brainwashing relentlessly inflicted upon me by many so-called religious leaders and teachers. From an early age I was bombarded with the ancient writings of old men, many cloistered in the dark, musty monasteries of the Old World, who wrote fantastical stories about Adam and Eve in the Garden of Eden with a talking snake, Noah and his Ark full of animals, Jonah riding about in the belly in a whale, and Daniel peacefully co-occupying a den with a pride of wild lions.

There were heroic stories of young David slaying a giant with a slingshot and Samson defeating an entire army armed only with a jawbone of an ass. Then there was Moses raining frogs down on the Egyptians, parting the Red Sea and leading his people, hopelessly lost in a desert for 40 years, in search of the Promised Land, with bread occasionally raining down from the heavens.

I remember being fascinated by the pictures in some bibles replicating the Renaissance paintings of Raphael, de Vinci, Michelangelo, Bellini, Titian and others. The depictions of cherubs and angels, devils, and a bearded God staring down from the clouds filled my young mind with wonder. I also remember being fascinated likewise by pictures of dragons and trolls in cousin Dolly's fairy tale books.

The God of the bible was depicted as bearded and white and all the male elders of the bible were similarly depicted because "man was made in the image of God." What of the people of colour, including my people, many of whom are beardless? The biblical image of a huge, black man wielding a sword at the beheading of John the Baptist stubbornly stuck in my mind for many years. The bibles may have since changed their depictions; however, the damage has been done.

Another group of men wrote of a teacher named Jesus Christ, many of the stories some 50 to 150 years after his death. It is not difficult to assume that facts could become somewhat muddled after such a lengthy period had passed before recording his history. It is also not difficult to assume how the stories became more fantastical with each telling before they were finally written down. I can believe there was probably a good man named Jesus who walked this earth preaching love and respect. However, the writings of ancient scribes going so far as to name him the son of God, becomes arrogantly presumptuous and loses me.

This collection of writings compiled into a book called The Bible and forced upon us from a young age, threatened us with eternal damnation in a fiery place called Hell if we dared question its authenticity. Other versions called the Torah and the Koran set off competing religions spawning the many conflicts of this world perpetuated in the name of Allah and God.

This is absurd. In fact, the heavy presence of so much unbelievable absurdity in these so-called holy books points to the well-known argument that god did not make man; man made god.

My Auntie Annie sowed the first seed of doubt about Christianity in my mind when she would angrily relate the story about the refusal of the Catholic Church to bury her father in the church's graveyard. Apparently, he had neglected to carry out his Easter duties of church attendance and participation in the rite of Mass.

My shaky faith was further weakened by the pathetic sights of weeping iconic preachers of the 1970s and '80s, Tammy Faye and Jim Bakker, who were caught pocketing funds blindly donated by their unquestioning congregation. In addition, the hypocritical Jim Bakker was wrapped in a sex scandal.

An even more pathetic sight was Jimmy Swaggart, who preached over a TV network of 3,000 stations and reached millions on a weekly basis, weeping and begging forgiveness for having availed himself of the services of prostitutes.

Oral Roberts, another renowned preacher, had convinced himself after reading verses from the Third Epistle of John in the bible, that it was acceptable to be rich. The only problem was that in striving for his richness, he participated in the quite legal scam of requesting and fleecing millions of dollars in donations from his aptly–named "flock." In late 1987, greed even drove him to announce to his sheep that unless he raised $8 million by March, "God was going to call him home." He was short of his target; however, miraculously he lived, and lived a rich life he did indeed.

My faith was forever and irreparably shaken by accusations of abuse and rape by so called holy "men of the cloth." I had met and befriended Ralph Rowe in Fort Hope, Ontario in the late sixties and early seventies when he was a pilot for the Anglican Church. He was a very likable man who enjoyed working with youth, and in later years, I heard he had become an ordained minister of the church. I was appalled, absolutely stunned and appalled, when a large number of Aboriginal men from northern Ontario, including a nephew, came forth and accused this man of unspeakable abuses involving rape and buggery when they were youth. He is now rightly in prison.

Similar accusations aimed at hundreds of priests of the Roman Catholic Church across Canada and the United States became common. I was further disgusted with the news that the church was complicit in protecting their priests by simply shuffling them off to different parishes where they could continue their abuses.

The Vatican, Jerusalem, and Mecca are huge businesses, generating countless millions of dollars in tourism dubbed as pilgrimages. The Vatican is a wonder of the world with its marbled opulence, much of it built and decorated and financed by gold plundered from the New World in the early 1500s. And yet these religious institutions, some incredibly wealthy, still enjoy tax exempt status wherever they are located.

Throughout the world the Roman Catholic Church is supported by one billion faithful, mainly the poor and the uneducated, especially in places like South America, the Philippines, and Africa. And the Roman Catholic Church is not the only religious institute preying on the poor and uneducated. There are far too many of these institutions on our reserves competing for the souls of our people.

I enjoyed the reading of several philosophers, none more so than the sharp wit of Voltaire and the wisdom of the ancients, Plato and Epicurus. Voltaire, an 18th-century French philosopher, had been a life-long atheist. When he became gravely ill, his Christian friends, fearing for his soul, implored him to renounce the devil. On his deathbed, apparently Voltaire murmured his response, "This is no time to be making enemies."

Epicurus was an ancient Greek philosopher who lived in a period about 300 years before the birth of Christ. He taught that "nothing should be believed except that which is tested through direct observation and logical deduction."

This declaration is best epitomized by his own following quote, which has become well known as the Epicurean Paradox:

"Is God willing to prevent evil, but not able? Then he is not omnipotent. Is he able, but not willing? Then he is malevolent. Is he both able and willing? Then whence cometh evil? Is he neither able nor willing? Then why call him God?"

Man has been able to replicate life through cloning, induce life through in-vitro fertilization of a human egg, and even create artificial life through synthetic DNA in laboratories; however, man has not yet been able to create life in its pure sense. Man knows the ingredients essential for life; we just need to figure out the appropriate process of putting all the ingredients together in the correct order. Is this possible? Who knows?

Nevertheless, I have learned to appreciate life, to wonder at the mystery of creation itself; to even ponder, still, if indeed there is a divinity responsible for life itself. This unanswered question in my mind makes me more an agnostic than an atheist. The existence of God as an absolute good-being and the existence of evil and suffering are contradictory and incompatible. On the other hand, no one, neither philosopher, theologian, nor scientist has been able to present a conclusive argument for or against the existence of God. The question always falls back on the existence of our conscience—that inner voice that expresses your moral values and guides you in determining right from wrong. Can the conscience be a product of evolution? Or was it designed by the hand of a Supreme Being? What I have concluded, without question, is that the God of the Bible, Torah and Koran is not the God I envision or embrace.

I find my solace in the love of friends and family, and I find my own peace in nature. Our planet is a life-giving miracle unto itself. It is all we have. I wonder at the infinite vastness of our universe. I marvel at the spectacular views of mountains, rivers, valleys, storm clouds, rainbows and sunsets. I appreciate the changing seasons of our northern hemisphere, the rainforests of our southern hemispheres, the vastness of our Arctic, the beauty of the Old World, the mysticism of Africa, and the wonderment of the Far East.

I have at times been in such awe of the natural beauty of this world that I have been moved to lay down some tobacco and sweetgrass in homage, out of an old habit instilled in me by our forefathers.

For As Long as The Grass is Green

Chief Samson Beardy was known as an exemplary leader. He is described in the *Keewatin* newspaper which reported his death on April 3, 1964 as "a big man physically, and of outstanding integrity and wisdom. As chief he signed Treaty No. 9 with the Canadian government in 1929. He was known as a first-rate leader, a chief whose rule was firm but just."

Samson was born somewhere around 1880, around the traditional territories of Big Trout Lake, Ontario, and in 1905 he married Nellie Bluecoat from Fort Severn. His children were Ellen, Eleazer, Enos, Rose, Georgina and my mother, Abigail.

In 1929 Chief Samson Beardy, on behalf of his people, entered into an agreement with Canada and signed the Adhesion to Treaty 9 which covered most of the northwest region of Ontario. The bottom had fallen out of the fur market in late 1929, and even though the market would bounce back, Samson realized the times were quickly changing. Gold had been discovered in the Red Lake area in 1926, and by the end of that decade, airplanes and prospectors were common sights in Samson's territory.

The people of Kichinuhmaykoosib Inninuwug never felt the same pressure experienced by the First Nations people of the prairies who had first entered into Treaty 60 years before. The disappearance of the great herds of buffalo, and the pressure of settlers moving onto the prairies had little effect on Samson's people at the time.

Paquetna and Wasakanoochie, traditional leaders in their own right, certainly had no thought ever of compromising the ownership of their territories. However, by 1929, Samson and some of the elders of Kitchinuhmaykoosib Inninuwug felt the pressure of the new age, and decided it was time to do the same.

Samson was an intuitive and far-sighted man. He wanted to ensure his people would be safe from disease and hunger from year to year. The annual four dollars per person, in addition to the other promises of the Treaty, were stingy, but adequate enough on a family basis. The collective amount for the family was sufficient to allow the purchase of such necessities as ammunition, traps, snare wire and a fishing net which would see them through the year.

The Treaty ensured that, in addition to the reserves set out specifically for their use, the people would have full use and access to their traditional lands for the purposes of hunting and trapping and maintaining the right to a livelihood they have always enjoyed.

Canada, the other party to the Treaty, wanted the territory for the purposes of settlement, trade, travel, mining, lumbering, etc.

The year was 1929. The value of the dollar was tied to gold, and gold had remained unchanged at around $20 an ounce for the past 100 years. How were Samson and all the many chiefs across Canada who signed treaties with representatives of the government to understand inflation? And anyway, why should they? Were they not given to understand that the Treaties would be good "for as long as the grass was green and the water runs"?

The Gold Standard, against which our dollar was tied, had been the rule since 1853. It was done away with in 1933. The value of gold began to rise, and currently it sits at about $1,400 per ounce. There was no adjustment to the dollar for this inflation. From $20 to $1,400 since the Treaties were signed, the value of gold had increased seventy fold.

The treaty payments were never adjusted. The $4 of 1929 that once was fair value to our people now barely purchases a loaf of bread. What is fair value today? $4 seventy fold is $280. Does Canada enjoy the fair value today of the territories provided by the Treaty? It can be safely assumed, yes, and much, much more.

Very recently, the personal diary of Daniel MacMartin, who was the Treaty Commissioner for the Province of Ontario when Treaty 9 was first signed in 1905, was discovered by historians at Queen's University archive. The diary, written over 100 years ago in MacMartin's own words, suggests that First Nations "leaders may have been misled by government negotiators as they were signing the Treaty."

Chief Samson Beardy

That is the understatement of the century. Our elders have always known and insisted that what was promised at the Treaty negotiations was not always included in the final documents signed by the chiefs. Those are the broken words and broken promises that our people speak about. In 1960, the former U.S. Supreme Court Justice, Hugo Black stated, "Great nations, like great men, should keep their word."

Canada's federal government has consistently failed its fiduciary obligations to First Nations. I believe Canada has a moral obligation to correct these historical wrongs. Canadians have for far too long been supportively shaking their heads at the grievances perpetuated on the aboriginal populations of this country, most often by our governments, but not doing anything about them.

I love our country. I love our flag. In 2015, the maple leaf flag is 50 years old. It is easily recognizable worldwide. Prime Minister Pearson did well by choosing a flag that does not bear reminders of the early colonialism by the French and English.

In 2008, Platinex, a mining company, was conducting mineral exploration on the traditional territory of my grandfather with no consultation—no permission from the First Nations. They were evicted from the area by the Kitchenumaykoosib Inninuwug (KI) Chief and Council. The company, like so many in a world gone mad, insatiably hell-bent on developing resources for the sole purpose of bolstering corporate share value, sued for access, and the Ontario courts found in favour of the exploration company. Chief Donny Morris and his five councillors refused to back down, the police were called in, and the KI First Nations leaders were jailed for their belief and principle that this land was not open for reckless development.

The province eventually had to resolve the issue on the side of the KI First Nations, and the KI leadership are now taking further steps to strengthen their position on this issue. There will be no further explorations or developments on KI traditional territory.

There can and should be reasonable development based on requirement and the national interest of our country. And most importantly, our Indigenous people need to participate fully in these developments.

In 1930, Samson had allowed the Department of Indian Affairs to take his youngest daughter, Abigail, to Sioux Lookout, Ontario, where she was enrolled in the Pelican Lake Residential School. The ominous four-storey building was located 10 kilometers west of the town of Sioux Lookout. Pelican Lake lay to the north of the property and along the south boundary of the residential school ran the transcontinental CN railway.

The school had been built in 1926 by Indian Affairs, and management agreements made with the Anglican Church to operate the institution. Children ran away from the school and tried to reach home by following the railroad track. Their bodies would be found along the track, in the dead of winter, frozen to death.

Word of these young deaths made their the way back to Big Trout Lake, and Samson, sensing something was wrong, travelled to Sioux Lookout. Confirming the stories, he asserted his authority as chief and took Abigail home with him.

One of the Articles to Treaty 9 that Samson signed states as follows: "Further, His Majesty agrees to pay such salaries of teachers to instruct the children of said Indians, and also to provide such school buildings and educational equipment as may seem advisable to His Majesty's Government of Canada."

Samson assumed a school would be built on his reserve, as promised; however this was not to be for many years yet. Abigail, with a grade one education, went on to self-educate herself with the assistance of her husband—my father—Horace Flett. She learned to read and write, and communicate by letter writing with her children who were boarded with relatives and others in the south for school. Abigail went on to become a respected lay reader and community leader for her church in Cumberland House, Saskatchewan.

The school Samson expected after signing the Treaty in 1929, was finally built long after his death. The Samson Beardy Memorial School was built at Muskrat Dam, Ontario in Samson's honour and memory. Chief Samson Beardy, my grandfather, the last of a long line of hereditary chiefs, died April 3, 1964.

Horace George Flett

Split Lake is a Cree community, today known by its traditional name of Tataskweyak. It is located on the north shore of Split Lake, Manitoba, which is on the boulder-strewn Nelson River system. Down river about 150 miles sits the port of Churchill. It was in Split Lake that my father, Horace Flett, was born on December 30, 1907, the son of a Métis fur trader. He was one of six surviving children born to Alexander and Edith Flett.

The main York boat transportation systems from Hudson Bay during the fur trade period relied on the Hayes River system up from York Factory. By appearance, the Nelson River had held promise as a river transportation route inland because of the large clear mouth. In actuality, the river proved passable for York boats only with Herculean effort. It is an extremely wild river with white-water rapids almost around every bend.

Today, many of these rapids have been harnessed to generate most of the electricity required by the province. There are generating stations at Limestone, Long Spruce, Kettle, and Kelsey with two more under construction at Conawapa and Keeyask.

Horace's father was in charge of the fur trade post in this location for 15 years from 1902 to 1917, almost to the end of the First World War. While in high school in The Pas, I met a young man who was from Split Lake. Remembering that my father had been born there, I asked my friend what Split Lake was like. He said the timber wolves used to come right into the community and attack their sled dogs if they were not driven away by gunfire.

The Mean Aunties

Horace was sent to his aunts in Selkirk, Manitoba once he reached school age. There, the two spinster aunts, Margaret and Elizabeth, better known as Maggie and Liz, lived together in a neat and tidy house their father James had assisted in acquiring for them. They were only too happy at the extra income to be derived from caring for their nephew. The following year he would be joined by Archie and later, by youngest brother Henry.

Horace, my dad, never forgot how lonely and hungry he always seemed to be. The arrival of his brother Archie lessened the feeling of loneliness but not the physical deprivation of hunger. I am not sure of the cause of their hunger. It may have been just the circumstances of the frugal, spinster Aunts or shortages caused by the war, or maybe both. Dad said they were just mean.

Aunts Maggie and Liz kept a few pigs and chickens and tended a large vegetable garden. Dad was forever either in the pigsty or chicken coop shovelling, sweeping and hauling water. When not in the sty or coop he was in the garden hoeing, weeding and hauling water from the well.

One day the aunts were set to baking and the kitchen was bustling with activity. The two women were kneading and punching a batch of dough in a large bread pan, adding more flour or water as needed. Once done the pan of dough was covered with a clean dishtowel and set to one side near the wood kitchen range to rise. The dough never did rise. Aunt Maggie decided the yeast had been defective and ordered dad to carry the dough out to the sty and feed the pigs.

The next morning dad found one of the pigs dead, its stomach bloated from the dough it had eaten. The dough had risen in the warmth of the piggy's tummy. Dad felt bad, however, he was well fed the next few days on pork roast and chops.

One day, on the way home from school, he fell in with a group of boys most of whom were slightly older. They were a boisterous group, laughing and joking and typically rough housing as they made their way down a back street of the village.

They were passing a chicken coop in a backyard when they noticed there was no vehicle or horse and carriage about. The house was quiet and no one appeared to be around so the boys decided to raid the chicken coop for some eggs. Dad, always hungry, joined in.

They squeezed themselves through the fence and into the coop and were busy filling their caps with eggs when a police constable happened by. The constable decided to check the commotion of squawking chickens coming from one of the yards. He spotted the boys and ran into the yard, shouting and hollering and threatening mayhem. The boys promptly took off in all directions, the bigger boys pushing by the smaller ones.

Dad panicked at the sight of the burly policeman and ran, carefully balancing the eggs in his cap at the same time, when he felt a hand roughly nabbing him by the collar. Later he realized he also could have outrun the burly, waddling policemen if only he had been willing to give up his ill-gotten eggs. He was escorted home by the constable, then whipped soundly and sent to bed by mean Aunt Maggie.

One day an uncle, dad could only remember the last name MacDonald, motored into Selkirk in a new Model T Ford. The black Model T, also known as the Tin Lizzy, was the first mass-produced vehicle produced by Henry Ford's innovative assembly lines. It could be purchased new for about $395. It had to be cranked to get the engine running and once the coughing and sputtering of the engine was replaced by a deep-throated hum, the car was ready to be driven. The vehicle could trundle down a gravel road at a top speed of 40 miles per hour, easily outrunning the horse-pulled buggies that were still the most common means of conveyance at the time.

Horace, Archie and Henry were fascinated by the vehicle. They inspected the wheels, the crank sticking out of the engine in front, and peeked in the windows admiring the upholstered interior. Uncle MacDonald told them to jump in—they were going for their first car ride.

Dad beamed and smiled as he related this story and recalled the thrill he felt. I realized this was one of the few joyous memories he had of his youth. Uncle MacDonald took the boys to a local restaurant where they ate so much dad recalled they had to loosen the string on their blousons. The blouson was a shirt-like garment that was tightened at the waist by means of a string.

Apprenticeship in York Factory

August 1, 1925, 17-year-old Horace was hired by the Hudson's Bay Company as an apprentice clerk. He started school late and simply outgrew his fellow students to the point where he told his father he was done. He had finished grade six and was much older and bigger than other kids in his grade. My grandfather Alexander, then, I am sure, used his influence with the company to get him hired at York Factory. Alexander had just finished a six-year stint as manager there and was moving to Big Trout Lake in Ontario.

Horace, in spite of his title of Apprentice Clerk, actually spent his first year looking after his manager's toddler boys and "eating like a horse" (his words) to fill his out his skinny frame. One time he sneaked into the kitchen which was against the manager's rules. No young men were allowed wherever the young ladies were working. It was a slow day and Horace thought he would go and flirt with the young girls who were at work scrubbing and cleaning floors, and preparing the evening meal. He was thoroughly enjoying himself and I guess the young ladies were also enjoying his company because their laughter caught the attention of the manager. The manager decided to go check up on all the commotion.

Horace and the girls heard the heavy footsteps of the manager approaching down the wooden-floored hallway and the girls frantically pointed to a closet which was covered by a curtain. Horace ducked behind the curtain and hid in the dark closet. When the manager reached the kitchen and asked the girls what all the merriment was about, Horace backed away from the curtain to hide deeper within the closet. Backing up, he tripped into a washtub filled with cold, dirty scrub water, falling into it with a tremendous splash. There was an uproar of laughter from the manager and girls when Horace sheepishly came out of hiding dripping wet.

Once old enough and big enough, he was put in charge of the company's team of dogs and, weekly, ran the dog team to Gillam for the mail and supplies. The railway to Churchill was under construction and at that time had been completed only to Gillam. It was approximately a 100 mile trip which Horace could complete in five days, there and back.

Gaining experience, Horace began "tripping" by dog team to Cree trapping encampments carrying sugar, flour, tea and other trade goods in his cariole and returning with furs. Cariole is the term for a canvas-sided toboggan that is pulled by a team of dogs. He carried only the minimum amount of flour and sugar as these were very heavy items and he tried instead loading up on lighter goods he hoped he could trade.

Tripping to encampments became necessary because a competitor had set up in the area trying to cash in on the booming fox business of the 1920s. During this period, silver and cross foxes could bring in small fortunes of up to two or three hundred dollars. When trappers came to the trading post and mentioned that another trapper on so-and-so lake or river had a large harvest of furs, it would set off a race between the dog trippers of the company and the competition.

The cariole was always loaded the night before with trade goods and dog feed and Horace's travel supplies were always at the ready. At daybreak the trippers were usually off on their way to the rumoured trapper with all the fur. At times a tripper would want to get a head start on his competitor and start hitching up before daybreak. The dogs would always get caught up in the excitement of harnessing up for a trip and the barking and yelping would usually wake the competitor.

Horace said he would often sleep with his moccasins on and mostly dressed when an important trip was to be made in the morning. The first tripper to reach the camp was always able to trade for most of the best furs. As somewhat of a consolation prize, the trapper always saved a few skins of lesser value for the slower tripper.

Horace's skinny frame filled out, and he became a lean, wiry man, quick on his feet and able to run or paddle for miles. His physique and stamina would remain unchanged the rest of his long life.

Horace prepared for his dog team trips by cooking up a large crock of home-baked beans with lots of salted pork. He would then pour the beans onto several tin plates and set them outside to freeze. Once frozen he would break the beans into frozen chunks, put them into a cotton bag and throw the bag into his "grub box," a wooden box that held his food and cookware. The bannock he had prepared beforehand was cut into meal-sized pieces and also thrown into a bag and added to the grub box.

On the trail, come mealtime, he set his frying pan onto the blazing campfire and threw in a handful of fresh snow. Once the snow melted then a chunk or two of frozen beans was added, and within a few minutes he had a pan of steaming beans. This he ate with his bannock which he had thawed next to the fire and downed with hot tea made from melted snow in his blackened tea pail.

Horace always made camp well before night fall because there was nothing worse, he said, then unharnessing dogs and tying them down in the dark. The traces and collars which made up the harness were made of leather and he had to be careful, storing them out of reach of the dogs, otherwise they would eat the harnessing. Once the dogs were safely tied down, he would throw a whole frozen fish to each of them.

He carried snowshoes and used one to shovel out a spot where he would bed down for the night. He cut spruce boughs and laid them down thickly for his bed on top of which he would lay his bear rug and then his sleeping bag. Several spruce saplings were then cut and strategically placed to act as a windbreak for his sleeping camp that was set in front of a blazing fire. He had enough wood to last the night.

Come daybreak, as soon as there was enough light he was up and harnessing the team. The dogs were eager to hit the trail and were yelping, barking, jumping and straining at the traces. Horace said there was nothing more exhilarating than striking out with a dog team first thing in the morning when the dogs were fresh and eager.

Bearskin Lake

In 1929, Horace was transferred to Big Trout Lake just as his father, Alexander, was leaving for his next posting in Fort Hope, Ontario. Horace had been promoted to Outpost Manager where he would be responsible for a small trading outpost also often referred to as a "camp trade" and reporting to the manager at Big Trout Lake.

He was posted first to Bearskin Lake, where the building which was supposed to be the outpost was so primitive, he rebuilt it over that winter using nothing more than a bucksaw and an axe to cut and hew the necessary logs. He spent two years there, a few years dog tripping out of Big Trout Lake, and another two at the outpost of Big Beaver House and back to Bearskin Lake in 1939. Under Horace's care, the outpost at Bearskin Lake had developed enough business to become an independent trading post. Horace was promoted and appointed its first store manager later that same year.

As had his father Alexander and grandfather James before him, upon promotion to store manager Horace married. On January 24, 1940, he wed Abigail Beardy, the youngest daughter of Chief Samson Beardy, in Bearskin Lake, Ontario. Marrying the Chief's youngest daughter was a proud and prestigious event for Horace, forever cementing the loyalty of Samson's people to Horace's trade.

Samson had earlier moved his family and several other families to Bearskin Lake as the growing population in Big Trout Lake was starting to exert pressure on the limited wildlife resources of the area. It was also said that a schism was created in the community of Big Trout Lake by Samson signing the treaty with Canada. To ease tensions within the community Samson decided to move his family and supporters to Bearskin Lake.

Once in Bearskin Lake, Samson decided the new community needed a church. He started construction on a small building which would eventually become an Anglican church and Horace took the time to assist the now elderly chief. People pointed the building out to me on my visit in 2001.

It was during this period that Horace fell in love with Samson's daughter. Horace had already impressed and gained the respect of Chief Samson so the blessing was received for Horace to marry the teenaged Abigail. She was fourteen years old when she married Horace who at the time was 32. That summer Abigail, at 14, gave birth to Glen Clarence Henry on August 17th, just nine days before her 15th birthday.

Shamattawa

In 1941, Horace and Abigail with their year-old son were transferred to Shamattawa, Manitoba located on the God's River. It did not take long for them to settle into their new home that summer. And it was not long before they had to make their first excursion to York Factory for some supplies.

Shamattawa lies approximately 50 miles up on the God's River from where it empties into the Hayes. From that juncture it is another 50 miles downstream to York Factory. They were able to cover that distance paddling their canoe in under two-and-a-half days nonstop except for the few portages that were necessary.

They took baby Glen and kept him swaddled in his tikinagan. There was no better place for a curious toddler in a canoe as he was now a year old, crawling and toddling about. Horace knew that territory and its rivers well from his apprenticeship and dog team days in York Factory.

On their first day of travel and by nightfall, Horace knew exactly where they were on the river and that there were no rapids or falls ahead. He put the canoe ashore and chopped down two fairly large and heavily branched spruce trees. These he and Abigail strapped to the sides of the canoe, and once secured, they pushed off into the current once again. They settled down for the night in the canoe and slept, drifting downstream in the dark, the large heavy branches pushing them back into the current whenever they drifted too closely to shore.

The return journey from York Factory was a different story as it was upriver all the way. The first leg of the trip from York Factory on the Hayes River to the confluence of the God's River was the most difficult. Many of the small rapids that Horace and Abigail were able to shoot on their way down were now just too difficult to paddle on the upstream.

Horace had to jump out and track the canoe, pulling on a long tow rope while Abigail with a pole and paddle, steered the craft and kept it moving along through the rapids. Where the size and wildness of the rapids made it necessary, they portaged the canoe and their supplies. It took them almost five days to reach home.

It was around this time that Dad met Tom Lamb. Tom was a pioneer bush pilot in the wilds of northern Manitoba. Born to fur trading parents in Moose Lake, Manitoba near The Pas, in 1900, he grew up speaking the Cree language of the area.

One day Tom flew into Shamattawa, and as the dwindling daylight made the return trip to The Pas impossible, Dad invited Tom to spend the night. Dad had to go to an elders' gathering that evening. He took Tom with him. Together they sat on the floor of the tiny church hall, next to a white-haired, very old First Nations gentleman of the community. Tom grew tired of the speeches and, turning to the old man, pleasantly surprised him and made him laugh loudly by saying in perfect Cree, "I bet you have eaten many rabbits in your lifetime."

Tom Lamb was a man of the north. He went on to build Lambair into one of the largest family-owned airlines anywhere. He had six sons who all became pilots and/or aircraft engineers. The summer of 1956 in Little Duck Lake, I met one of his flying sons, Dennis. I was surprised when he spoke to me in Cree, and he quickly switched to English when he saw I was struggling with the language. I sat with him on our community dock for about an hour or so as he waited for his passenger to complete his business. I was 14 and completely enthralled by his stories of bush flying. I so wanted to become a bush pilot. Lambair was later purchased by Calm Air.

In The Land of Little Sticks

Little Duck Lake is in "The Land of Little Sticks," so called because of the stunted trees that grow in this semi-tundra area which lies on the edge of the barren lands. In 1946, Horace was transferred to Caribou Post, on Little Duck Lake, 140 miles inland northwest of Churchill. He would spend ten memorable years there.

Little Duck Lake is adjoined to Nejanilini Lake by a short but breathtakingly beautiful stretch of the Wolverine River. The Wolverine also flows south to the Seal River which in turn flows east and spills into Hudson Bay just north of Churchill.

The trading post of the Hudson's Bay Company was called Caribou Post because the buildings had been relocated to Little Duck Lake from its original site about 50 miles away. The Company kept the post name.

Little Duck Lake, just 65 miles south of the Nunavut border, is the lonely site of the white buildings with the red roofs typical of the old

Hudson's Bay Company. Its combined store and residence sits along-side a warehouse and powershed on a peninsula of gravelly land. Its only neighbour is the Anglican church building built of small logs.

The powershed was nothing more than a shed which housed a set of sixteen wet-cell batteries. The batteries provided thirty-two volts of electrical power, enough to brighten a light bulb and power a small two-way Morse code radio. Alongside the powershed stood a 15- to 20-foot tower atop which sat a propeller-driven wind charger.

When required, Horace always took advantage of the constant wind to keep his batteries charged and bubbling. The wind had to be just of the right velocity. Too gentle a wind would not drive the pro-pellers to the proper speed required to generate electricity. A fierce gale would likely topple the tower or blow the charger right off the structure. I can remember my father struggling with the ropes which operated the braking system on the wind charger whenever the wind suddenly came up and started blowing with hurricane force.

The late Farley Mowat, a great Canadian author, wrote in his best-selling novel, *People of The Deer*, of finding a group of starving Inuit while he was travelling inland in the area of Nueltin Lake north-west of Churchill around 1947. He swung his dog team south and pro-ceeded to Caribou Post 150 miles away, which would have been his closest point of communication with the outside world.

He writes of the "half-breed" fur trader wiring off Farley's des-perate message for help in Morse code on his antiquated telegraph radio. After the message was sent off, Farley Mowat arranged for a toboggan load of emergency supplies that he would take back to the starving camp of Inuit.

The fur trader had been given the mailing address for a govern-ment department in Ottawa and Mr. Mowat affixed his signature to the invoice that the trader had written out in detail. The half-breed fur trader, of course, was my father Horace. Dad said the invoice came back because the purchase was unauthorized. He had thought that Farley was a representative of the government as he had certainly acted as if he were one.

"That bugger still owes me $229.65!" is all that Dad ever had to say about Farley Mowat. The book mentions another half-breed trapper that made the dog team trip to Little Duck Lake, however, Dad insists it was Farley himself.

Horace was now in Dene country, the traditional land of the Sayisi Dene. His family consisted of me, Jim, Frank and Linda and of course our mother, Abigail. The people were of the Chipewyan tribe and as Horace was not familiar with the language, he was provided with an assistant who also acted as translator.

Pat Hislop was a versatile man, fluent in Cree, his mother tongue, and Chipewyan. He also had a working knowledge of English. However, Horace was fluent in Cree so that was the language in which the two men conversed. Horace depended upon him greatly that first season. Not only was there the issue of a strange language, but Horace also lacked the rudimentary skills of coping with life on the edge of the barrens.

First thing that fall, they had to lay up a supply of wood for fuel. They travelled by canoe down the Wolverine River and from the wood stands they found scattered along the river, they cut their supply of wood. Some of the wood was brought back to the trading post with their canoe which was propelled by a two-and-one-half horsepower Firestone outboard motor.

It was rather a primitive two-stroke engine with the gas tank built into the top part of the motor. The motor was started by wrapping a cord around the flywheel on top the engine and then yanking to spin the flywheel until the ignition caught. Once running, the operator had to ensure he kept his hand off the open spinning flywheel.

Most of the wood was piled standing up in the form of a teepee to be brought back to the trading post by sled in the winter. The company had a large wooden sled and three dogs used mainly for hauling wood and water in winter.

They also came in handy for the occasional hunting trip to replenish the caribou meat stock for the dogs and family. However, that meant dog feed also had to be stocked. Horace and Pat set a fish net

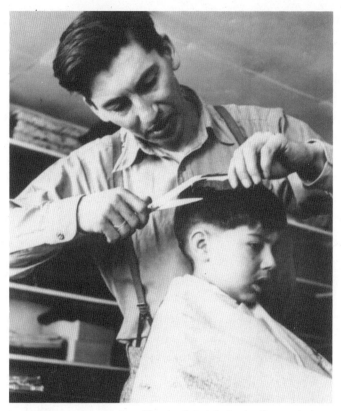

Len's father, Horace Flett, cutting Len's hair in the trading post at
Caribou Post, Manitoba. PHOTO FROM HBC ARCHIVES.

as there was a plentiful supply of suckers and white fish in the lake.
They did their fishing late in the fall when the air was freshly cool
and crisp. The fish would be put up in sticks of ten. A stick would be
passed through the gills of ten fish and together they would be hung
in a shed to freeze.

Horace hauled the wood back to the post in winter in a very unique
manner. In the barren lands, the cold constant north winds packs the
upper layers of snow into a hard cement-like surface. Snowshoes are not
required unless a lot of time is to be spent in the tree stand areas at the
southern edge of the barrens where the caribou cows have their calves.

With the right wind conditions, Horace would hitch up his dogs
and drive to his wood stands. There he would pile his sled up with the

wood poles and tightly lash his load down. He would then set up his canvas sail and literally sail his sled home with his dogs guiding and pulling the load as required. In the dead of winter the barren lands can look like a snowy version of the Sahara Desert. Dad always took extra care in knowing his exact whereabouts at all times.

When the sun or the stars were not visible, Horace, like the Dene and Inuit, had learned to identify the general direction of north from the frozen riffles in the snow caused by the prevailing north winds. He would occasionally stop his sled, take his ax and chop down through the snow. When he hit ice he confirmed he was on Little Duck Lake. He then followed the contour of the territory until he spotted the buildings of the trading post in the distance.

The caribou were on their last migration of the season, just ahead of the snows, which were now starting to fall more frequently. The excitement of the fall hunt to be conducted by the Dene would be palpable in the air. They needed to stock up on a substantial supply of caribou meat to see them through the unforgiving winter. Canoes were hidden at the ready. Harpoons were sharpened and the shafts checked for durability. Rifles were cleaned and ammunition counted. Small herds were now evident almost every day; however, the villagers continued to wait for the main herd before launching their canoes.

Finally two young Dene men who had been camped several miles north on a high gravelly esker keeping watch for the main herd came running back to the village. The great herd was on its way.

The geography of the land with its eskers of sand and gravel that ran mainly north and south and parallel to Nejanilini Lake and the Wolverine River suddenly narrowed toward Little Duck Lake. This acted as a natural funnel for the massive caribou herds that were unstoppable as the moving mass behind would force the forward animals into the water.

Little Duck Lake was the natural crossing point for the herds and the Dene took full advantage of this unique location to stockpile their food source. As the caribou swam the lake, the Dene hunters launched their canoes. One man or woman paddled and steered the craft through the swimming swarm while the hunter picked his targets and deftly harpooned one caribou after another.

The killing stopped only when most of the herd had reached the opposite shore and scrambled to safety. Hundreds of caribou were to be seen floating lifelessly in the cold water, the draining blood from the carcasses staining the bay a deep red. The hollow hair of the caribou fur, an excellent natural insulating material, kept the dead animals afloat for a short period of time. Once the carcass itself started taking in water through its mouth and wounds, the animal would slowly slip under the surface of the water. The Dene now quickly set to work hauling the dead animals to shore, lassoing the floating caribou by the antlers, tying to the canoe, and then laboriously paddling beast and craft to shore. On shore it appeared the entire village was at work, hauling the best and fattest of the kill onto shore, then skinning and butchering what was immediately required.

The bones containing the fatty marrow were cracked and the marrow carefully removed. Some of the more choice carcasses were slit along the stomachs and gutted, removing hearts, kidneys and livers.The cleaned carcasses to be later butchered for the meat were then submerged in the frigidly cold water by large rocks placed in the stomach cavities. They would be removed from the water before the lake froze over.

All the animals were slit under the chin areas and the tongues removed. The marrow and tongues were not only delicious, they were the main source of fat that the Dene required for their diet. The rest of the carcasses were then left on the shore to freeze and be covered by drifting snow. Should the hunts become difficult when they were out on their traditional wintering grounds, the people would always have this source of meat to fall back on.

Horace and Pat did not participate in the harpooning of the caribou. This appeared to be strictly the domain of the Sayisi Dene who had been practising this method of harvesting their caribou from time immemorial. Dad and Pat instead trekked out onto the land and shot the caribou they required for themselves and their dogs. They would shoot up to 50 caribou and gut and clean the carcasses, leaving the guts for the wolves and foxes. They would then cache the caribou carcasses under piles of rock, out of reach of marauding Arctic wolves.

After each day of hunting they would cut the hindquarters from one of the animals to carry home. At the post that summer, Dad had hired a number of Dene men to dig a large underground cellar about ten feet by ten feet and about six feet high. It was dug right into the permafrost and accessible only by a trapdoor and ladder. The frosted walls and ceiling were supported by beams and poles and in this freezing cellar, Horace and Pat hung carcasses of caribou. The cellar was cold enough to keep the hanging meat frozen right through the hot summer months.

Abigail was also keeping busy during this period. Blueberries and cloudberries grow abundantly in the taiga, semi-tundra geographical area. In August she could go for a walk and return with a pail full of berries in each hand within an hour. She would find a good picking spot and then just start pulling handfuls of blueberries off the bushes. She loved canning and she put up numerous jars of blueberries and cloudberries. Cloudberries are close relatives of raspberries except that they are orange in colour and more succulent.

Mom also canned caribou meat diced into mouth-sized pieces that, once canned, we found most tender and delicious. She also canned caribou tongues and this had to be the ultimate in tundra cuisine. In addition to the cooking, Abigail busied herself sewing caribou hide clothing for her children. She had the assistance of several Dene women who were only too pleased to show Abigail how to prepare, cut and sew caribou hides.

As children, we wore caribou hide parks and pants with the hair out. For added warmth, sometime in extremely cold weather, we also wore caribou vests with the hair in. The Inuit of old wore two suits of caribou clothing. The inner suit was worn with the hair in against the skin. The outer suit was worn with the hair out. Nothing else was needed as this was the most comfortable, efficient and lightweight attire required for the harsh unforgiving Arctic conditions.

The parkas that Mom made for us had the sleeve opening sewn shut so we had no need for mittens. This eliminated the possibility of us losing mittens and freezing our hands in the minus fifty weather that we played in. It was a little frustrating at times trying to pick things up using only our arms, but we got by. The constant wind at Duck Lake piled up huge drifts around our buildings that we used for sliding. We didn't need sleds. We would just take a short run then flop ourselves down on our tummies and slide about like penguins in our caribou hide clothing.

Once I turned seven, Mom fixed my caribou hide parka with open sleeves so that I could wear mittens. This was important as I needed to be able to hold, aim and shoot at the snowbirds I hunted around the post with the slingshot that Dad had made for me. One day a small flock of snowbirds flew down before me and alit behind some willow brush. I sneaked up to the willows, blindly aimed over the brush and fired my slingshot.

Len Flett—far left—with his siblings dressed in caribou hide clothing made by their mother at Caribou Post.

The tiny flock flew off and when I poked around where the flock had been pecking at some seeds, I found a dead snowbird laying on its back, tiny black feet sticking up into the air. My first kill! Excitedly, I picked up the dead bird and ran home as fast as my little legs would carry me, all the while yelling, "Mom! Mom!" I ran into the house and showed my mother the dead bird and she beamed with pride and gave me a big hug. It was years later that, with laughter, she told me the bird was frozen stiff and had been dead for months.

Once the dead of winter set in, we barely saw the sun. It would simply peek over the horizon and set again around midday leaving us in a perpetual state of semi-darkness. The winds were always vicious and if fresh snow was falling the result was often a "white-out."

The wind would pick up the snow and whip it about so that you could not see beyond your nose. Dad had cords running from his back door: one to the outdoor toilet, one to the woodpile, one to his power shed, and a fourth line to his warehouse. Following the cords back to the house during a "white-out" ensured he did not wander out onto the tundra wilderness by mistake.

Around the woodpile there was a stand of willow brush. Dad strung a fishing net amongst the willows and every so often he would "fish" out the odd ptarmigan that got caught up in the netting. The ptarmigan was always a welcome change to our steady diet of caribou. Ptarmigan is a beautiful white feathered game bird, the Arctic version of the common grouse.

During the winter small herds of male caribou, numbering anywhere from six to a hundred would often wander by. Normally they travelled about in groups of ten to twenty. The larger groups seemed to be less fearful of man as they would often pass right by our house. We boys naturally would get all excited and want to go out and chase them around; however, our mother would have none of that. They are, after all, wild animals and if for any reason they began to stampede there was no stopping them.

One day Dad and Pat spotted a small herd of caribou approaching from over an esker. They donned their parkas and grabbed their rifles intending to shoot a few caribou to freshen their supply of meat. They scooted, in a bent-over run, to a nearby ridge and then lay in wait for the herd to come by. As the lead caribou passed by the ridge, Dad and Pat noticed that the herd every so often would stop and peer back over their haunches. After a moment, satisfying their curiosity, the herd would continue moving on.

Puzzled, Dad and Pat craned their necks to peer over the ridge to see what was bothering the herd. There was my sister, Linda, barely three years and fully dressed in her caribou hide parka and pants, running behind the herd as fast as her little legs could carry her. The men put their rifles down and remained hidden so as not to spook the herd. They waited until the caribou had put a safe distance between themselves and the pursuing toddler before running out to bring my sister back to safety. Frank, Jim and I were playing behind one of the warehouses, oblivious to the fact that our sister had wandered away.

A memorable character from that area of the far north was a white Norwegian trapper named Ragnar Jonsson. He trapped an area around Nueltin Lake which straddles the Manitoba and Nunavut border. His range had to cover several hundred square miles.

Ragnar, from what I was given to understand, first entered the area as a young man. He lived and trapped there his entire life with a brief sojourn in the tiny community of Brochet. He had retired to Thompson; however, around 1980, there he was in a newspaper photograph loading supplies and his team of dogs into an aircraft bound for, once again and probably for the last time, Nueltin Lake. He had to be around 80 years old. He is now buried in the quietude and beauty of the land that he so loved.

I remember him from Caribou Post because Dad often invited him into the house for tea or coffee. Ragnar was a short, stocky man, clean shaven and always with a ready smile. His uniform, it seemed, was a heavy red woolen shirt, black woolen pants held up with a wide dark green pair of suspenders, the type that were fastened on to the pants by buttons.

I saw him a number of times and viewed many pictures of him. Never had I ever seen him bewhiskered. Every other white trapper, prospector, or trekker who have been in the barrens for any length of time simply stopped using razors.

Ragnar put at least five or six teaspoons of sugar into his tea or coffee. As a young impressionable boy my eyes never failed to openly stare at him in awe as he piled his sugar into his tea or coffee. I would turn to look at my mother as she always yelled at me if I tried to sneak a second spoonful of sugar onto my porridge. But Ragnar got away with that. And he always smelled of his dogs.

Ragnar loved his dogs. He was one of the very few dog mushers I met who treated his dogs as pets instead of work animals. He had names for every one of his dogs that he himself had taken great care in breeding and raising. He favoured the name "Tootsie" as two or three of his dogs would bear the same name at the same time. They were huge and the malamute breed in them was evident.

There was also good reason for Ragnar smelling of his dogs. They were like family to him, and like a good family they lived, ate and slept together. Ragnar gave a young dog to Dad. To be given a dog by Ragnar was a great honour because for him to part with one of his dogs was like putting up a child for adoption. We named the dog Rags. He fitted easily into Dad's team along with an all white Siberian called Polar and a mutt named Sabotchee.

Sabotchee was an on-the-moment made-up name that our late brother Glen had given one of his puppies. In Shamattawa, when Glen was about three or four years of age, he had walked into Dad's trading post hugging a puppy to his chest, his arms wrapped around the pup's torso under its front legs. The pup's lower torso and hind legs dangled from Glen's arms.

"What is your puppy's name?" asked one of the Cree trappers who was waiting to be served.

"I don't know. Sabotchee, I guess." Glen said.

Since then, it was in Glen's memory that Dad named every mutt he owned "Sabotchee."

One stormy, blustery winter day we were in our kitchen when we heard dogs yelping and barking and someone hollering "Whoa, whoa, whoa!" We ran and looked out the window and there was Ragnar with his parka front unzipped and flying out behind him like a cape as he circled the house two or three times trying to get his excited dog team under control. He was finally able to bring his team to a halt. We are not too sure why he always seemed to lose control of his dog team around the trading post but we think the dogs probably caught the scent of the caribou carcasses that Dad had hanging in his permafrosted cellar.

Horace opened the trading post for Ragnar and within a few minutes Dad was back in the house (the store remained unheated unless trappers came in with loads of fur) and Ragnar was off once again in the blizzard. He was camped at one of his winter shelters an hour or so away. He was making the round of his trapline and he needed a few supplies.

Dog mushing in Duck Lake had its particular drawbacks because dog teams espying or catching the scent of caribou always presented a serious problem for their handlers. A runaway dog team in the barrens could very well result in death for the handler so great care was always taken when travelling. Some mushers utilized a caribou antler hinged onto the back of their sleds. When a team of dogs became excited and would not stop to yelled commands, the driver would simply slip his foot under the antler brakes and flip the antler over. The musher would then jump on and apply his entire weight on the antler, sinking the antler's many tines into the snow. The sled would slowly grind to a stop, in spite of the dogs jumping and straining at their harnesses.

Another method of braking an unruly dog team, and this always elicited laughter from the Dene hunters, would be to run a rope from the back of the sled to the harness of the wheel dog, and then through the harnessing of all the dogs right up to the leader. When the team started bolting after caribou, the driver would reach down, grab the rope and with one mighty tug, trip his lead dog and the team following would end up in an entangled ball. It was a home-fashioned emergency brake. Of course, it would then take the driver about an hour to untangle this mess of dogs, sled and harnessing. Crude, funny, but effective!

Ragnar Jonnson and Horace Flett at Caribou Post. PHOTO FROM HBC ARCHIVES

The Dene loved telling stories. When a group came in together to the post to trade, Pat would do the meet and greet and pass out some tobacco while Horace fired up the 45-gallon drum that served as the heater for the store. In about thirty minutes the tin stovepipes that guided the smoke up and out of the building were red hot and the trappers were now backing away from the heat emanating from the drum.

Parkas were now coming off and serving as cushions on the floor or on a serving counter that separated the customers from the merchandise. The trappers quietly puffed on their pipes while Horace measured each pelt, stroked the fur, and carefully examined for any damages or defects. He would then make a notation on a pad he kept on his work table. Once done with a trapper's catch, Horace would quote the price he was willing to pay, and then wait for the trapper's reaction. Usually there would be a quiet discussion and Horace would quote another, usually higher, price. A smile would break out on the trapper's face or there would be a stoic positive nod of the head.

Horace would then post a credit to the trapper's account and Pat would take over to provide the trapper with whatever he required in the form of trade goods while Horace dealt with the next trapper and his furs. Once all the fur-buying and shopping was completed, Horace would pass around more tobacco and pull out his own pipe or deftly roll a cigarette and join the trappers in sharing a smoke and a story or two.

One of the Dene trappers related how he had come upon a herd of caribou while out with his dog team checking the traps on his line. Of course his team had taken off in chase at the first scent of the caribou and it was some time and with great difficulty that he managed to get his dogs and sled under control. Standing on his antler brake, he reached into his sled and pulled out his rifle as the small herd was still well within his range. He decided to bring back a freshly killed caribou.

His excited dogs were jumping and straining at their traces. When the herd stopped momentarily to peer back curiously at them, as they are often wont to do, he took the opportunity to fire a shot at a buck he had picked out of the herd. At the exact moment he pulled the trigger, his lead dog chose that inopportune moment to leap excitedly into the air resulting in it taking a bullet to the back of the head.

Dad and Pat first expressed shock at the loss of the dog, then chuckled along with the storyteller who was laughing at his own misfortune. The group of men, all experienced dog drivers, understood the importance of the lead dog to a team and could only imagine the problems the storyteller had trying to get home with his leaderless team.

Horace's first encounter with the Inuit took place that winter at Little Duck Lake. Two young Inuit men making their way to Churchill pulled into the trading post with their dog team. They spoke only Inuktitut but Dad recognized two words. They pointed to the northwest from whence they came and said "Padlei," and then they pointed to the southeast, the direction they were travelling, and said, "Churchill."

They had a few white fox pelts with them to trade but certainly not enough to provide them with the provisions they would require for the rest of their journey. Dad provided them ammunition for their rifle, tea, pilot biscuits, rolled oats and sugar. He then went down into his permafrost cellar and provided them with a carcass of caribou that they would need for themselves and their dogs.

Dad had been sawing wood when they arrived, so out of gratitude they offered to saw the wood for him. They picked up the bucksaw and to their great amusement tried to emulate what Horace had been doing when they arrived. Let us not forget there are no trees in the Arctic, thus little need for bucksaws. Dad gave them instructions on how to handle the saw with a man on either end and soon they were sawing like professional lumberjacks.

Horace then decided he should feed his guests. He had always heard that the Inuit ate raw meat so out of curiosity he served up two plates of raw and bloody caribou steaks. The young Inuit men laughed at him and pointed to the stove. They preferred their meat cooked—and well done at that.

Sometime later Horace watched the men as they were feeding their dogs with the frozen caribou he had given them. Using axes they were chopping up small pieces and throwing them to their dogs. Every once in a while they would chip off a sliver of frozen meat and pop it into their mouths. Yes, raw meat when frozen is much easier to eat than chewing on a rubbery piece of fully thawed meat.

Padlei was the location of a small Hudson's Bay Company trading post south of Eskimo Point in what was then the North West Territories but now Nunavut. The manager was a part-Inuit gentleman named Henry Voisey who was full of stories about Farley Mowat. Mowat had spent the better part of a winter living with him when he was researching and writing his *People of the Deer* novel. The renowned Arctic photographer Richard Harrington also spent several months with Henry, shooting photographs for his coffee table book *Padlei Diary 1950*.

Mail day skeds (scheduled flights) were special and exciting days at Caribou Post. Once a month, Arctic Wings' bush pilots Charlie Webber or Gunnar Ingerbritson would come flying in from Churchill in their antiquated Anson or powerful Norseman aircraft delivering a bag of mail and a case of beer. They always stayed for dinner and stayed up late into the evening drinking beer and telling stories. I was in complete awe of these men and their flying machines.

I absolutely had my mind made up that when I grew up, I too was going to be a bush pilot. Later, when I was going to grade school in Powerview, I read with great pride about Gunnar Ingerbritson and his heroic exploits rescuing stranded travellers from icefloes. Unfortunately, some time later I also read about his untimely death as a result of a plane crash.

That same winter I witnessed a wondrous event. Tractor trains! The United States Armed Forces had a strong presence in Churchill during and after the Second World War. One winter they experimented with tractor transportation in Arctic conditions and departed Churchill with a train of tractors and various equipment destined for Nueltin Lake.

They arrived at Little Duck Lake with great fanfare late in the afternoon or early evening as I remember it was getting quite dark. The lead tractor shot flares into the air. It had to be a signal for the tractor drivers to stop because the entire train ground to a halt. The train appeared to be a mile long through my eyes; however, I was an impressionable six years old at the time. Soldiers in full winter gear milled about with lamps and flashlights checking their equipment and shouting instructions to each other.

Dad took me, Frank and Jim down to the lake where the train had parked within walking distance of our trading post. I recall the hum of the many engines and the smell of gasoline and diesel in the air. The commanding officer invited us into one of their cabooses that doubled as sleeping quarters and eating area. The cook was preparing the evening meal for the officers and we were invited to sit and have a bite to eat. It was my first taste of beef steak. Delicious!

Over the ten years that my parents spent at Caribou Post in Little Duck Lake my mother made a lot of money sewing gloves and jackets. These she sold to the members of the U.S. Armed Forces for their wives. Abigail had learned from the Dene women, Nancy French in particular, how to process caribou hide into a soft white leather. Most hides were processed by smoking which produced a soft brown leather permeated with a smoky odour.

This tanned leather Mom used for men's and boys' mitts and parkas, but it was the white leather gloves and jackets for women that was in demand and commanded such an attractive price. She adorned the white ladies' gloves and hip-length ladies' jackets or coats of soft white caribou leather with intricately beaded designs. Once a month on their mail runs, the bush pilots of Arctic Wings, Charlie Webber and Gunnar Ingerbritson would bring in envelopes of cash with written orders for gloves and jackets and on their return flights deliver boxes of the finished goods.

Horace kept his dogs tethered within sight but some distance away from the house as at night they often sat on their haunches and bayed at the moon or howled in answer to the distant call of Arctic wolves. Dad often chopped large pieces of frozen caribou that he would throw to the dogs for feed. When the dogs had eaten their fill, they would jealously guard the remainder of their meat.

One day Horace's attention was caught by the snarling and growling of his dogs. He looked about and noticed four snowy white Arctic wolves warily approaching in the direction of his dogs, probably attracted by the scent of the feed caribou. Dad ran into the house for his rifle and then quietly started creeping in the general direction of his tethered dogs.

As he neared his dogs, Horace poked his head up searching for the wolves. They had disappeared, or so he thought, until he was able to just barely make out the shape of four shadowy figures laying in wait, hidden in the backdrop of the snowdrifts. They had covered their dark noses with their white furry paws folded over their faces, making it almost impossible for Horace to spot them.

Dad stayed frozen on all fours while he sized up the situation that he suddenly found himself in. The hunter had become the hunted! He became unnerved, jumped up and fired a shot. The wolves scampered off unharmed.

The darkness of winter was now slowly being pushed back by the ever increasing boldness of the sun. The sun rose higher and higher each day, quickly melting the snow and ice of the tundra.

Finally around the date of the spring equinox, the sun would just barely set, sometime after midnight. And by two or three in morning it would begin its daily rise in the sky. The interim between the setting and rising of the sun was so short that the sky never really darkened. It was more like evening or dawn—not dark, and yet not fully light.

This was the signal for the people to leave their winter lodges and make their way back to their traditional summer home: Little Duck Lake. Almost overnight, it seemed, the lonely trading post became a neighbour to a village of tents set up in the vicinity of the rustic Anglican church.

There, the Reverend Sandy Clippings, with his blustery booming voice, was the unproclaimed leader of the Sayisi Dene band of First Nations people. His son Jimmy was one of my childhood friends, and Mom took us to church every Sunday when Reverend Clippings was in the community.

I can remember being frightened and intimidated by the Reverend and his loud voice when he became animated and passionate during the delivery of one of his sermons. He preached in the Dene Chipewyan language, which I no longer understood. His body language, however, unmistakably conveyed his displeasure.

During these sermons, the Reverend would glare wild-eyed at his tiny congregation, and his face would darken and become contorted with anger. In a rage he would pound his fist on his pulpit.

The Sayisi Dene band was at that period in an odd transition; from a timeless age of tradition, with spiritual beliefs rooted in animism, yet moving into a new period of Christianity precipitated by the arrival of missionaries and the construction of the first church in the area. Those missionaries coached and taught Sandy Clippings and, upon his ordination to the ministry, they left the community.

The Reverend Sandy Clippings was a self-important man, and he often chastised Horace whenever and wherever he found reason to do so. Over the years he and Dad had an on-going tiff, minor in nature, but still an irritation to both men. They simply did not like each other.

But one spring day, an opportunity for a little payback presented itself when the Reverend Clippings came in from his winter trapping grounds with a toothache. He went straight to the trading post and requested Horace pull the troublesome tooth.

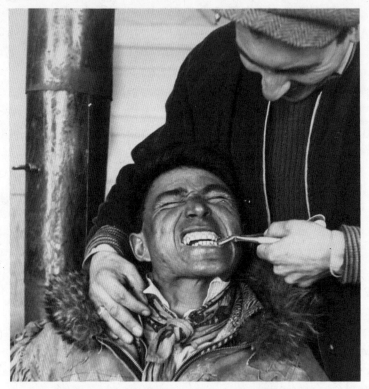

The Reverend Sandy Clippings having a tooth extracted by Horace Flett at Caribou Post. PHOTO FROM HBC ARCHIVES.

In those days, the Hudson's Bay Company provided a medicine chest at all its trading posts that included a basic supply of various medicines and drugs. It also contained equipment such as scalpels, sutures, and bandages. The small dental section provided toothache drops made of oil of cloves and a selection of extraction forceps. A large medical reference manual was included for the do-it-yourself practitioner. There were no anesthetics.

Horace sat Reverend Clippings in a chair in the middle of the trading post floor, with a number of Dene trappers looking on with immense interest. Horace looked at the various implements in the medicine chest, and, like a dueler choosing his weapon, he selected the heaviest, sturdiest and most intimidating set of extractors.

"Okay, open wide—here we go," he said.

"EEYYAAHH!!" cried the Reverend.

Horace struggled to keep a straight face as he unnecessarily gave the forceps an extra little twist.

"EEEYYYAAAHHH!!!"

Out popped the tooth. Horace gave Reverend Clippings a wad of gauze to stick in his mouth to stanch the flow of blood.

The Reverend, a large and obviously very tough man, slowly rose from the chair. He looked Horace straight in the eye, extended his hand, and after a handshake quietly left.

The Reverend treated Horace quite civilly thereafter.

That spring, as the people gathered after a long winter of solitude, friendships were renewed, gifts exchanged, and feasts prepared. The warm summer evenings heralded the start of drumming, singing, dancing and feasting. The hand drums of taut caribou rawhide would be warmed by the bonfires and their resonance tested by gentle tappings with their sticks.

Once satisfied with the tone of his drum, the lead singer would begin his song, soon to be joined by anywhere from six to 12 other drummers and singers. Mom and Dad would join the celebration after they had put us to bed in the care of a young babysitter named Deoshazzie.

As the village of tents and site of the drumming and dancing was only a short walk from the trading post, the throbbing beat of the drums resonated through our bedroom. To this day, the sound and beat of Dene drums stirs my heart and jogs my memory of Little Duck Lake and its people.

One of the dances involved the men dancing in a group and when two men came together dancing face to face they exchanged gifts which they carried in their pockets, usually leather pouches of tobacco, or articles of clothing that they were wearing.

The men all wore brightly coloured handkerchiefs around their necks and these were the first to be exchanged. Jackets were next and when the men started stripping their shirts and exchanging without skipping a beat in their dance, the women howled with laughter.

Dad always left the house for these dances dressed in his best attire, which made him a very popular dancing partner indeed. Often he would be set up by the dancing group with a male partner dressed in apparel that had seen better days, to the great amusement of everyone. We kids would laugh with glee at the sight of Dad in his strange clothes on his return home.

On a number of occasions, I and my siblings would become confused by the early sunrises. We would get up, get dressed and start making our way for the door when our mother or father awakened. They would look at the alarm clock ticking away by the bedside and notice that it was only three or four o'clock in the morning. They would then have to get up to chase us back to bed.

During the day, usually late afternoons, Dene hand-games would break out, either in the village of tents or most often, in front of our trading post. Two groups of men sat on the ground, each group facing the other. Each group consisted of the game players, sitting on their knees with their legs tucked under them, facing the opposing game players. Behind them were the drummers, sitting, kneeling, or standing.

The game players would pass a stick between them, but hidden under blankets or jackets that covered the men's laps. The drummers would pound their drums and chant their songs while the players would bounce and occasionally whoop to the beat and exuberantly pass the stick between them covertly.

The drumming and chanting would stop on cue from an opposing player, who would now guess who held the stick. If he was correct, the player would claim the stick. If he guessed incorrectly, he had to give up one of his sticks.

At the end of the game, the sticks were tallied and money or property exchanged between the players. The Dene loved gambling and a considerable amount of property, including rifles, ammunition, traps, dogs, sleds, and canoes, would often change hands. Not to worry. There would be other games tomorrow or the next day and a chance to win it all back.

5

LEONARD GEORGE FLETT

FIRST DAY OF SCHOOL

My first day of school in a strange town where the people spoke a strange language was not so much traumatizing as it was puzzling.

The teachers were Roman Catholic nuns. I had never seen or even heard of nuns, so I had no idea who these women were, or why they were dressed like crows and magpies. Sister Amy was my first teacher.

I was bilingual; fluent in both Cree and Chipewyan. Powerview, where I was to live for the next seven years, was also bilingual, but in French and English. Powerview sits in southern Manitoba be-tween Pine Falls, an English-speaking community, and St. George, a French community. A few miles north of Pine Falls lies Fort Alexander, now called Sagkeeng First Nations, an Anishinabe (Ojibwe) -speak-ing community.

That summer of 1949, Mom and Dad were due a vacation and it was also time for me to begin school. A young relief manager, Pete Clark, flew in with Arctic Wings and the return flight to Churchill carried our family. From Churchill we took the CN train to Winnipeg thence to Pine Falls.

My first memory of Winnipeg is not the huge buildings or the clogging traffic of automobiles but of the pigeons and sparrows that hopped about on the sidewalk not more than four or five feet away. To boys that had been raised hunting birds with slingshots, this was just too much. Frank and I were frantic with excitement as we scrambled around on the sidewalk looking for stones to throw at the birds. From Winnipeg we took a train to Pine Falls. The train was loaded with picnickers and vacationers bound for Grand Beach. Frank, Jim and I would stand on the platformed vestibules between the railway cars and as the train wound its way around bends, the chugging locomotive, belching black and grey smoke, would come into view. We would stick our heads out for better views and our faces would be peppered and become blackened by the grime and cinder dust spewed out by the coal-fueled engine.

At Pine Falls, we piled into a taxi and motored out to Flett's Corner to spend the summer with my grandfather Alexander.

Arrangements were then made to leave me with my Uncle Archie and Auntie Annie for my schooling years. At the end of that summer I would stand at the Pine Falls train station with Auntie Annie and wave goodbye to my parents and siblings: Jim, Frank, Linda, and baby Don. I would not see my family again for three years.

It was 1949. I was seven years old and would turn eight in February. On my first day of school, I looked down at my five- and six-year-old classmates with some disdain because I was older and bigger than they were. They returned looks of scorn because they thought I was mentally challenged, since I couldn't speak or understand French or English. By ten-thirty that morning, I had had enough, and as soon as we were let out of class for recess I went home.

I was greeted at home by Uncle Archie, who remembered enough of the Cree language to be able to ask what I was doing home so early. I advised him in Cree that I had given school a try, and that it was something that I was no longer interested in pursuing. Therefore I decided I would just stay home and play, or maybe go hunting birds with my slingshot (or words to that effect).

"Kee chisk!" (your ass!) muttered Uncle Archie as he took me by the hand and marched me right back to the school that I had just left. He accompanied me back to the grade one classroom and rapped on the door. Uncle spoke to the teacher in English, the students twittered in amusement, and next I knew I found myself sitting at my desk absentmindedly singing the alphabet song along with the class: "AB CD EFG ..."

My cousin Edie was the same age I was; however, she was in grade two. She took full charge of me. She loved playing school and of course she was "teacher." I was the ideal student because I knew nothing and she knew everything. I gradually came to realize that not only was I spending full days in school five days a week, I was also stuck with Edie's schooling on evenings and weekends. However, my learning experience was greatly accelerated, and I quickly learned English and adapted to my new way of life.

The name of our school was, ironically, Leonard School. A few Aboriginal kids that overflowed the Fort Alexander Residential school in Sagkeeng were bussed to Leonard School. Phil Fontaine, a former Grand Chief of the Assembly of First Nations, was two grades behind me.

I loved my Auntie Annie. She had only one eye. She wore a pair of glasses with one of the lens frosted so you could not see the empty socket where her eye should be. She told me how she had lost her eye on a fishing trip. My knees weaken whenever I think of that fish hook.

Auntie Annie was very popular. She was fun, witty, and always the life of the party. She had a wide circle of friends and she spoke both French and English. She was a wonderful dancer and she loved to dance. She gave me my first dance lesson that New Year's Eve when she hosted a small family party at her house.

Auntie Annie had a ready laugh and I loved making her laugh. My learning the English language was always a source of comedy. Auntie and I were almost a comedy pair, as whenever company was present, she would ask of me, "Leonard, say something sweet."

I would answer in my affected Cree accent, "Syrup!" and that made everyone laugh. I only had a literal understanding of English then, therefore I did not understand what was so funny. But because it made people laugh, I always answered the same way.

One other time that first year as I struggled with my English, my older cousins, Clarence and Bruce took me to the movie theatre in Pine Falls to see a Bob Hope movie. The movie featured an old song called "Baby, It's Cold Outside" and I guess the song and words stuck in my head because one wintry day I walked into the house to be met by Auntie Annie and my comment to her, "Baby, it's cold outside," was met with a burst of laughter.

The Pine Falls movie theatre was my first experience with the fact that somehow I was different because of my colour. I had some taunts and name calling thrown at me by kids at school, but there was enough diversification that I did not feel singled out. The kids in Leonard School came in all shades, many were Métis and some First Nations. The white kids were either French or English. All kids can be mean to one another at some point. A fist fight here and there quickly settled differences.

The theatre was different in that discriminating behavior was being exhibited by adults. They actually practised a form of segregation, no different from the segregationist policies of the deep American South, that prevented Blacks from drinking at "White Only" water fountains or using "White Only" restrooms. All First Nations people were made to sit on the left-hand side of the theatre, separated from the others by an aisle. Ushers attempted to sit me on the left side with the people that looked like me; however, I was not to be separated from my cousins. I glared at the ushers as I sat in the middle section, the only brown face there, with my cousins and friends. I did not fully understand my feeling then; all I knew was that it was not right and it was not a pleasant feeling.

Uncle Archie and Auntie Annie were of Cree-Métis heritage. My cousins Clarence, Bruce and Edie were lighter skinned but that did not spare them from the cruelty of racism. In Powerview we lived in poorer neighbourhoods disparagingly called either Bannock Town or Tin Town so we were all looked down upon by white people.

Uncle Archie was a pulp cutter for the Pine Falls Paper Mill. The mill had been in operation since 1920, around 30 years then, and logs for pulp were no longer in easy distance of the mill. Many of the loggers stayed in camps in the bush for weeks at a time. The work was hard and the pay was poor and subsequently we were poor. However, most of the people in Powerview were in the same boat so we did not feel singled out.

We never starved. Auntie Annie was expert at stretching her dollar. Often a few days before payday, when our money started running out, she would send me to Allard's store with 50 cents to purchase soup bones from Mr. Sands the butcher. Mr. Sands was my grandfather's neighbour and good friend. He always threw extra bones into the bag and he also ensured there was some meat on the bones. With macaroni, barley, a can of tomatoes and a head of cabbage, Auntie could make a delicious pot of stew from the bones, accompanied always with fresh bannock.

Our home was modest and located on the main street facing the bakery and tiny shoe repair shop next to it. At one corner of the street was a grocery store with an adjoined soda fountain shop where I had my first banana split. Across the street was Fatty's Taxi. Uncle Archie must have been experiencing some tough times because the following year, we moved into a shanty behind the Bargain Store.

"Blindman" Jack was a regular fixture sitting out in front of the Bargain Store where he played his harmonica for loose change. He had a tin cup in front of him and whenever a coin was dropped into his cup, Phil and I swore that we spotted him peeking out of the corner of his eye from behind dark glasses, without interrupting his music, to see how much he had earned.

The shanty carries a wonderful memory with it. I and my cousins excitedly went to bed because we were told Santa Claus never came while the kids remained awake. We kids all slept in one bed; Clarence, Bruce, me and then Edie. It was difficult falling asleep when overcome with anticipation. I saw Santa Claus for the first time sitting in a chair in front of The Bay store at Pine Falls. He was surrounded by assistants shepherding kids through a line to see him. He said "Ho ho ho" to me and gave me a bag of candy and a candy cane. I just gawked, completely speechless, and was absolutely amazed.

Finally, exhaustion set in and we all fell fast asleep. I was awakened by a bump on the head. I opened my eyes and there was my beloved Auntie with her forefinger on her lips signaling me to keep quiet. I looked around and realized she had dropped an orange on my head while she was filling our socks with Christmas treats. We had hung our socks at the head of our bed on the heavy metal frame, fully expecting the arrival of Santa Claus in the middle of the night with all his goodies. And there was Auntie smiling at me, shushing me to be quiet. I helped her fill the rest of the stockings, feeling quite smug at the conspiracy of it all.

Sometime that year, Clarence, Bruce and I happened to be standing in front of the Bargain Store when a First Nations person approached us and requested we purchase a bottle of extract for him. He had a one-dollar bill and he said we could keep the change as the extract cost 75 cents. Clarence and Bruce declined because they did not want to get into any trouble. The extract being sought was vanilla extract and the content was high in alcohol. Everyone then turned and looked at me. I was sufficiently innocent-looking to get away with this. The issue was that by legislation First Nations people were not allowed into beer parlours or liquor stores or even to possess any alcohol. That piece of legislation would not be repealed until 1960.

I agreed to make the illicit purchase as the change promised, 25 cents, was sufficient for a movie and a box of popcorn. Clarence and Bruce told me to simply ask the clerk at the checkout for extract and give her the money. I took the dollar bill, confidently strode into the store, made my purchase, and then walked out. I handed the First Nations person a small package of Ex-lax. He looked at the package with puzzlement and burst out laughing, exclaiming "Extract! Not Ex-lax! Extract!"

Also at this time Uncle Archie had a truck that Dad, to help out, had purchased for him. Uncle could now haul in his own pulp wood for a better price. He also had a gravel-box built of wood that was custom constructed to fit his truck. The bottom opened like a trap-door by pulling on a set of chains for offloading the gravel. Uncle now had an all-season working truck, hauling wood in winter and gravel in summer. In summer, Uncle Archie often piled us kids into that rear gravel box, and with auntie Annie in the passenger seat, off we would go for a picnic to McArthur Falls or Great Falls. He loved his truck and he even had a name for it—Violet.

In spite of the truck, we still had to move one more time. This time we ended up in a shack about a mile or two out of town, across from the Tardiffs, on the highway south of Powerview. The shack, lined with cardboard for warmth, was frigidly cold in winter. We rode to school in a bus, but there were many times we walked the highway, especially weekends, in the freezing cold.

The following summer I eagerly awaited the arrival of my mother and father and siblings that I had not seen for three years. My brother, Frank, meanwhile, had been enrolled in a school in The Pas the previous year. My family arrived at long last and Dad took us to Grandfather's house where we would spend the summer. It was a joy-ful reunion full of tears and laughter.

Grandfather had given us the upstairs part of his house for our use. It was roomy, bright and open. That night I heard my mother quietly weeping in bed. Mom and Dad whispered to each other in Cree but I could not understand. To my Dad's surprise and my mother's immense grief I had entirely forgotten my languages. I could no longer converse in either Cree or Chipewyan. Mother spoke little or no English, and Dad had to interpret any communication we attempted that summer.

That summer, before returning to Little Duck Lake, Dad purchased a house for Uncle Archie, and that enabled us to move back to the vil-lage of Powerview. This time I was joined by my brothers Frank and Jim and sister Linda. However, we could not stay together as Uncle Archie and Auntie Annie already had a large family, including me. Frank and Linda went to live with our grandfather and Auntie Islay, and Jim was taken in by Auntie Annie's sister, Dora, who lived just a few blocks from us. Frank and Linda lived out in the countryside so it was somewhat strange only seeing your brother and sister at school but we did get to visit some weekends.

Aunt Dora and Matt loved Jim. They had a single child, Margaret, but everyone knew her as Dolly. Aunt Dora, like her sister Annie, was fluently bilingual but Matt St. Croix struggled and was barely understandable with his broken English. He had a good job in the paper mill and thus they enjoyed the good life. Edie would often go to visit and play with Dolly. I loved to go along and when there, I would sit quietly in their living room and read all of Dolly's large collection of fairy-tale books. I was captivated by tales of dragons, princesses and ogres.

Both Jim and Linda are challenged but functional in life. They can read and do arithmetic only at the primary grade level. Jim has a remarkable memory in spite of his challenge. At a little over three years of age Jim had slipped off a dock in Duck Lake. No one knows exactly how long he was in the water before someone noticed him floating face down in the water. A Dene man jumped off the dock into three or four feet of water, and lifted Jim onto the pier. Dad performed artificial respiration until Jim vomited water and then started breathing.

Linda has a deep scar on her forehead from falling onto the corner of a cast iron stove as a baby. We are not sure whether Linda and Jim were born the way they are, or if their challenges are due to the childhood accidents. They were just treated and accepted no differently from anyone else. Linda was a very quiet, shy little girl with a very gentle spirit. Jim was a happy boy, always had a big smile for everyone, and because he did not start school until he was nine, he was called "Big Jim" by everyone. Mom and Dad kept Linda in school for two years and Jim for four.

That winter I received my first letter from Mom. As soon as they had returned home to Little Duck Lake from their vacation, Mom sat down with Dad to learn not only to speak, but also to write English. She was an amazing woman. Once a month we eagerly awaited her letters and I wrote as often as I could.

Big Jim was a popular playmate with the neighbourhood kids. One winter day I saw him and cousins Butch and Nibby playing stagecoach, or something along that line, because Jim had a rope around his chest and Butch was "driving" him around.

"Whoa, Horsey," said Butch. Butch then tied his horse to the back of a car. He turned his back to draw his pistol on Nibby. Suddenly the car drove off dragging his "horse" behind. "Stop! Stop!" they screamed as they ran after the car. The driver must have noticed the frantic kids or heard the screaming, because the vehicle came to a halt and the driver stepped out with a puzzled look on his face. Imagine the look of horror on his face when he saw Jim, still tied to the bumper of his car, struggling to his feet and brushing the snow off his coat. And then Big Jim's face broke out into a huge smile. No bumps, scratches or bruises—the roadways were seldom cleared and over time the surfaces became snow and ice packed. He had just had the ride of his life.

The slippery conditions of the local roads made possible one of our favourite winter pastimes—bumper sliding. There were few street lamps, and the winter sun set early. All the cars of the forties and fifties had large steel bumpers sticking out of the rear end, providing ideal handholds. Strategically hidden in the ditch near a stop sign was the best place to successfully hitch a ride without being seen.

If the driver spotted you sneaking up to his vehicle you could be assured to have a stream of swear words and curses directed at you. If too many riders hitched the same car, it was possible for the driver to feel the drag and he would slam on the brakes and sometime jump out of his vehicle. We would simply scatter in all directions.

There were few women drivers then, if any. If you were lucky enough to hitch a bumper ride with a teenaged or young male driver who knew you were there, you could be in for an exciting ride if vehicle, driver and bumper riders all managed to stay on the road.

Winter weekends were spent at Campbell's outdoor rink. We would spend the entire day playing pick-up hockey. We used Eaton's catalogues, held in place by sealer jar rubber rings, as shin pads. Thick woolen toques were always worn. No other pieces of equipment were to be had, and for the most part were not necessary, as slap shots and raising of the pucks, if we had the ability to do so, were simply not allowed.

Later in the evenings, after a day of hockey, I can remember sitting in our house next to the cast-iron wood stove, holding and rubbing my tingling feet; crying and sobbing while they took forever to thaw.

Our house was poorly insulated. The frigid wind just blew through the drafty home. The single-paned windows were always heavily frosted, making it difficult to look out. We had to melt a spot in the window with our hand so we could peer out. Once enough snow fell, I would spend hours outside shovelling and banking the snow up against the walls. This pleased Auntie Annie, and I enjoyed pleasing her.

I would also spend hours chopping and splitting our wood. If Uncle Archie wasn't around with his chainsaw, Bruce and I would end up sawing our wood with a bucksaw and sawhorse. Then it would have to be split before hauling into the house and stored in our wood-box.

We had no running water. A 45-gallon drum with a wooden lid sat in the corner of our kitchen. When water was required, a red sign was hung in the window and the water-man, spying the sign, would drive his water truck to the door, drag a hose into the house and fill the barrel.

Sundays were bath nights. Auntie Annie had a large copper container called a boiler that she used to heat water atop the cast iron stove. Come evening she would fill a round washtub with warm water. She placed the washtub on the living room floor next to the stove. Edie, the "ringleader" we called her, was always the first in the tub. Two or three chairs with a blanket draped over them acted as a screen for privacy. When she finished, I and the rest of the boys took our turns.

Mondays were wash days for Auntie, and the clothes, sheets and towels were hung outside on a line to freeze. Once the line was full, it was raised and kept in place by a long pole. The first day the laundry would be hanging stiffly on the line, but in another day or so the laundry would soften and start flapping freely in the wind. It would then be deemed dry enough to bring into the house.

An outdoor toilet sat on the back corner of our lot. The cracks between the boards that made up the walls were wide enough that one could sit and watch the going-ons in the neighbourhood, if one were so inclined. A ragged Eaton's Catalogue sat on the seat, its pages used in place of toilet paper. In winter, the turds would freeze, one on top the other, until a stalagmite of frozen excrement threatened to poke up through the toilet hole. We would knock it down with a length of two by four. Next to the toilet was the slop pit where the slop pail, mostly grey water, was emptied every day. A blackened 45-gallon drum sat nearby for burning garbage.

Clarence had left home at an early age the year before. He and Uncle Archie never got along, especially after Uncle had had a few drinks. Bruce, the next oldest, now had to assume the male role in the house when Uncle was away cutting pulp wood. He had the least desirable chore in the house, and that was lighting the morning fires. Auntie Annie would be the first to awaken, and she would begin calling out for Bruce to rise and start the fire. The mornings were so bone-chilling, I never blamed Bruce for feigning sleep. If you stuck your head out from under the blankets, you would see your frosty breath hanging in the frigid morning air.

"Bruce!" "Bruce!" "Bruce!" nagged Auntie Annie.

Finally he could take no more, and he would just literally explode out of bed, covers flying. He would put on his socks, and angrily stomp out in his underwear to the kitchen to light the fire in the range, and then into the living room to get the old cast iron stove blazing. He would come stomping back into the bedroom, and when I heard him coming I would put my head back under the covers. If he spotted me eying him, he would invariably cuff my head on his way back to his own bed.

The winter gradually turned to spring, and green grass and weeds slowly replaced the snow. Sometime that spring my brother Frank went missing from school for two weeks before someone followed up and called our Aunt Islay.

"No, Frank is not ill. He is on the bus for school every morning," informed Auntie Islay.

"That is odd. He has not been in school for two weeks." countered the teacher.

Frank's two weeks of hookey from school was abruptly cut short. He was met at the bus by a school monitor for the rest of the school year.

The summer of 1954, Mom and Dad once again vacationed, and we got to spend the summer with them in Powerview after not seeing them for two years. For that school year, I was joined by brother Don at Aunt Annie's. Frank was moved to Aunt Dora's with Jim, and Linda went home with Mom and Dad.

Back to the Land of the Midnight Sun

1956 was an extraordinary year. We were actually going home to Little Duck Lake for the summer. It would be my first time home in seven years. We were taken to Winnipeg and put on the long train ride to

A Dene hunter with his freshly killed caribou. PHOTO FROM HBC ARCHIVES.

Churchill. Near Churchill our train came to a stop for an hour or so to let a herd of caribou, migrating northward, pass over the railway track. In Churchill, we were met by representatives from Arctic Wings, the town's bush plane operation, and we were reunited with Jimmy Clippings and other students who had just arrived from Prince Albert Indian Residential School. We were all flying to Duck Lake together in a rickety Norseman aircraft loaded with some freight for the Hudson's Bay Company. There were no seats or seatbelts. We sat on boxes and crates wherever room was available.

The roar of the aircraft was deafening and the smell of gasoline was overpowering. We weren't very long in the air before most of us were gagging into little waxed paper bags supplied by the pilot. The flight lasted about an hour and a half and it was with great relief that we finally landed on the glassy smooth water of Little Duck Lake.

The aircraft taxied to the dock where we could see Mom, Dad, little brothers and sisters and members from the community anxiously waiting and waving with excitement. My heart started thumping, first with a sense of thrill, and then over-washed by a sense of anguish at finally seeing my family for the first time in two years. The emotions were confusing; I had missed my family so. My body began convulsing involuntarily as I sobbed in my seat.

The pilot cut the engine, hopped out onto the pontoon, and with rope in hand, the other end now fastened to the pontoon, jumped onto the dock. The men on the dock simultaneously grabbed the strut of the wing and pulled the heavy aircraft to a stop alongside the dock. The plane was lashed securely to the dock and the doors finally opened so that we could spill out into the fresh air.

I took a deep breath, wiped my tears, and bravely stepped out of the plane. After the hugs and tears I looked around to reacquaint myself with my old home—it had been seven years since I left for school. Dene friends of our family who remembered me came up and tried speaking to me in Chipewyan. They were surprised when they found that I no longer understood them. However, they politely shook my hand and welcomed me home.

After the aircraft that had brought us home noisily took off for its return flight to Churchill, I watched the plane disappear into the distance. I was then struck by the strange quietness: no cars, trucks, horns, whistles—just the voices of the Dene people being carried over the water interspersed by the odd barking or baying of dogs.

After two weeks home, Frank and I were in the trading post watching our father conduct business. The trading post stocked an assortment of basic groceries; Fort Garry Tea, Marvin's Pilot Biscuits, Carnation Milk, Hubay Flour, Rogers Syrup, Burns' Lard were some of the few products neatly displayed on shelves along two walls. They were separated from the customers by counters behind which Dad worked to serve them.

A third wall displayed some clothing , all neatly folded on shelves: men's and boys' denim overalls, brightly coloured flannel shirts, Stanfield underwear, and heavy woolen work socks. The women's and girl's section contained only brightly coloured head scarves, navy and red socks, beige stockings, and pink or white Balbriggan bloomers. The selection was sparse as the women sewed most of their own clothing.

Aluminum washtubs and pails, aluminum and tin pots and pans, enameled cups and plates, pewter utensils of knives, forks and spoons made up the houseware department. The hardware section contained a few hammers and screwdrivers, some wrenches and pliers, an assortment of nails and tacks, swede saw blades, a wide variety of traps and snare wire, some guns, and a wide assortment of ammunition.

The area of the counter where Dad served his customers accommodated a weigh scale—the old type where the goods were placed on a pan and then the weight calculated by sliding the metal weight along a calibrated metal arm. Once the arm hung in perfect balance with the goods being weighed, Dad would note the weight calibrated on the arm.

Next to the scale was a large roll of brown wrapping paper about two feet in length, set in a stand with a weighted cutter. Dad would pull out the required length of paper and then deftly lift up against the sharp weight that would cut the paper from the roll. Above the roll of wrapping paper hung a cone of white string that unravelled as

Dad wrapped the purchased goods into a parcel, tied a knot into the string and snapped the string with his fingers. It would be several years yet before paper bags would be introduced and decades yet before the advent of plastic bags.

There was no cash register; the cash from the few cash transactions that were made was kept in a sliding drawer under the counter. Most transaction were on "credit," the details of which were painstakingly recorded by hand, item by item, in a book or pad of counterslips measuring about three inches by six. The record of the purchase was duplicated by means of a sheet of carbon paper.

The purchaser received the carbon copy of the transaction and the original was deposited into the "sortergraph." A sortograph was a metal container measuring about 12 inches by 24 inches and divided into two compartments lengthwise. Each compartment contained a row of about 25 heavy pressboard dividers each labeled with a customer name. The counterslips were deposited into the appropriate slot after the balance owing was brought forward and the total of the new purchase added. The average trading post had sortographs occupying about two feet of counter space accommodating up to one hundred customers. Larger stores had sortographs taking up to six feet of space depending upon the number of customers.

Right next to the customer checkout space was the drug and liniment section, which I always found fascinating. In addition to the Bayer's Aspirin could be found Dodd's Kidney Pills, Smith Brothers' Cough Medicine, Dr. Thomas' Eclectric Oil (a type of liniment good for anything that ailed you), Dr. Carter's Liver Pills, Phillip's Milk of Magnesia, Minard's Liniment (good for man or beast), Perry Davis' Pain-Killer, and an old favourite currently making a comeback, the foul-tasting Buckley's Cough Syrup.

In the middle of the floor was a converted 45-gallon drum which served as a wood burning heater, with stove pipes running upward and disappearing into the ceiling. Two Dene men were purchasing some supplies for a short fishing trip they were planning. They looked at Frank and me and asked if we wanted to go fishing. We looked at Dad.

"Please. Please," we pleaded.

Dad asked the men where they were going and for how long. It was just to a day trip up the Wolverine River to the rapids and then onto Nejanilini Lake to fish some nets they had set a few days before. They would be back before dark.

Yes! Arrangements were made for us to meet Sandy French and John Duck at the dock at seven the following morning. Mom packed some lunches and put extra sweaters into a backpack for us. Dad found a couple of fishing rods and put together a small tackle box for us to share.

The next morning Frank and I were standing on the dock in the early morning mist when a canoe with two men put-putted up to the dock. Their dark green canoe was propelled by an ancient two-stroke Firestone outboard motor. As the craft approached the dock, Sandy shut off the engine and tilted the motor out of the water. John used his paddle to expertly steer the canoe alongside the dock and come to a stop. John and Sandy were right on time.

We hopped into the canoe and pushed some fish tubs around to make room so we could sit comfortably on the floor. The canoe smelled of fetid fish. Soon we were underway, the breeze mercifully wafting the odour away. We reached the north end of Little Duck Lake and the mouth of the Wolverine River by midmorning. Plying up the swiftly flowing river was slow but steady progress was made.

Gravelly eskers ran parallel to the river and around one bend we came across a young bull caribou, splendidly antlered, standing majestically on a rise and cautiously watching our progress. Sandy pointed to the animal and smiled.

Around midday we reached the rapids draining Nejanilini Lake. Tea time. Sandy pointed the canoe toward shore and about a canoe length from the shore, cut the engine and flipped the outboard forward out of the water. The canoe nosed onto the shore and came to rest sufficiently out of the water that we did not have to do anything except simply step out of the boat. The men decided we would climb the gravelly bank to the top where a breeze would keep the blackflies down.

A fire was quickly made and a blackened tea pail filled with water and hung over the fire. Frank and I pulled sliced roast caribou sandwiches out of our bag. John and Sandy pulled dried caribou, lard and salt out of theirs. After we ate, John peeked into our bag and with a big smile pulled out an orange. This was, after all, a culture of sharing. He shared it with Sandy. Afterward they pulled out their pipes and tobacco and smoked and chatted away in Chipewyan while reclining around the fire. Frank and I couldn't understand their conversation and we soon grew bored. We decided to go for a walk, just a short distance to the top of the rapids.

The view from the top of the ridge was breathtakingly beautiful. The sandy-topped purple green eskers decorated with violet and yellow blooms and stretching endlessly out into the horizon was typical of the tundra setting. The rapids below churned and splashed with white water spilling over rocks and then swirling into eddying pools. The gravel and rocky banks of the Wolverine River rose steeply on both sides of the rapids. We sat on boulders to rest and take in the view of the rapids when an idea popped into our heads. What a great place for an avalanche!

We found a log which we used to lever one of the boulders free and set it on its course plummeting downhill. It smashed into other boulders on the way down and soon we had a small avalanche splashing spectacularly into the water.

As the dust settled, the two Dene men came running, their eyes wide with fear. They admonished us in a mixture of Cree, English and Chipewyan saying we were not allowed to do what we did— that the wind spirits were going to be very angry with us. In fact, that was almost the end of our fishing trip that day. They extinguished their fire and made their way to the canoe. We followed in silence.

When the canoe was readied, the men decided they had to fish their nets. The nets had been set too long without checking and any caught fish could begin to spoil. We boarded and the men proceeded upriver the short distance to Nijanilini Lake. On the lake they located and quickly emptied and reset their nets. Barely speaking and with worried looks on their faces, they turned the canoe around and immediately struck for home.

About halfway home, our outboard unexpectedly clanged and clunked and abruptly stopped running. Sandy, with a panicky look on his face, quickly stood up in the canoe and scanned the horizon. Was he on the lookout for the wind spirits? He then sat down and with a few words in Chipewyan to John the men paddled the short distance to shore. They chose a flat rock outcrop on which to stop and pull up the boat.

Sandy spread a tarp out on the rock, removed the outboard and laid it on top the oily canvas material. With nothing more than pliers, wrench and a screwdriver Sandy soon had the entire engine apart and spread on the tarp. He found the problem which he repaired by binding with snare wire. Sandy then put the motor back together and re-attached it to the canoe. We all got back in and once we were in deep enough water, Sandy lowered the engine, wrapped a string around the flywheel, and pulled. The engine coughed and sputtered to life and soon we were on our way again.

At home that evening we related to Dad what had taken place. He told us to never do anything like that again and that he would speak to the men. Later that evening, we heard the rhythmic beat of a pair of Dene drums, and chants of atonement. We listened carefully as we recognized the voices of Sandy and John.

Years later I mulled that incident over in my mind several times and I grew to understand that people like Sandy and John, in spite of their conversion to Christianity, were still governed in their daily lives by the deeply rooted teachings and beliefs of their ancestors. The old teachings, similar to that of my grandfathers Wasakanoochie and Paquetna, unexpectedly came to the surface for Sandy French and John Duck. Nothing must be done to change or harm what has already been laid out by the Creator.

The reaction by John and Sandy to what Frank and I had done to the rapids in the Wolverine River is the same deep down negative visceral reaction experienced today by First Nations peoples anywhere in the country wherever power dams, pipelines, mines or any developments threaten to tear at the flesh of mother nature. The people are abhorred by the desecration and disrespect of all that created by the Great Spirit to sustain ourselves. When First Nations elders today refer to our people as "Keepers of Mother Earth," they make this statement in reference to the inherent values taught to us by our forebears. This basic value is still carried today by many of our traditional people.

I awoke to gentle prodding one early morning from my father. He then awakened my brothers Frank and Jim and with a finger to his lips, signalled we be quiet so as not to as awaken our younger siblings. He led us downstairs. In the kitchen, Dad pointed out the window and at first glance there didn't appear to be anything to see. Suddenly, I realized the hills were moving and, once focused, I could make out the teeming mass of a caribou herd in migration.

We opened the door and went outside to get a better view and the pungent smell of barnyard wafted in the air. There was an oddly muffled sound of multi-clicking as the tendons in the caribou's hind legs flexed within. The cool still morning air was further disturbed by the grunts and bellows of the bulls and cows and the bleats of calves in the herd.

"We will go out after breakfast to do some hunting," promised my father. I was so excited I was bursting inside. The village of tents lay between us and the caribou, and we could see the Dene crawling out of their tents, standing and stretching in the early morning, and calling to each other. They pointed toward the sandy and purple-green eskers which were alive, quivering and undulating with the caribou mass.

It was early summer in the far north and by eight the sun had already been in the sky since shortly after two or three o'clock. It would set briefly sometime around midnight. I found the concept of time to be chaotic in this part of the country at that time of year as the people could not plan or live their life to the cycle of the sun. They simply went to bed when they were tired and arose when they were rested. They ate when they were hungry and worked when it as necessary.

For practical reasons, the people, when at home in the seasonal tent village, adjusted their days to the opening hours of the trading post. I think we were the only family in the area with an alarm clock.

By midmorning Dad, a 30-30 Winchester rifle in hand, was tramping out onto the tundra with his boys, Frank, Jim and me, 12-, 13- and 14-year-olds. He chose an esker that he knew was one of several that the caribou were following northward in their migration, driven by the ceaseless harassment of mosquitoes and blackflies. They were headed for the tundra flatlands where cooling winds from the Arctic ocean would offer some relief from the heat and bugs.

We found a suitably dry and comfortable location where we could lie in wait and out of sight to ambush the unsuspecting caribou. Dad chose this time to explain once again the lever action of the Winchester rifle, the safety catch, and the sighting line. He knew that my heart was pounding, so he made me take deep breaths and listen carefully as he explained that I had to focus. I had to ensure I made a clean shot to avoid undue suffering of the quarry in a hunt.

I was told not to take my eyes off the animal if the targeted caribou was not brought down on the first shot. I would have to reload for the next shot, if need be, all the while keeping my quarry in sight. If I took my eyes off my animal even for a moment, I would probably lose the caribou in the mass of the herd. The animal, now impossible to track or follow, would then probably travel several miles with its wound before it dropped.

A wounded game animal on the run pumps adrenaline directly into its bloodstream, imparting a gamier taste to its meat. Digesting all this information that Dad whispered into my ear, I tried my best to calm down and focus, but this was such an unbelievably remarkable moment.

After what seemed an eternity, the caribou came into sight. Magnificent bulls, white throated and massively antlered, led the herd. I raised my rifle and took aim but my father placed his hand on top of the gun barrel and whispered, "Not yet. These are the wise ones. The leaders. We do not shoot them. Neither do we shoot the cows at this time of year as they have young ones."

We waited until the main part of the herd arrived in sight, and then Dad pointed to the young bulls and told me to chose one for my first kill. My heart was in my throat and my chest felt like it was about to explode. I took a deep breath, held it, and gently squeezed the trigger. Boom! The thunder of the rifle reverberated through my head as I saw the legs of the buck I had shot buckle under him. I looked at my Dad in wonder and he flashed me an approving smile. I felt ten feet tall.

Frank insisted it was now his turn but Dad said, "No, not for another two or three years. You are still too young to handle a rifle."

I felt not only proud but quite smug about myself. The crack of the rifle had stampeded the herd away from where we lay hidden.

We arose and followed Dad to the dead caribou and watched as he gutted the animal, steam and stench rising from innards. That done, he then proceeded to cut the head, antlers and all, from the carcass.

I and my brothers had gathered dry wood under Dad's instructions and this Dad lit, and soon we had a roaring fire to take the morning chill out of our bones. Dad lifted the caribou head by its antlers and carefully placed it on top the fire. He placed some extra wood on and around the head and said this will be our lunch and that it should be ready in a couple of hours or so.

We gathered rocks to pile on the caribou carcass to thwart the ever-present wolves that followed and harassed the herds. He then led us away and we trekked toward the eskers to do more hunting. In actuality, Dad just wanted to show us the beauty of the land as the carcass of the one caribou I had shot was more than enough for us boys to carry home.

I, my brothers and father were not the only ones out hunting. There were a number of Dene families and groups also hunting and subsequently the main herd of caribou had broken up into a number of smaller herds. We were crossing a valley from one esker to another when we heard the crack of a rifle in the distance. Soon after we saw a herd of caribou bearing down on us. Dad quickly shepherded us behind some large rocks in the boulder-strewn valley, and within a few minutes hundreds of caribou were frenetically stampeding around and past us. It is difficult to imagine a more scary but unforgettable moment.

As the herd disappeared into the distance, Dad rose from his crouch behind a boulder and looked around. Once it was safe he signalled for us to follow him and we made our way over the gravelly eskers back to the site of our campfire. The fire had died down to little more than ashes and warm embers. A set of blackened antlers stuck out of the ashes from which a few wisps of smoke lazily rose. Dad grabbed the antlers and lifted the charred head of the caribou out of the dying fire. We boys stared at the burned nondescript clump hanging from the end of the antlers and similarly thought, "This is lunch?"

Dad took out his hunting knife, scraped as much of the charred fur and hide as he could from the head, cut through the burned hide and stripped it back, unloosing a delicious aroma and revealing the steamy succulent cooked meat of the cheek. Once the meat was sufficiently cool to handle with fingers, Dad cut strips and handed each of us a piece. I cannot remember a more delicious and satisfying lunch.

Time to go home. Dad extinguished what remained of the fire by kicking dirt onto the ashes and we helped but once started we got carried away. We exuberantly kicked dirt not only onto the ashes but at each other until Dad barked at us to cut it out. We sheepishly smiled at him as he attempted to put on display his meanest scowl.

We ran to our buried caribou and started uncovering it, throwing rocks every which way. Dad then cut the carcass into four pieces—two front quarters, the rib cage, and the haunch with the two hindquarters still attached. Frank and Jim each hoisted a front quarter onto their shoulders. Dad pulled dry moss which was everywhere and padded my shoulders before fitting the rib cage onto my back. The moss offered some padding from the bones and also absorbed any blood still dripping.

He then threw the haunch onto his shoulders, one leg sticking out on each side of his head, and led the way home. We were greeted at the door by our mother who had patiently been waiting for the safe return of her young "hunters." We excitedly told her of our experiences while she hugged and kissed each of us in turn.

Dad took the caribou and hung the pieces in his underground permafrosted cellar. The cellar was packed with meat as several Dene families shared the space. It was still too warm for the Dene to kill more caribou than they could preserve by smoking and drying. They would kill just enough to last them the two or three months before the caribou returned in the late fall.

Most of their hunting at this time of year would take place by the lake. Once gutted, the extra caribou would simply be placed in about two to three feet of the frigid lake water anchored down by placing rocks in the stomach cavity. Here the carcasses could safely be stored for short periods of time until there was room in the smoke tents and on the drying racks.

This was a time of plenty for the Dene, cause for celebration and feasting. The evenings were marked by bonfires, food, drumming and dancing. I and my friend Jimmy Clippings would go to eat and watch the dancing. Everyone attended the feast with their own cup, bowl and utensils. We would sit in a big circle and the men would come around with kettles of stewed caribou that they would ladle into our bowls. They were followed by young men or women carrying baskets of bannock and kettles of tea.

After we had our fill of caribou and tea we would stay for the dancing. Both Jimmy and I were too shy to join the circle of dancers, even though several of the young pretty girls motioned with a come-here flip of their hands for us to join them in a tea dance.

As the sun started to set close to midnight, the mosquitoes became more voracious and, as there was no breeze to keep them in check, this was the signal to end festivities for the night.

Several days later Sandy French asked if I wanted to go on another trip with him and several other men to fish Nejanilini Lake. Sandy's wife Nancy was Mom's best friend and Mom treated both as family. After Dad had spoken to him, Sandy had apparently forgiven me for my stupidity involving the small avalanche at Wolverine Rapids. The outing was to be a day trip but there was room for only me this time so Frank had to sit this trip out.

I checked out my fishing rod and tackle box to ensure I was fully equipped. Mom threw an extra sweater, a can of juice and some biscuits into a brown canvas rucksack. I anxiously went to bed and after staring wide-eyed at the ceiling for some time, finally became sleepy enough to close my drooping eyes and dream of humongous lake trout.

Sandy French and John Duck were sitting in the canoe tied to the dock when I approached them. They pointed to the other canoe behind them where sat John Solomon and Simon Duck. Simon called for me to jump in with them. It made me wonder whether Sandy and John were still irked with me, but on the other hand, Simon spoke good English and I looked forward to asking a number of questions that I knew I couldn't ask Sandy and John. And better yet, Simon's canoe smelled of fresh pine. Shortly we were off chugging our way across the small, serene Little Duck Lake.

Near the mouth of the Wolverine River, we stopped to lift a fish net that had been set several days before specifically for this trip. It was filled with a substantial catch of suckers, bottom-feeding rough fish that the Dene used for dog feed, almost filling a tub to the rim. The two canoes pulled next to each other and John Solomon offloaded half of the catch into the other canoe.

Once underway, with Simon manning the outboard motor and John Solomon up front with me in the middle riding passenger, John tugged the half-tub load of suckers closer to him and took out his knife from its sheath. He cut a fish deftly in half, and reaching into a can in front of him he pulled out a huge black fish hook which had to be at least six inches long bent into a lethal barbed hook obviously targeted for huge fish—the majestic northern lake trout.

John skewered the half fish onto the hook, took a threaded needle out of his box of supplies and firmly sewed the carcass of the half fish onto the hook. He baited about a dozen hooks similarly. I peered over to our companion canoe being driven by Sandy French and noticed that John Duck was busy doing the same.

We made our way up the swiftly flowing Wolverine, and Simon expertly guided our canoe through the white water of the rapids. I guiltily glanced over to the area where Frank and I had avalanched a rubble of rocks into the rapids a week before. I averted eye contact with everyone and remained silent, staring stoically straight ahead. We finally arrived at the top of the Wolverine River and before us lay the dark, deep and frigid waters of Nejanilini Lake. My feeling of guilt eased and my breathing became easier.

We pulled the canoes to shore and the men gathered about two dozen pieces of wood each about 12 to 18 inches long for each of the canoes. They also gathered about a dozen rocks for each canoe and each rock was about the size of a grapefruit. Underway once again, John Solomon proceeded to the final step of completing the lake trout sets.

He pulled a roll of heavy green cotton fishing line from his box and cut 12 lengths of line each about 20 feet long. At one end of a length of line John tied a baited hook. He then ran out about eight feet of line and tied one end of a piece of wood to the line. He did the same thing with a second piece of wood about six feet further down the line. Finally, at the end of the line he secured a rock.

Once thrown into the water, the trout set would float U-shaped in the water buoyed by the two pieces of wood. The first piece of wood buoyed the rock which kept the set from floating away too quickly. The other piece of wood held the baited hook in place, bobbing up and down enticingly with the waves. Once a fish grabbed the bait and tugged at the line, the piece of wood would stand upright in the water, dancing to the tugs of the fish.

John Solomon had completed 12 trout sets for our canoe and John Duck the same number for their canoe. A small group of rocky islands somewhere close to the middle of Nejanilini Lake came into sight and both canoes headed in that direction. At the destination, the men chose an island around which all the trout sets were thrown out.

The men then pulled into shore, secured the boats, and built a fire upon which they put a small blackened pail of water to boil for tea. They lunched on strips of dried caribou dipped into containers of rendered caribou fat and marrow or into a container of lard purchased from the Hudson's Bay Company trading post. They washed their lunches down with copious amounts of tea and when done they pulled out their pipes and tobacco. They spoke in Chipewyan, a language I no longer understood and they laughed, but in an inclusive way, as if I should also know what the laughter was all about. Frustrating!

I walked around the tiny rocky island casting my rod out, but not a nibble. I could not cast my line far enough to reach the deeper waters where the trout lurked. I grew bored, extremely bored, and swore if there had been a suitable hill nearby I would surely have considered another avalanche. Someone finally noticed that there were several sticks standing upright in the water waving about and occasionally disappearing below the surface.

Simon stood, stretched and motioned for me to join him. We jumped into one of the canoes and paddled to the first dancing stick. Simon told me to pull the empty tub close to me as I would be pulling in the first fish. He told me to grab the dancing stick and pull the line in with the fish. I grabbed the stick, pulled it to the side of the canoe, took a firm hold on the fish line and started to haul in the fish.

A tremendous tug on the line nearly jerked me into the water, and the line which I had wrapped around my hand was now cutting into my flesh and bone. I was in excruciating pain. I threw myself to the side of the canoe and grabbed the line with my other hand taking the pressure off my bound hand sufficiently to free myself. I let go the line and rubbed my sore hand as the dancing stick dove underwater. It bobbled back into view several feet away.

Simon laughed, speculating on the huge size of the fish, and threw me a pair of leather gloves. He also pointed to another stick in the canoe about three feet long which had a short branch forking from it. It was an improvised gaff cut from a sapling which would be used to snag the fish by the gills. This would make easy work of hauling the fish into the boat.

I hauled the fish nearly to the surface when it decided to dive again; the leather glove saved my hand from serious rope burn. I held firmly onto the line, slowing the fish's dive, and gradually it came to a stop. I started again to haul it in and could not believe the size of the lake trout once I had it near the surface, the water magnifying the overall size. I held the line firmly with one hand and maneuvered the gaff in my other hand until I was able to pull the gaff firmly up into the trout's gills. I then hauled the struggling gasping fish into the boat, whereupon Simon smacked it between the eyes with a billy—a stout short club cut from a shaggy spruce and dried into a knotty weapon.

The monstrous fish was about 40 pounds. It would prove to be the biggest fish of the day with the rest averaging about 20 pounds each.

On shore the men poked the trout eyes out with their fingers and popped them into their mouths before gutting and cleaning the fish. They noticed me staring at them in surprise and one of them popped a fish eye and offered it to me.

"Suweechees," John offered.

He laughed at his attempt for the Cree word meaning "candy." To their great amusement they noticed me blanch as I politely declined the offer. They continued cleaning the fish, saving the bladders and major intestines by squeezing out all the contents and swirling in the cold fresh water. By early evening we had several tubs full of fish but there were also still a few empty tubs.

The men decided they did not have enough fish and would spend the night to get in another day of fishing. Simon explained that the lake trout fed in the early mornings and late afternoons. He thought that a few hours of fishing in the morning would easily fill the rest of the tubs and then we could return for home.

Did I hear correctly? A sudden panic gripped my spine as I absorbed the fact that we would be spending the night on Nejanilini Lake. Where were the tents, cots, sleeping bags, mosquito bars? Are these men in their right minds? What are we going to eat? Where are we going to sleep? A number of questions buzzed through my head but I was too scared to ask. Or maybe I was too proud because the men so easily broke into laughter and I did not want them laughing at me. I was fourteen. They were grown men. I had to swallow my fear and put my trust in the men.

We pushed off in the two canoes and headed in the direction of the sinking sun. The waves gently lapped and splashed about the canoes and the cool air felt fresh against my face. As we approached shore I looked about me in wonder at the vastness of the land. In the short few weeks I had been home I was coming to realize that this land was not as void and empty as it looked. It was teeming with life.

The misnomered barren lands and tundra exploded into a profusion of life with the melting of the spring snows. Caribou, wolves, foxes, wolverines, rabbits, mice and moles roamed the land. Owls, geese, ducks, loons, swans, hawks, ptarmigan, and tiny snow buntings flew everywhere. The lakes, rivers and creeks abounded with fish. And last but not least, this land supported mosquitoes, ticks, blackflies, sandflies, deer flies, and every creepy crawly imaginable.

The canoes approached shore and John Duck pointed to a likely landing spot. Sandy shut down the motor at the last possible moment and tilted the engine out of the water as the canoe glided to shore. John jumped out of the bow of the canoe and the momentum of the craft carried the boat right up onto the shore. John Solomon and Simon did the same with our canoe and soon we were about the shore gathering firewood for our evening fire.

With the fire blazing and the blackened kettles hanging with water to be boiled, the men took two fish, split them lengthwise down the middle, and set them on sticks to broil over the open fire. They also took several of the bladders and intestines which had been thrown into one of the tubs and suspended them on long willows to roast alongside our lake trout. They quickly shrivelled and turned black but the men ate them with gusto. Northern hors d'oeuvres, I guess. The men offered me a sampling to taste but I quickly shook my head and indicated I was waiting for the fish. The broiled lake trout was delicious.

After the men ate and smoked their pipes, they got up, stretched, looked around and chose a spot on the ground where the moss was thick and dry. They simply flopped themselves down, curled up and went to sleep. I was too apprehensive to follow suit and sat up for some time by myself, absentmindedly feeding wood into the fire. I wondered about my parents. Would they be worried that I had not yet returned?

Would they know I was about to overnight in the wilderness without a tent or sleeping bag?

I did not appreciate that my father knew well the hunting habits of the Dene. He knew if they felt they needed more time to complete what they had set out to do, they would take the necessary time to do so. The weather was absolutely fine, so Dad would have no problem in that area. He also knew our party included two canoes with four experienced huntsmen. Mom and Dad would sleep soundly that night. I, on the other hand, faced a number of issues.

The sun started to slowly sink into the horizon and I realized the mosquitoes were becoming more active and annoying. I decided I better get some sleep. I got up and walked down to the lake to wash my face in the refreshingly cold water. I walked back to the campfire, looked about, and found a suitable place to lay my head, apart from the snoring men but still close enough to afford some sense of security.

I emptied my rucksack which held a sweater, a can of juice and some biscuits. I flattened the rucksack and laid it on the ground for me to sleep on. I rolled up the sweater and tucked it under my head. It was fairly comfortable and the night air was warm. However the persistent buzzing of mosquitoes around my head grew more annoying as the sun set deeper into the horizon. It wasn't long before I was flailing at the bugs around my head. It became impossible to sleep.

I sat up and peered at the men in the semi-darkness of the northern night. They were all fast asleep and snoring in unison like a tandem of chainsaws. I looked at my canvas rucksack and estimated that it was just wide enough to squeeze my shoulders into. I opened it up and crawled into it to escape the voracious mosquitoes. I left an opening at the flap just large enough to allow a bit of air to flow. It worked; no bugs. My eyes drooped and I fell into an exhausted fitful sleep.

I awoke, less than two hours later, my face and body drenched in sticky sweat. The sun was already beating down on my canvas bag. I was slowly cooking and quickly asphyxiating. I pulled my head out of the suffocating bag and gasped deeply for air. The mosquitoes quickly went on the offensive and called in the blackflies for reinforcement. I swatted and batted away futilely.

Now fully awake I glanced over at the still snoring men. I looked at my watch. It was almost three and the summer sun was quickly climbing from its brief sojourn below the horizon. I walked over to the campfire, fed it some small dry branches and coaxed the still hot embers into flames by gently blowing at it. I threw on more wood and then gathered some green weeds from around the shoreline. The weeds I threw onto the fire quickly withered on the fire and emitted a thick smudge of smoke.

I sat in the smoke, bleary-eyed from lack of sleep, occasionally choking and coughing uncontrollably. The mosquitoes and blackflies backed off, hovering just outside my smoky cloud waiting for me to show myself. Finally a morning breeze started to pick up, and as if responding to a retreat signal, the tormenting gnats disappeared.

Around five o'clock one of the men stirred, sat up, yawned and stretched his arms up into the air and then got to his feet. It was Simon. He saw me sitting by the fire, waved, and flashed me a quiet smile. We didn't speak as Simon did not want to disturb the others who were still asleep. He picked up a shotgun and a bag of shells and motioned for me to follow.

Once out of ear range of the sleeping men, Simon told me we were going to get breakfast. We walked along the boulder-strewn shoreline of sand and gravel that were reminders of the long ago receded glaciers of the Ice Age. We reached a point of land that jutted out into the cold blue water of the lake.

Flights of ducks were flying about in the early morning air. Simon collected some dry driftwood which he heaped into a small pile. I assisted. He then lit the wood and soon an impromptu campfire was blazing brightly on the small point of land. We squatted down out of sight behind several nearby boulders.

It wasn't long before a flight of six or seven ducks flew within firing range, drawn out of curiosity by the lonely fire. Simon took aim, pulled the trigger, and two ducks dropped out of the flight, wings flapping wildly as they spun out of control and splashed heavily into the water. Simon whispered to stay down and out of sight as he quickly reloaded his shotgun.

I watched the small flight fly off into the distance and then slowly they looped around and returned for another flyby over the fire. Simon poked his shotgun out from behind a boulder, fired, and brought down another duck. The flight continued their suicidal fly-bys over the fire until Simon brought down the last duck.

Simon and I gathered the seven ducks that had by then floated to shore and we started back for the camp. We climbed a few short steps up from the sandy shore onto firm land which made for easier walking. As we trudged along some tall grass and weeds a duck suddenly took off from nearly under my feet startling the living daylights out of me. Simon poked about in the grass until he came upon a nest full of eggs. He was extremely pleased with his find as he gingerly filled his cap with the eggs.

Back at the camp the rest of the men were now up and about, no doubt awakened by our shotgun blasts. A couple of kettles were on the fire boiling water for our morning tea. Simon, John and I plucked and cleaned the ducks. Both Simon and John snickered at my initial attempts to pluck the waterfowl; however, they were also patient and interested enough to teach me the finer points of plucking. Once done, four of the birds were put on spits and propped up closely to the campfire.

Within minutes the fat on the ducks was crackling in the heat and a delicious smell wafted through the air. The other three ducks were cut up and along with the eggs thrown into the largest of our kettles hanging over the fire and bubbling with boiling water. In about half an hour we were feasting. The miserable night I had spent was now forgotten, a vague bad memory replaced by the extraordinary morning adventure experienced with Simon.

Forced Relocation: All for Naught

In mid-August 1956, a twin engine PBY Canso—commonly known as a flying boat—broke the peace and placidness of Little Duck Lake as it roared noisily into view of the tiny community. This was during the period of the Cold War with the Soviet Union under the provocative leadership of Nikita Khrushchev. All Hudson's Bay Company establishments in the far north were, in a small way, part of the Distant Early Warning system. It was surmised that should the Soviet Union attack North America it would be by way of the Arctic polar region.

In the early 1950s the United States under President Dwight Eisenhower collaborated with Prime Minister Louis St. Laurent of Canada to build a string of American radar stations across northern Canada. This was the Distant Early Warning system, commonly called the DEW line.

As a supplement to the DEW line, every Hudson's Bay Company post was provided with a booklet which contained information about every aircraft being flown by the Soviet forces and also every aircraft being flown by the Canadian and American forces. The booklet included silhouetted drawings of what the flying aircraft would look like when viewed from the ground.

Dad had given me the booklet and made it my responsibility to check out every aircraft that passed through our area. As the strange aircraft approached our community that early morning I quickly referred to my booklet which I always carried in my back pocket and identified the plane as one of ours—a PBY Canso.

The Canso circled once as the pilot and co-pilot closely scanned the waters of the planned landing area to ensure there were no rocky reefs or floating hazards. Coming in on the approach for the landing, the aircraft throttled back and slowed in its descent. Once the Canso broke the surface of the water with its belly, the pilot throttled up on the engine to ensure the craft stayed "on step" until it was close enough to the dock to begin throttling down. Once throttled down, the aircraft slowed and clumsily settled deeper into the water.

It was now plowing and splashing water like a clumsy old tub as it made its way toward the dock. The pilot expertly maneuvered the aircraft through the water by throttling up on one engine and down on the other until the craft slowly turned in the direction desired by the pilot. Approaching the dock, the pilot shut down both engines and the huge aircraft propelled by its own momentum drifted toward the tiny pier. A hatch door on the nose of the aircraft suddenly opened and the co-pilot popped his head and shoulder out of the hole like a gopher and directed my Dad and other men waiting on the dock to grab the wings and bring the entire machine to a stop against the wharf. The pilot and co-pilot then scrambled out of the plane and secured the craft to the wharf with rope.

The year prior, an Arctic Wings Norseman chartered by a photojournalist had flown into Little Duck Lake. As the aircraft taxied toward the dock, the journalist was shocked and appalled by the sight of hundreds, if not thousands, of caribou antlers and bones littering the shore of the tiny lake. She snapped photographs of the antlers and bones from the aircraft and once landed, she walked the shore of the lake taking numerous pictures.

She never bothered to enquire and find out that the antlers and bones were an accumulation of numerous decades, if not centuries, of hunting by the Sayisi Dene. The Sayisi Dene had hunted in this exact location for millennia. The unique location and delineation of the eskers and lakes, a quirk in geography, funneled the migration of caribou to cross this tiny lake in this exact location.

The vulnerability of the animals in the water was an opportunity for the Dene hunters to spear the caribou from their canoes. There was an annual fall harvest of the life-providing animals in this very location, year after year after year. It was one of the few constants in the lives of the Sayisi Dene; it could be said this was very much the "buffalo jump" for these people.

The pictures of the caribou bones and antlers featured in magazines and newspapers across the country caused an uninformed and misguided concern for the perceived slaughter of caribou. The greater Canadian public demanded some action be taken to protect the caribou herd from the savage Dene. My mind boggled at the thought that it would eventually be at the expense of an innocent, self-sufficient small tribe of First Nations people with little knowledge of the outside world.

The pilot and co-pilot harangued the people on the dock and said they were there to pick up and transport the first group of people to Churchill. There had been meetings, talks, discussions, debates ever since the Indian Agent had arrived some two weeks before to inform the Sayisis Dene that they were to be relocated to new homes in Churchill very shortly.

Other than Simon Duck, who had lived for a short period in Churchill working at the grain docks, the rest had only a Utopian vision of Churchill as a white man's place of ease and wonder. Most simply believed the promise of the Indian Agent of a simpler and better life in Churchill. No one could imagine the eventual living hell to which they were being condemned.

The first few hours were one of chaos as the people had never decided beforehand who would be the first to go. Eventually, several families stepped forward and volunteered. It did not take them long to dismantle their tent homes and pack their meager belongings. They hauled their possessions to the dock including dogs, toboggans, and canoes for which the pilot said he had no room.

Much debate and argument ensued but the people insisted there was no way they would abandon their dogs. They would leave their toboggans and canoes but not their dogs. The pilot eventually relented once he realized the people were firm in their decision not to part with their dogs.

"All right. Load the dogs!" barked the pilot.

The people had already decided amongst themselves right there on the dock that the younger men would return in the fall by canoe to retrieve the canoes and toboggans being left behind.

Over the next five days all 58 members of the band present in Little Duck Lake were airlifted to Churchill. That morning, on the fifth day of the expulsion of the Sayisi Dene from their ancestral homeland, I watched the Canso lumbering noisily down the lake with the last members of the band. I had shaken hands with my good friend Jimmy Clippings before he stepped into that plane. Fifty years would pass before we would next meet.

As the aircraft clumsily lifted into the air, I remained frozen on the dock and just stood and stared as the plane disappeared into the distance. I remember the eeriness of the quietude. Not a voice or a bark anywhere. A crow cawed in the distance and brought me back to the present. I walked slowly up the embankment from the dock back to the trading post to assist Dad with packing the remainder of the trade goods.

The fateful decision to relocate the band caught the Hudson's Bay Company off guard. They had sent in an entire year's supply of trade goods by tractor train earlier that winter. Most of the goods would be shipped back to the company's store in Churchill. The exception were the bulky heavy goods which were too costly to transport by air. The flour and sugar were thrown into the permafrost cellar dug into the ground just a few steps from the store.

The plane returned around noon for the next load. Our personal belongings were loaded and then topped up with cases of goods from the trading post. The plane departed carrying our belongings from the home we had known for the past ten years. There was now nothing left except to await the return of the same plane for the final trip.

By late afternoon we finished loading the last of the trade goods into the Canso which had returned for us. Mom and my brothers and sisters had already boarded and I was next. I stepped into the aircraft apprehensively and looked around at the sparseness of the interior. It was divided into several compartments and actually looked unfinished. The aircraft was designed to patrol our coastlines and hunt for submarines.

I chose a seat next to my brothers Frank and Jim and through a small port window watched Dad and the co-pilot untie the craft from the dock. Dad boarded the plane and the co-pilot shoved the craft away from the dock. I could no longer see him but I imagined he hopped onto the nose and boarded the plane through the little hatch.

The engines whined and with a pop and a puff of black smoke each engine finally caught and started chugging and then purring. The pilot expertly steered the craft to the middle of the lake, nosed into the wind, and then throttled the engines wide open for take-off. The plane plowed through the water and nothing could be seen through the port windows except the stream of water thrown up by the Canso. The pilot coaxed the huge craft up onto "step" and now the plane was speeding along on the surface of the lake. The windows were now clear and we could see the shoreline speeding by.

Finally the plane lifted its bulky body off the water and quickly climbed into the blue sky. From the air I took one last look at the bones and antlers lining the shore of the lake and I managed a final glimpse of the trading post and the tiny log structure that was Sandy Clipping's church. The community and lake faded into distance behind us.

The hour and thirty minute flight to Churchill was torture for me as I had not yet developed my "flying" stomach. The heat and smell of gasoline was soon overpowering and the constant roar of the engines reverberating through the un-insulated compartments was deafening. As soon as my stomach started heaving I reached for a stack of water pails that were part of the trade goods being sent to the Churchill store. For the next hour I vomited into this stack of pails that I held firmly between my legs.

The large airport of Churchill, with its several long runways to accommodate the American air force, finally came into view. The Canso lowered its wheels in preparation for the landing. This amphibious aircraft was also capable of landing at an airport. Once landed and taxied to our disembarking point I was struck by how high off the ground the plane sat. A stepway was rolled up the aircraft so we could deplane.

Moving is an experience that brings with it mixed emotions. There was the heavy gloom of having left a place that had been home for ten years. There was also the excitement of a new place, a fresh start. I was not then familiar with the outcomes of the deportation of the Sayisi Dene from their homelands. I thought their move would be similar to mine—sad in leaving a familiar place but excited about the prospect of a new experience. One could not know how far from the truth that actuality would prove to be.

A few short years later, controversy surfaced about the relocation of the Sayisi Dene and my father was summoned to Churchill (if I

remember correctly) to testify at a hearing. My father took the opportunity to visit his friends in their new community located on the outskirts of Churchill and was shocked and dismayed at what he found
and learned from his friends.

The people were for the most part destitute and drunk. They were
greatly disillusioned and had lost their purpose in life. They lived in
un-insulated one-room shacks, blankets hanging in place of doors
and windows. In some houses the people were sitting on the joists, the
flooring having been torn up and used for firewood. Churchill sits on
a barren shore miles from any tree stands.

The people related to Dad that when they first arrived in Churchill
there were no homes waiting for them as promised by the Indian Agent.
Instead, a few truckloads of building material were dumped on the
desolate shores of Hudson Bay where the people had been told to set
up their tents. This was in August. In a few short weeks the cold winds
of winter would be arriving.

The people were not carpenters. They never lived in constructed
houses. They moved with the seasons and lived in tents in the summer
and in lodges dug partially into the ground, built in wood stands of
poles, chinked and covered with moss for the winter. How were they
to survive in Churchill? Many did not.

Former Chief Ila Bussidor, born in Churchill during this period of
hell on earth for the Sayisi Dene, describes in her book, *Night Spirits:
The Story of the Relocation of the Sayisi Dene*, how she survived by
rooting in the garbage behind the Hudson's Bay Company store for
decayed produce, spoiled meat and dairy, stale and moldy breads, and
any other still edible goods thrown out by the employees.

How could this be? Where was that photojournalist then? Where
was the concern of the greater Canadian public for fellow human beings? Were governments and their bureaucrats really that ignorant,
inept and callous? How could the Indian Agent, a representative of the
federal government and thus trusted by the Sayisi Dene, lie bald-facedly
to the people supposedly in his care? I decided to review the Annual
Reports of Indian Affairs for 1956 and 1957 in search some answers.

I examined the Annual Report for 1956 and under "Housing" the report boasted of 904 new homes built on reserves, up from 837 the year before. I surmise these new homes were built in southern locations, the prairies for example, where logs were simply not available and sod homes no longer acceptable.

The housing program on northern reserves at that time consisted of framed doors and windows and rolls of tarpaper shipped in by tractor trains. The people lived in log homes built by themselves and supplemented by the doors and windows provided by Indian Affairs. One of the first few framed houses that I saw on a northern reserve was one built by my father in 1959 or 1960, assisted by me and my brother Frank, for Phillip Morin in Southend. It is not a huge stretch of the imagination to surmise that the housing for the Sayisi Dene in Churchill in 1956 was minimal at best.

I continued to comb through Indian Affairs' Annual Reports, this time for the year 1957, looking for some mention of Little Duck Lake and the Sayisi Dene. Who made the disastrous decision to relocate these people and why? I continued my search. Nothing. It was like the Sayisi Dene never existed. Under "Wildlife and Fisheries" I did find the following nebulous entry which hinted at a possible reason:

> Big game, particularly moose and deer, continue to increase and provide much needed supplies of fresh meat in isolated areas, although further declines have been registered in the numbers of barren land caribou. An intensive survey of the component parts of the caribou herd have been started by the special committee of federal and provincial representatives appointed to investigate the situation and the survey will continue.

Huh? What is this goobleygook about "an intensive survey of the component parts of the caribou herd"? And what do federal and provincial bureaucrats know about northern wildlife and caribou in particular? I would bet my life that not one member of that "special committee" had ever so much as seen a caribou.

I turned my attention to a more recent report published jointly by Environment Canada and the Beverly and Qamanirjuaq Caribou Management Board (BQCMB). The Board consisted of not only wild-life biologists but also Dene and Inuit elders who were experienced hunters. The following statement relative to the Beverly Herd caught my attention:

> Government biologists have determined that caribou counts in the spring and winter ranges from the late 1940s to the 1960s did not provide adequate information for determining whether the herd was increasing or decreasing.

I wondered where the information that the caribou population in the mid-1950s was in steep decline originated. Further down the same report was the following statement:

> Calving ground surveys from 1971 to 1980 suggested that the herd was declining.

Was it not the assumption that the caribou population would increase substantially after 1956 once the Sayisi Dene were removed from their homeland part of the rationale for the relocation?

I was not able to find any definitive answers to my questions about why the Sayisi Dene were uprooted from their homeland and deposited on the desolate shores of Hudson Bay and then completely and purposely forgotten about. The decision for the removal of the "Indians" was easy and convenient for unfeeling incompetent bureaucrats to make and it more than hinted at their complete lack of respect and consideration for a First Nations people. And, according to the joint report of Environment Canada and the BQCMB, all for naught.

Gateway to the North

With the closing of the Hudson's Bay Company's trading post in Little Duck Lake, the company decided to transfer Dad to Southend, Saskatchewan.

Southend is a Cree First Nations community located aptly at the extreme south end of Reindeer Lake. My parents had determined that The Pas, Manitoba would be a better location for us to attend school. It would be close enough that we could go home every summer once school was out.

They found a boarding home operated by Mary Trynacity, who was willing to board all five of us together: me, Frank, Jim, Don, and Islay. Harold would also arrive the following year. I was enrolled in The Pas Collegiate Institute, now known as the Margaret Barbour Collegiate, named for the long time no-nonsense teacher. Miss Barbour spent her entire career teaching in The Pas and she taught several generations of families. I got along well with her and thrived under her tutelage. She treated me no differently from the other students and she demanded and expected the best from me. My younger siblings were enrolled in The Pas Elementary School.

Mrs. Trynacity was of Ukrainian heritage, hence we were introduced to the new tastes of garlic, dill, sour cream, and the traditional Ukrainian dishes of puttiha (perogies), holupchi (cabbage rolls), kovbassa (garlic sausage), beet borscht and head cheese. We learned to say "duscha dobra" (very good) when excusing ourselves from the dinner table.

I had found an evening and weekend job at Guy Hall pin setting in the bowling alley. There were four lanes and we pin setters were responsible for two lanes each. We sat up on a seat straddling the ball-return between the two lanes. Friday and Saturday evenings were the most exciting as young men on dates attempted to impress the girls with their bowling prowess. They would hurl the 5-pin bowling balls with all their might to send the pins flying, causing us to duck and dodge as best we could. When hit we would yell out "ouch!" to the great amusement of the bowlers. We yelled out "Ouch!" quite often even when not hit as this assured a good tip from the bowlers.

One Saturday afternoon I had stepped outside for a cigarette during a break from setting pins. I was coolly puffing and hacking on a cigarette when I noticed two groups of kids on the nearby bridge throwing rocks and cursing at each other. The bridge crossed the Saskatchewan River, which separated The Pas First Nations reserve from the town of The Pas. One group of kids was from the reserve and the other from the town. I looked closer and noticed that my kid brother Frank was with the group from town throwing stones at the First Nations kids. Suddenly the kids stopped fighting and in the lull the First Nations kids yelled, obviously at my brother:

"Hey, Indian boy, why are you throwing stones at us?"

"Sorry. I go to school here and I have to live with these guys." I heard Frank yell back.

The stone throwing resumed. And such was life for us. We often seemed conflicted with our station in life. There were very few schools built on First Nations reserves other than residential schools in select locations. My father was not a status Indian and my mother, a daughter of Chief Samson Beardy, had lost her treaty status when she married my father. Hence, we, the children, were not recognized as Status or Treaty Indians and as such were not eligible to attend Indian Affairs Residential Schools. As history would later prove, this was a good thing. (We subsequently had our Treaty Status returned to us in 1985 following an amendment to the Indian Act.

Even so, we did not live through the height of the residential school era unscathed. We still had to leave home in order to be educated. We were still without our parents for years at a time. We suffered the same pangs of loneliness and we were also shocked by the racism directed at us.

We lost our languages. We were subjected to the same racist curricula. And we were subjected to the same superior attitudes of our teachers and religious leaders. And most of all, we missed being consoled and comforted by our parents when we needed them.

Our parents sent us to school in white communities because there were no other options until the early sixties. In 1960, Indian Affairs constructed an elementary school in Southend that enrolled students up to grade eight. My younger siblings were thus able to attend school without having to leave home. This made a big difference in that they were able to retain the Cree language as their first language and learned English as a second language. For those of us who attended elementary school away from home, English became our first language.

In the early spring of 1957, my grandfather Alexander died at the age of 87. He had slipped and fallen on an ice patch during one of his daily walks and broke a hip. He never recovered. My parents arrived in The Pas after we had completed the school year and arrangements were made for a last visit to Pine Falls and Powerview. Dad still had his brother, Archie, in Powerview.

We travelled to Winnipeg by CN passenger train and as there were now a total of eleven of us in the family, I remember this as our last travelling vacation together. On arrival at the Winnipeg train station, we had to take two taxis to the St. Charles Hotel on Notre Dame and Albert, where we were booked into adjoining rooms for the next few days. Dad would always need to call down to the restaurant in our hotel an hour ahead to ensure two adjoining tables were available for us.

We also had to go through the family routine of medical and dental checkups that the Hudson's Bay Company arranged for us whenever Dad took his vacation. Dad chose to take his vacations every two or three years following company policy.

Our company-appointed dentist, Dr. Brown, was elderly with unsteady hands. As far as I remember Dr. Brown never did fillings, caps, root canals or such. He just performed extractions with his shaky old hands and the more times I visited him, the fewer teeth I came away with.

On each of these vacation trips, Dad was obligated to pay a visit to the company head office on 77 Main Street. He owned one suit strictly for this purpose, although I do remember him donning his suit occasionally for funerals. The morning of his company appointment he carefully laid out his suit, white shirt and tie and carefully polished his shoes. After shaving and showering he realized he had no fresh underwear and time was too short for a quick shopping trip.

He dug around in one of the suitcases and found one of Mom's summer cotton balbriggan bloomers that he put on without a second thought. He dressed, checked his tie in the mirror, put on his fedora and away he went. Mom cautioned him, for god's sake, to be careful and do not become involved in an accident. I think Mom was picturing Dad in a hospital room, his pants being stripped away, to reveal her bloomers. To this day, in my mind, I can still picture this tough little fur trader appearing before his superiors at the venerable Hudson's Bay House on Main Street, dapperly dressed but secretly attired in Mom's underwear.

After our unmemorable vacation in Powerview (it was just not the same without Grandpa) it was time to return home and to school. As our train trip to The Pas was overnight, Dad had booked us into sleeping berths which we found exciting. The train conductor would pull our seats together into a bed, pull the overhead bin out which would unfold into the upper berth, draw a set of heavy curtains, and presto!, we had our bedroom.

During the evening prior, Mom, Dad and the younger siblings proceeding on to Flin Flon were moved to another sleeping car. I and the brothers and sister destined for The Pas were in a car that would be separated from the rest of the train on arrival at The Pas during the night. When we awoke, Mom, Dad, and the rest of the family were already gone and chugging their way through the boreal forests to the mining town of Flin Flon. There, a bush floatplane awaited to fly them to Reindeer Lake.

My brother Harold, at six years, had reached school age, therefore he was in our sleeping car that had been dropped off in The Pas, unbeknownst to him. He awoke, looked around, and asked for Mom and Dad. Don gleefully and sadistically told him they were gone and that he was never going to see them again. Of course Harold began to wail loudly and uncontrollably. I boldly took charge of the situation, slapped him up the backside of his head, and told him: "Shut up! I'm your daddy now."

Junior high and high school in The Pas is memorable mostly as a painful and fearful period for me. In Powerview, I had cousins Edie, Bruce and Clarence who kept an eye out for me, my Auntie Annie who loved me, and even Uncle Archie who in his gruff way ensured I stayed on the straight and narrow. In The Pas I was not only alone, I had a sister and four younger brothers who had only me to turn to for comfort and security. I felt ill-equipped to provide these as I myself was still in my early teen years. However, somehow we managed and to this day there are times I reflect on our family and attribute the closeness of my brothers and sisters to those early experiences.

Throughout the history of our country, a First Nations reserve situated next to a white community never bode well. In fact, an amendment to the Indian Act in 1905 allowed the removal of First Nations people from reserves that were located too closely to white communities with populations over 8,000. The Pas did not have the necessary population to remove the reserve. In addition, the town and the reserve were separated by the Saskatchewan River. Next to the reserve was the Métis community of Umpherville that added to the racial tensions in the area.

The late fifties was a booming period for The Pas. The Moak Lake mine had been discovered and Thompson was on its way to being developed. The Hungarian Revolution had been brutally suppressed by the Soviet Union with the loss of 2,500 Hungarian lives. 200,000 Hungarians fled their country and hundreds found themselves in The Pas, some elbowing their way in with the Ukrainians and finding employment on the Hudson Bay rail line. Others made their way to the port jobs of Churchill, and many more flooded the new mining community of Thompson.

The Pas was the El Paso of the north, filled to capacity by transients. Several rooming houses like the Flin Flon Rooms and Rupert House were hastily thrown up to handle the overflow from the many hotels in this small frontier town. The Pas at the time and to this day still calls itself the Gateway to the North.

The beer parlours of the Paskoyac (now Gateway), Avenue, Cambrian and Alouette Hotels without fail offered the nightly entertainment at closing time as First Nations, Métis, Hungarians, Ukrainians and others came spilling and hollering out of the pubs and into the streets. Fights between First Nations allied with the Métis against all others kept the RCMP and their paddy wagons busy. Boots and fists flew in these fights accompanied by loud curses, swearing and uncomplimentary remarks about each others' mothers.

There was the occasional board ripped off a conveniently located picket fence that would be used as a club but that was about as lethal as the fisticuffs would get. There were few if any deaths. Knives and firearms were never resorted to and fights never involved stomping anyone to death.

Still, the relations between First Nations, Métis and the white community were atrocious and little respect accorded to anyone of Aboriginal descent. On one of my mother's visits to The Pas she took me along with my brothers and sister to the downtown Princess Cafe for lunch.

After several long minutes of sitting at a table being intentionally ignored by the serving staff, all of whom were white, Mom stood up and loudly asked if Indians were served at this restaurant. She remained standing until a waiter or waitress, I can't remember which because I was so embarrassed, came scurrying with menus. I think that was my first experience of seeing my mother angrily and courageously dealing with racism head-on. It was a lesson well learned and never forgotten.

The brewing hatred and disrespect in the community would culminate ten years later in 1971, years after we had already left the community, with the heinous rape and murder of Helen Betty Osborne. This level of disrespect had been allowed to grow and fester to a point where white youths and men cruising about in their cars would simply snatch First Nations and Métis women off the streets for the purposes of rape and degradation. They would laughingly refer to these acts of debasement as "squaw humping."

Although I did not fully understand the turbulent dynamics of the community at the time, I did communicate my concern to my father and in the summer of 1961, I and my siblings were moved to Prince Albert, Saskatchewan.

Helen Betty Osborne was a young dynamic Cree girl from Norway
House, Manitoba who was attending the Margaret Barbour High
School in The Pas. Her dream and ambition of becoming a teacher
were snuffed out when her body was discovered one late fall day on
the popular beachfront of Clearwater Lake, about 20 miles north of
The Pas. Her clothes had been savagely ripped off and she sustained
some fifty stab wounds from a screwdriver to her young body. Despite
a supposedly thorough investigation, no suspects were uncovered.

Some 15 years later it would be revealed that many townspeople
knew who the perpetrators were but remained tight-lipped on the issue. The murderers, their tongues loosened by alcohol, spoke openly
about the grisly deed in the local pubs, yet no one took the initiative
to approach the RCMP with this information. The closed-mouth position adopted by the town spawned the book, *Conspiracy of Silence*,
authored by a journalist, Lisa Priest.

In 1983, RCMP Constable Robert Urbanoski of the Thompson
Detachment undertook the cold case and with a simple ad of appeal
in the local paper to the public uncovered several suspects; James
Houghton, Norman Manger, Dwayne Johnston, and Lee Colgan.
In 1986, the RCMP laid charges and a year later Dwayne Johnston
was convicted of murder, Colgan walked away with a plea bargain,
Houghton was acquitted, and Manger had been too drunk to remem-
ber anything and in the end was never charged.

I remember the Houghtons from my school years and never imagined that James could ever have become associated with such a heinous act.

Until there is at least a modicum of respect developed for our people, the ongoing prevalent contempt will continue to manifest itself in
the rape and murder of our women.

Reindeer Lake

With the completion of school in The Pas in 1961, we packed our meagre belongings, bade Mrs. Trynacity a final goodbye, and boarded a
train for Flin Flon.

In Flin Flon, a representative of Parson's Air Charter Services picked us up and transported us to Bakers Narrows where a pontooned De Havilland Beaver aircraft awaited to fly us to Reindeer Lake. We boarded the floatplane, strapped ourselves into the seats, and the dockhand pushed us away from the pier. The pilot cranked the engine and the motor responded with a few coughs and sputters as the aircraft cleared its throat. Finally the engine fired up and the pilot steered the aircraft into several circles not too far from the dock in case he had to paddle the plane back.

With the nine-cylinder Pratt and Whitney now warm and purring smoothly, the pilot confidently nosed the Beaver into the narrows and headed for the area designated for take-offs and landings. The air was still and the water glassy smooth so it made no difference from which direction we took off. The pilot muttered a few inaudible words into his crackling two-way radio and a response, undecipherable to us but apparently understood by the pilot, signaled the all clear for take-off.

The pilot pushed the throttle forward and the aircraft picked up speed as it smashed its way through the water. The pilot pushed forward and then pulled back on his control stick and he repeated this procedure several times. This caused the aircraft to gently rock forward and backward in the water as the pilot attempted to get the plane onto "step" to no avail. With no wind to assist the aircraft, the pilot decide to abort the take-off attempt. He throttled down and the plane settled back heavily into the water.

We taxied back to the wharf where the pilot and dockhand emptied several heavy boxes of freight destined for a fishing camp on Reindeer Lake. With a lighter load, the pilot repeated his take-off procedure. This time the aircraft climbed out of the water and sped down the glassy surface of the narrows gaining enough speed to eventually lift off and soar into the air.

It was June 30th and the temperature was a hot humid plus thirty degrees Celsius. It was not long in the roaring loud, stuffy and gas smelling aircraft before my stomach started heaving. Bush plane flying sounds exciting and romantic but at the time I hated it. I invariably

became violently ill on every plane ride therefore, in anxious anticipation of a flight, I stopped eating at least the day before the trip.
Nevertheless, I still got sick.

It was only a year or two later that I found my "flying" stomach.
I had boarded a plane on a full stomach and it had not been to my
planning. The plane had arrived a day early and I had no choice but to
board. To my pleasant surprise, I did not become ill, and it fact it was
my most enjoyable flight. I learned I could not fly on an empty stomach.

But not today. I heaved into a little bag, provided by the pilot, for
most of the trip. I was never so relieved to spot the white buildings of
the Hudson's Bay Company with their red roofs in the tiny community of Southend. As we neared our destination we could now make
out the log homes of the Cree community.

The pilot eased back on the throttle and trimmed his ailerons as the
plane slowly banked toward its landing target. He expertly landed on
the Reindeer River which drains the immense lake only a few hundred
yards away. The pilot opened the window in the cockpit allowing a rush
of cool air, fanned by the propeller, into the cabin of the Beaver aircraft.

I wiped my brow and dabbed at the sour taste clinging to my mouth
with a Kleenex I had found in my pocket. I spotted Mom and Dad and
my little brothers and sisters, Linda, Georgina, Brian, Kimberly and
baby Alex in Mom's arms standing on the dock and a sudden yearn-
ing ache gripped my heart. Tears filled my eyes and I suddenly found
it difficult to breathe. I inhaled deeply to control myself and the ache
quickly turned to joy when I saw the smiles on the faces of our waiting family. I turned to glance at Jim, Frank, Don, Islay and Harold
and I could see they shared my feeling of coming home.

The big event of that summer was the construction of the Indian
Affairs school in Southend. I quickly landed a summer job as a labourer
and labour I did. There was no heavy equipment except for one small
Caterpillar that did most of the excavating for the foundation of the
building. Everything else was done by hand. The concrete was mixed
in two small mixers and we wheelbarrowed the cement up-ramps and
dumped our loads into the concrete forms.

I and Alex Clarke manned the wheel barrows and in order to get the wet heavy loads up to the top of the forms we had to run at the ramps. I began running constantly with the wheelbarrow. I was a wiry 19-year-old and I wanted to build up my body and muscles. Run and dump. Run and dump. Day after day. Alex was a man in his early thirties, married to Rosalie, already full-bodied and muscled; however, he could not just walk with his wheelbarrow if I was running with mine. He also had to run.

Soon the white carpenters were shaking their heads in wonder at the sight of these two Indians running with heavy wheelbarrow loads of wet cement from sunrise to sunset. Al Pitzel, the project foreman of the small construction company from Rosetown, Saskatchewan mentioned to Dad over a glass of scotch one evening that he had never seen such hard workers as me and Alex. Dad told me that statement had made him proud.

We started work at six in the morning and broke off at eight for breakfast. The cook had platters of eggs, bacon, ham, sausage, steak, pancakes, French toast, pan fries of potatoes along with fruit and vegetables and pots of steaming coffee. After breakfast it was back to work for another two hours.

Ten o'clock was coffee break time and that turned out to be another full breakfast as the cook had laid out all the remainder of the food from our first meal along with fresh-baked buns. Lunch and the afternoon coffee break were again full sit-down meals.

The work day ended at six. Both Alex and I chose to go home to sup with our families. With the tremendous food and caloric intake that summer neither Alex or I put on any additional weight. I guess all that maniacal running with the fully-loaded wheelbarrows managed to burn off all the extra calories.

Riverside High School

That fall Frank, Don, Islay, Harold and I moved to Prince Albert for school and I enrolled at Riverside High School. Georgina and Brian enrolled in the new school at Southend, under the tutorship of principal Ken Passler and his teacher-wife Lorraine.

Alex Robertson was the manager of the Hudson's Bay Company Fur Department in Prince Albert and he made all the arrangements for a boarding home for us. He would later have a dispute with the company, quit his position, and move to Lac La Ronge where he would found Robertson's Trading, a highly successful fur and merchandising business thriving to this day.

Florence and Doug Macdonald had a three-storey home on Thirteenth Avenue East that made an ideal rooming house with its eight bedrooms and semi-finished basement. Doug was a hard-working carpenter often on jobs away from home. We would see him mostly on weekends. Interestingly, one of his projects was building a retirement centre in Cumberland House that to this day bears his name. Cumberland House is the community to which Dad would eventually move to with his family and where he would work the final years of his career with the Hudson's Bay Company.

Florence was an easygoing, happy-go-lucky landlady with a propensity for burning her meals. Nobody complained about the charred food she served us as she always had a cheerful smile and time to chat with all of us. Florence and Doug's son, Bobby, had just finished high school and was busy learning the trade of carpentry. He and his friends broke the monotony of our school year with a case or two of beer every Saturday evening for *Hockey Night in Canada* followed by *Ponderosa* starring Lorne Greene and his TV sons.

The school year was non-memorable with the exception that I remember there was only one other First Nations student in the high school. I was in grade twelve and Daniel Sasakamoose from Sandy Lake or Ahtahkakoop Cree Nation was in grade eleven. My brother Frank was just entering junior high school. Daniel wore the same heavy black-framed eyeglasses, standard Indian Affairs issue, that I did. I often say that Daniel and I were the first nerds of the Indian world. I do not recall the First Nations high school graduation rate at that time but I do know there were only 60 First Nations students, Canada-wide, enrolled in post-secondary education in 1960. My yearbook states I was the Einstein of my class. I was clever but not overly intellectual.

Toward the end of the school year and as the graduation date neared, my classmates were excitedly making plans; the girls about what they would wear and the boys about where they would party. Several days before the graduation date the graduating students assembled for rehearsals for the big day. I found an excuse not to attend.

My homeroom teacher, Mr. Costello, noticing that I did not appear to be excited about graduation like the other students, suspected something and questioned me closely. I told him I would not be attending the ceremony. Mom and Dad knew nothing about graduations and beside that, they were too far away to attend even if they knew about and wanted to attend the ceremony. It was just not a part of our lives then and on the whole, graduation ceremonies at that time were simply not part of the First Nations culture. I certainly wasn't excited by the concept although, years later when my own girls were graduating, it became an all-important event in my life.

I also did not have a suit that I could wear for the ceremony. Mr. Costello was aghast at the thought that I would not be attending my graduation ceremony because I did not have a suit. He immediately offered to lend me one of his suits; however, he was several sizes larger than I so I politely declined his offer. He then offered to approach and take up a collection from the rest of the teachers at my school but that only served to embarrass me further. In the end, I simply skipped school the day of our graduation.

I still had no idea at that time how I was going to make my own way in life. There were few role models to emulate. There were no Aboriginal resources to which to turn. In fact, there were very few First Nations people in Prince Albert.

The migration of our people into the cities had not yet begun. Since the North-West Rebellion in 1885, which culminated in the hanging of Louis Riel and the imprisonment of Chiefs Poundmaker and Big Bear, and the land rush to the West that started soon after Manitoba became a province, the government severely restricted the free movement of First Nations people by imposing the pass system. The pass, issued by an Indian Agent, identified the bearer, noted where he or she was going, for what purpose, and specified when the bearer had to return. The pass system became more strictly enforced with the surge of settlers from the East who did not want the Indians competing with them in farming.

It was only in 1951that major changes were made to the Indian Act, including the lifting of restrictions on attending and practising age-old spiritual ceremonies were also finally lifted.

Other amendments extended the right to frequent public places such as poolrooms; however, First Nations people still could not visit beer pubs or purchase alcohol from liquor stores nor vote in Canadian elections. That right would not come until 1960, under the leadership of John Diefenbaker (who incidentally was from Prince Albert), when Indians were extended Canadian Citizenship and granted the right to vote in federal elections. The Indian Act restrictions to alcohol were also lifted that same year.

Notwithstanding the legislated changes granting new freedoms, it would be at least another decade before First Nations people felt confident enough to throw off the long-standing, suffocating cloak of oppression and venture from their reserves to seek new opportunities in urban areas. It amazed me that Canada could be so indignant about the apartheid regime in South Africa and yet turn a blind eye to what was happening in our own backyard.

It was during this period of gradual easing of the atmosphere of oppression and depression that I found myself, as a First Nations person, attempting to make my own way quietly without stepping on any white toes. It did not cross my mind to attempt finding employment at the local Eaton's, Simpson's or Woolworth stores or at any of the four major banks that occupied all the four street corners of Thirteenth and Central. There was not one face other than white in those establishments.

Today, the population of Prince Albert, at more than 40,000, is 34 percent First Nations and Métis. There are numerous First Nations organizations and numerous First Nations businesses, the largest of which is the Northern Lights Casino and Hotel located on the southern edge of the city.

Prince Albert was also one of the first major cities in Canada to accommodate an Urban Reserve within its boundaries. The success of the Urban Reserve concept in Prince Albert is such that the many other mainstream businesses in the city welcome the dollars brought to the city by First Nations and Métis residents and visitors. This is a massive change in a relatively short period of time, my lifetime, not without its social problems, but nevertheless a colossal step in the right direction.

The Fishing Guide

After graduation, I went home to Southend as there were always some summer jobs on the lake, whether it be building resorts, guiding, commercial fishing or, if you were lucky enough, a job with a survey or diamond drilling crew. Around the end of June, arrangements had been made for us to catch a bus to La Ronge, overnight there, and then board an SGA scheduled aircraft for Southend. The only problem was that on the morning the bus departed for La Ronge, I had one final exam to write. I had no other choice than to stay behind, write the exam, and then hitchhike to La Ronge to catch up with my siblings.

I got into La Ronge that evening, went to look for my siblings, and found out that the aircraft had immediately taken them to Southend upon their arrival in La Ronge. The next scheduled flight to Southend was two weeks hence. Now what? I had about two dollars in my pocket.

I went into the Lac La Ronge Restaurant and ordered coffee, not knowing what else to do. An affable young man sat down on a neighbouring stool at the coffee counter and started a conversation. I told him my predicament and he told me he would try to assist in finding a place for me to stay. He took me to Olson's Camps, who as it turned out, were friends of my mother. Mom had boarded there for several weeks over the freeze-up period for her last pregnancy where she had given birth to my little brother Alex. The Olsons, with no hesitation, provided me with an unoccupied cabin where I was to stay for the next two weeks.

There were basic groceries in the cabin such as coffee, tea, sugar, margarine, cooking oil and my new-found young friend loaned me his fishing gear and showed me the good fishing spots. He also introduced me to Joe Roberts, a First Nations person from the reserve who, with a stiff leg, walked with a limp. Joe took me under his wing, often inviting me to his house for meals of fish or moose. Joe was a generous, kindly gentleman, one whom I have never forgotten.

I finally made it home and after a few days I ran into some First Nations friends, Herman and Obert Morin, who were happy to see me back in Southend. We caught up on the news and they made me laugh when they told me about a hunting incident on their way back from spring trapping a few months before.

Herman and Obert had accompanied Norvil Olson to their trap lines south of Southend in the Harriet Lake region. They had been away for over two months and were returning by canoe heavily ladened with furs and equipment down the Harriet River when they spotted a moose. It was a cow with her calf.

The trappers were low on supplies and they had been living solely on beaver and muskrat for the past few weeks. They would love some moose; however, their little canoe was heavily loaded and they realized there was no room for the moose. The meat would just go to waste. They decided instead to shoot the calf which would provide them enough food for the two days of travel they needed before arriving at Southend.

Obert, who was at the front of the canoe, lifted his rifle, fired, and the calf dropped on the willowy shoreline. The cow moose, surprised by the shot, whirled and ran into the heavy brush. Norvil, manning the outboard motor and the senior of the group, knew enough to listen closely to the cow moose as it ran through the willows. The rustling of the willows and brush did not last long so Norvil knew the cow had run only a short distance into the brush. She was standing alert and watching over her fallen calf.

Norvil whispered to Obert and Herman, "One of you is going to have to jump out the canoe to grab and throw the calf on board."

"No way. Not me." said Obert. He further suggested, "Herman, you are smaller and faster than me. You go and I will look after the front paddle."

After much prodding and coaxing, Herman agreed to retrieve the dead calf, fully and painfully aware that the cow moose was standing vigilant a short distance away in the willows.

Obert and Herman switched positions in the canoe, leaving room for the calf and for Herman to leap back into the front of the canoe if required.

Norvil quietly paddled the canoe toward shore and when close enough, Herman jumped out of the canoe and grabbed the calf. A loud grunt and snort and crashing of willows and brush told Herman the cow was attacking. Herman hastily threw the calf into the canoe as Norvil and Obert were already frantically back-paddling. Herman was in a foot of water and desperately pushing the canoe back before he leaped head-first into the canoe, just ahead of the thrashing front hooves of the cow moose.

Only when they were safely out of reach of the cow moose did the men breathe sighs of relief and break out into fits of laughter.

At the time, Obert and Herman were guiding at Birch Point some 20 miles up the lake. They encouraged me to come with them and apply for a job as a fishing guide as they knew the camp was short of guides. I reminded them that I did not know the lake and that I had never guided before.

"No problem. Just follow us around. We will teach you what you need to know. Besides, they pay good money and the Americans tip well." offered Herman.

My friends hit all the right buttons when they mentioned the money as I hoped to save enough money to finance my return trip to Prince Albert. I planned to return to the city that fall to look for a job. I agreed to give the guiding job a try and went home to throw a few changes of clothes into a packsack. Within an hour after a short boat ride, I found myself walking toward the building that my friends had pointed out.

I entered a combined office/store with displays of lures and fishing equipment along one wall and soft drinks and junk snacks along the other. A very short but well-built man, obviously the camp manager, rose from behind a desk.

"Hi. My name is Hans. What can I do for you?" said the man behind the desk.

I answered, "My name is Len Flett. I am from Southend and I am looking for a summer job. I heard you were looking for guides."

I could tell from his quizzical look that he was impressed with my command of the English language which had no trace of a Cree accent. That seemed to be enough for him to make a positive decision. Guides who spoke good English were always in demand. It turned out that Hans was also new to the area and he naturally assumed that I, obviously a First Nations person and being from Southend, knew the lake and was an experienced outdoorsman.

He hired me on the spot. He told me to go camp with the rest of the guides on the point of land just beyond the main lodge. The lodge was log structured and behind it, a dozen or so log cabins were laid out neatly in a row.

I found my friends in one of the tents and claimed one of the cots that was unoccupied. A single engine De Havilland Otter aircraft buzzed over the camp, made a lazy semi-circle over the lake, landed smoothly on the water, and began taxiing toward our camp dock.

"It's our American guests for the next six days. We have to go and help unload." said Herman, one of my tent mates.

The next morning we arose around six thirty. Herman and Obert each took soap, towel, toothbrush and toothpaste and padded down to the beach in bare feet. I followed suit. We removed our T-shirts, waded a short distance into the water and splashed refreshingly cold water onto our faces and chests followed by the brushing of our teeth.

Once dressed, we made our way to the lodge, took a table at the rear intended for the guides, and we were served a hearty breakfast of bacon and eggs. I asked the cook to turn my eggs over easy. Frostily, she looked me in the eye and told me I would eat whatever she served me. Lesson number one. Never mess with the camp cook.

By seven thirty we were on the beach, launching our assigned boats into the water and paddling over to the dock. We loaded our gas tanks into the aluminum boats, attached the hoses to the engines and then squeezed the rubber bulbs on the lines to get the gas flowing to the motors. After several tugs on the starter cords, the engines coughed and sputtered and then came to life and began running smoothly.

We would run the motors for several minutes until they warmed up and then shut them off to complete our preparations for the work day. While some of the guides worked the boats and motors, others were lugging the grub boxes from the lodge down to the dock. Each boat was loaded with a grub box, life jackets for the guests and guide, a paddle, gaff, fishing net scoop and a fish tub.

Around eight o'clock, the guests came down carrying their assortment of rods and tackle boxes. Hans and the camp cook were on the dock directing and giving instructions. The cook told us everything we needed for our shore lunch was in the grub box.

The most avid fishermen were assigned the most experienced guides. I was assigned two super-sized Americans toting super-sized tackle boxes. I eyed my boat, which suddenly appeared tiny. As I had no idea where we were going, I worried that we may not be able to keep up with the others. I sidled up to Herman and reminded him to not lose me. He grinned and told me not to worry.

My guests introduced themselves and asked how the fish were biting. I assured them that the fishing was great and that they were in for the treat of their lives. Of course I did not let them know they were entrusting their lives to someone completely inexperienced with the wilderness.

Six red and white boats spectacularly roared away from the dock at the same time. At the end of the narrows, three boats turned and headed north, while Herman and Obert turned and headed in the opposite direction. I followed Herman and Obert as closely as I could, my engine throttle wide open for maximum speed; yet, my boat was steadily falling behind because of the extra weight. I was feeling pangs of anxiety, if not panic, and I wanted to scream at the top of my lungs for Herman and Obert to wait for me. They were caught up their own race for the best fishing spot, visualizing huge tips for the biggest fish, and completely forgot about me.

I could see the white splash of water off the gunwales of their boats in the distance as they raced through the water. I was now imagining search planes and helicopters when suddenly they stopped near a group of rocky islands and set to trolling. After several minutes I caught up to the boats and nonchalantly waved at them as I sped by, pretending for the benefit of my guests that I knew exactly where I was going. However, it was only to the next rocky island, well in sight of the other two boats.

We spent a pleasant morning catching fish, weighing and measuring the big ones, mugging for pictures and deciding which fish to keep and which to release. I was now worrying about the shore lunch because I had no idea how to clean and filet fish. If worse came to worst, I thought that I could just chop the fish up and boil it in a pot of water. However, I just knew my guests were not going to be happy with that.

I kept a close eye on my watch and as the time neared noon, I trolled the boat in Herman's direction. Once abreast, I suggested to Herman that we have shore lunch together, and he agreed. Everyone reeled their lines in and we proceeded toward shore and a suitable site for our shore lunch. As we neared the shore, I gunned my engine to ensure we were the first boat ashore. I jumped ashore and shouted to Herman for him to clean the fish while I got the fire going.

I managed to think my way out of that problem, and now I watched Herman closely as he expertly fried his fish. I copied his every move. When done, I was quite proud of my fried fish, which was not only surprisingly edible but also quite delicious. We boiled steaming pots of tea and everything was going smoothly without a hitch until one of my guests requested coffee.

I got up and dug around in the grub box and found another tea pail and a further search located a jar of ground coffee. I filled the tea pail with water and set it on a pole over the fire to bring to a boil. I looked at the jar trying to determine how much coffee I should put into the boiling pail of water. I remembered the words of the camp cook telling us that everything in the box was sufficient for one shore lunch....or something like that. I dumped the entire jar into the tea pail.

The pot boiled and frothed and there was a wonderful aroma of coffee in the northern air. I took out two cups and poured coffee for my guest and myself. The coffee suddenly looked suspiciously dark like mud. My guest took one sip and immediately spat it onto the ground complaining that it was much too strong.

I feigned surprise and hurt as I advised my guest to just add some hot water to his cup if he found his coffee a mite strong. I sat there stoically drinking my coffee, masking my grimace, under pretence that this was how we northerners preferred our coffee. I imagine that American is still talking to his friends about the unbelievable potency of our Canadian coffee.

Before heading out for the afternoon of fishing, I told Herman about my over-weighted boat and that if he left me behind again I threatened to beat the tar out of him back in camp. He laughed at my threat. I don't think he realized how serious I was.

"Don't worry!" he assured me.

I followed him to another group of islands and we found Obert and his guests already there. It turned out to be fun spot and I joined my guests with my own rod. After several hours of unusually enjoyable fishing I had lost track of time. I suddenly thought to look up and around and my heart dropped with cold fear when I realized we were alone—utterly alone in the wilderness of northern Saskatchewan.

I looked around, sizing up our situation, and realized I didn't even know north from south. I had absolutely no idea where we were or how we were going to get back. We were surely going to die.

I thought of two options other than screaming and crying out of panic. Admit to my guests that I was no guide, that we were lost, and that we should pull into the nearest shore and wait to be rescued. I thought to myself it might be a day or two before they called for search and rescue planes. The second option: pretend all was well and set off in search of Herman and Obert or anyone for that matter.

"Reel it in, guys. I want to try the other side of Big Moose Island for a while. We caught a monster fish there last week." I lied with a straight face.

We arrived at some nondescript, unknown island.

"Here we are. Big Moose Island. Better put on your biggest lures." I advised.

We caught nothing. I didn't care. I was desperately in search of another boat.

"This is very odd. Not one nibble. Let's try the mouth of Yellow Dog Creek which is just beyond that point of land called Old Woman's Point," I stated quite convincingly to my guests. I imagined my guests were in awe of my detailed knowledge of this huge northern lake.

I was pretty safe in looking for a creek as there were creeks everywhere draining into Reindeer Lake. We rounded the point and much to my relief there were Herman and Obert. With a big grin Herman waved as if there had been no problem at all.

"Forget Yellow Dog Creek. We'll fish here with these guys." I announced confidently to my fishermen.

That night back in camp, I read by candlelight and waited until Herman was soundly snoring in his sleep. I picked up my pillow and silently tiptoed over to his cot. I pushed my pillow roughly into his face and he screamed in terror as he awoke, but my pillow muffled his screams. Once wide awake, his eyes round like saucers, he realized it was just me and he started fighting back. I wrestled him to the ground and got him into a choke hold.

"Uncle!" he cried out.

"Say you are sorry," I growled.

"I'm sorry," pleaded Herman.

"For what?" I grilled him.

"For snoring?" Herman asked.

"No. What happened today?" I asked to jostle his memory.

"You got lost," offered Herman.

"Yes. You left without me," I reminded him.

"I'm sorry," he apologized.

"And...?"

"And I won't do it again," he promised.

Only then did I release Herman and let him get up. Obert was laughing in great amusement from his cot. Obert was older and I never roughhoused with him. Herman, on the other hand, was my age and one of my best friends.

Someone not very pleased with all the tomfoolery yelled from the next tent. "Gagatoh! Neepaw! Mamaskats!" (Shut up. Go to sleep. For heaven's sake!)

The following weeks were quite enjoyable. Herman paid closer attention and I became somewhat more proficient in my job. The boys were right. The Americans did tip well, especially if they "caught the big one."

Billy Boy, the most experienced guide in our group, received a brand new 30-30 Winchester rifle (purchased for protection from bears but never used) from one his American guests along with a total of one hundred and twenty dollars in tips. His regular salary for that week—seventy dollars. I collected one hundred dollars in tips for that week.

Billy Boy was one of the sons of Sidley Clarke, a rough and tough boisterous offspring of Lawrence Clarke, a Hudson's Bay Company fur trader from Orkney, Scotland. Sidley was also known as "Chummy," a cute name for someone who enjoyed brawling after he had downed a few drinks. Sidley raised a brood of brawling boys, all rough and tough men like himself.

Sidley's brother, William Clarke, a quiet, honourable man quite unlike his brother, and his wife Mary are the grandparents of my first-born daughter, Sandra.

Co-op Point is the common name for Kinoosao, Saskatchewan. Kinoosao is Cree for "fish." It is located on the eastern shore of Reindeer Lake about midway up its length. It was ideally situated because the fish plant served both the Cree fishermen to the south and the Dene fishermen to the north. From Co-op Point a graveled road ran to Lynn Lake on which the fish, filleted and frozen, was trucked for trans-shipment to southern markets.

The plant employed mostly young women for the filleting processes. At peak periods there were up to fifty young women involved.

One particularly slow weekend at the lodge, Herman and I had free time to ourselves. We were sitting at a campfire and the smell of the smoke emanating from the fire was firing my imagination. As all homes at that time were heated by wood stoves and outside fires quite common, my first loves in Southend exuded a faint delightful aroma of woodsmoke, a scent that to this day still kindles excitement in me. We were not expecting any guests for a few days so when Herman suggested we go visit Co-op Point he got little argument from me. The only question I had was, "How are we going to get there?"

Herman gave me his standard, "Don't worry about it. Just leave it to me. We will leave after sunset."

So, it appeared we were going to slip away in the dark. That should have been my first hint that Herman was up to some mischief.

As the evening sunset got underway, Herman rolled up and tied his sleeping bag. He advised me to do the same with mine. He then stuffed them both into one of our waterproof duffle bags along with a change of clothes for both of us and our soap, razors and toothbrushes. Herman told me to wait and he slipped away into the semi-darkness.

In about a half-hour, I heard him softly call me. I stepped out of our tent and followed the trail of his voice to the water's edge. He was in a camp boat and motor spirited from the lodge. The first image that flashed in my mind was of myself being led away in handcuffs. I weighed that thought against the girls of Co-op Point. I chose the girls.

I handed Herman our duffle bag and quietly stepped into the aluminum boat. We paddled about a half mile until we finally rounded the point and entered the narrows that would lead us out to the main body of the huge lake. Once we were out of earshot of the lodge, Herman tugged on the starter cord several times until the engine coughed and sputtered into life. The lake was calm and the moon was out. Herman had made this trip many times before in the dark.

I steadied the outline of the dark horizon to imprint the route firmly in my mind as Herman described the approximate location of

various islands, points and other landmarks. We slowed as we neared
Floating Island. This was a boggy mass of swamp grass, reeds, willows and moss about the size of a football field and held together by
the intertwining of the roots of all the plants. Our passage through
the narrows was dictated by the direction of the wind, which pushed
the island back and forth within a narrow strait.

Once we passed Floating Island, we were on the final leg of our
journey to Co-op Point. It was about a two-and-one-half-hour trip
from Birch Point so we arrived just before midnight. Upon our arrival,
there were a number of young women around the dock and Co-op Store
area, as this was the only part of the tiny community lit by a streetlight.

Herman waved to a small group of girls to come over while we
were pulling our boat up to secure for the night. Herman introduced
me to the group that included a strikingly beautiful, young Charlotte
Sinclair, the mother of my beloved daughter Sandra. I fell in love.

Shaking Hides

That fall I boarded an aircraft for La Ronge and then bussed to Prince
Albert. I found a room at Macdonald's where my brothers Frank, Don,
and Harold and sister Islay were boarding for school. One of the first
jobs I landed was at the now defunct Burns Foods plant in Prince
Albert. Part of the plant at the time included an abattoir, which is a
nice word for a slaughterhouse.

Cattle would be delivered to the plant and one by one unloaded
from the trucks, down ramps attached to the rear of the trailers for
this purpose. The animals would be prodded along wooden chutes,
accompanied by much mooing from the beasts and shouts from the
men until they arrived at the killing area. There they were administered a coup de grâce with an iron bolt shot directly into the head.

The carcass was then ungracefully dragged from the area by a
winch and hoisted upside down on hooks in the skinning and cleaning area. The stench of manure and blood hung heavily in the humid
air. The dead steer would be beheaded, skinned, and then eviscer-
ated. After a thorough hosing with cold water, the naked carcass,

still hanging from the same hook, continued its gruesome journey, along with other carcasses, slowly moving to the cutting floor to be butchered.

Hooves, skulls, horns, bones and other odds and ends from the evisceration of the steer were sent to the "rendering room." The hide would be bundled up and thrown down a chute where it would land with a heavy splat in the "hide room." It was there I found my first part-time job.

The "hide room" was active only when slaughter was being carried out and slaughtering was done only until the plant had enough carcasses to keep its cutting floors busy. The carcasses were cleaned and cut into halves, quarters, and smaller cuts packed into block-readies for the butcher trade. Leftovers were destined for the hamburger and wiener rooms.

Our job in the "hide room" was to pick up the raw hides that would come sliding down the chute into our work area. As the wet hides weighed over a hundred pounds and were awkward to lift, it took several men to safely handle a single hide. We made sure never to stand in the vicinity of the chute mouth when the hides came crashing down onto the concrete floor.

We would pick up the hides and spread them out on the fleshing tables where the "fleshers," men with razor-sharp butcher knives, would cut and scrape any remaining traces of flesh or fat off the hides. We spread and lay the hides out, one on top the other on the hide piles after they were liberally salted down, and then they were allowed to cure for several weeks.

I gagged and dry-heaved numerous times the first few days on the job until my stomach and nose became impervious to the rancid, semi-putrid odors that hung in the heavy, humid air in this particular section of the plant.

As we handled and dealt with the fresh hides coming down the chute, there were a number of piles of salted and cured hides that had to be readied for the next stage of the process. The salt had to be removed from the hides and this was done through the "shaking" process.

Very simply, a hide was removed from a chosen pile, laid out hair down on a rack about 10 feet by 12 feet which consisted of evenly spaced metal pipes. The hide was then hoisted into the air by a crew of six men and slammed back down onto the rack with all our might. This was enough to dislodge most of the salt encrusted in the hair side of the hide. Any salt on the raw side was simply scraped off with a large scraper.

It would take a number of days of "shaking" to complete all the piles of salted hides. The completed hides would then be rolled up, tied into bundles, and trundled to and loaded into railroad boxcars sitting on sidings next to the plant loading docks. The boxcars of cured hides would be shipped to factories where they would be tanned and processed into marketable leather.

Shaking hides was back-breaking, hot, sweaty work. The sweat would begin rolling down your face after several minutes of lifting and slamming the dead weight of salty smelly hides in the warm humid room. When you absentmindedly wiped your brow with your hands, your eyes would soon begin to sting from the salt accidentally transferred. It would be necessary to run to a nearby tap to flush your eyes with cold water while the next hide was being loaded onto the rack.

By the end of the day, the rancid stench of death—blood, sweat, manure, and rotting flesh— permeated your clothing and your entire body. As I walked home, I hoped I would not meet anyone I knew. As I passed the odd person out for a walk, he or she would turn to stare at me as I passed, their nose and face wrinkled up in disgust. Dogs would growl threateningly at me as if to say, "Keep your distance."

Finally home, I would quietly and furtively slip through the back door like a burglar and jump straight into the shower to scrub off the stench. My clothes would go into a garbage bag and sealed or go directly into the washing machine.

After several months of working on and off in the hide rooms I received a call from the plant and was asked if I would be interested in working night shifts, four to midnight, in the Dry Feeds department. I was definitely looking for more steady hours so I readily accepted.

That job offer came as the result of a recommendation from someone who had observed my work in the hide rooms. I enjoyed the new job. Most of my co-workers were farmers who, during the summer months, worked their fields, or in winter completed their farm chores and then commuted to the city to work this shift.

This department of the Burns plant processed commercial dry feed mainly for the livestock and poultry industries but also some dry pet foods for cats and dogs. They also processed dry mink feed for the mink ranches that abounded throughout the northern half of the province at that time. The pet and mink foods depended upon the plant's supply of by-products such as blood and bone meal.

Dried peas, soy beans, corn, silage, blood meal, bone meal, various additives and supplements would be run through various hoppers, chopped, ground, blended and then bagged, sewn shut and carted off and piled on pallets. Chicken starter, pig starter and calf supplements seemed to be the main products.

The department had what we referred to as the "cook book." This book contained the ingredients and amounts required to produce one ton of any product. Upon our arrival for our shift there would be orders in the in-basket of our tiny office calling for various quantities of product such as five-and-one-half tons of chicken starter, three-and-three-quarters tons of pig starter, one-and-one-half tons of dog feed, etc.

As I was the one most proficient in maths, it wasn't long before I was directing my co-workers in retrieving the specific number of bags of each ingredient required to manufacture and fill our orders. The bags of various ingredients would be hauled in on hand trolleys and stacked next to the proper mixing hoppers. I would conduct the final check on the formula, double check the amounts of the various ingredients on hand, and then give the go-ahead on the production.

The mixers and hoppers would groan, clang and whine as only old machinery can, until the specific allotted time when the machines would grind to a halt. By this time the finished product had been automatically conveyed to the sewing hopper area. Our crew of four to six men would line up for the final stage of the production. One handled the empty paper sacks, opening and fitting them under the spout of the hopper. The other would handle the mechanisms that filled the sacks to the proper weights. Another would move the filled bag through the sewing machine where the sack was sewn shut. The others then loaded their trollies and wheeled the product out to be stacked in the warehouse.

I enjoyed this work, so much so that I decided not to attend teachers' college, where a seat had been reserved for me under a scholarship. The scholarship had been arranged by Bishop Dumichel after he had met me in Southend. He laughed when I had proudly told him I was a guide.

The bishop said, "You are no guide. You should be a teacher. Let me make some calls when I get home." A week later a telegram arrived, advising that a place for me at Teachers' College in Saskatoon was being held for me.

Being young, single, and stupid, I thought I had the world by the tail. I was gainfully employed, making fairly good money, and saving to buy a car.

It was early winter when my world crashed. Unionized workers within the Burns plant had caught wind of my rise through the ranks. It was not long before I was "bumped," a union term for replacing a non-unionized employee with a union member. It did not matter that I offered to join the union because my position would still have gone to another unionized worker with more seniority.

I was now unemployed. However, it would soon lead to the beginning of my 41-year career with the Hudson's Bay Company and The North West Company.

Okemasis – "Little Boss"

A short article in the *Prince Albert Herald* about Rose Valley Construction being awarded a contract for the construction of a geological laboratory in La Ronge caught my eye.

It was late February in 1964 and I had just finished reading the "Want Ads" in the local paper. I combed the paper every weekend, weeding through the job opportunities, looking for something that was appropriate for me.

Rose Valley Construction was the same company that built the elementary school in Southend and for whom I had worked a couple of years ago. I picked up the phone, called the company, asked for Al Pitzel and surprisingly, I got him on the line. Al remembered immediately who I was and he replied positively.

"Yes, by all means, I would be happy to have you on my crew. We are still only in the planning stages, but we expect to start the middle of March," he advised.

"Thank you. I will be there," I replied appreciatively.

Three weeks later I was on an early bus to La Ronge, arriving shortly after noon. After getting directions I walked to the site, which was only about two or three blocks from the hotel where the bus had dropped us off. On arriving at the proposed location for the lab, my heart dropped as there was only a lone caterpillar tractor to be seen, struggling to knock down some trees.

The site was only now just being cleared. The company was obviously at least two weeks from starting the actual construction. There was still a ton of snow on the hard frozen ground. Once again I found myself stranded with only a backpack of work clothes and a few dollars in my pocket.

I decided to walk over to the Hudson's Bay store because I had met the manager, Vic Mckay, previously on trips through La Ronge. The store was bustling with out-of-town trappers, fishermen, outfitters, surveyors, miners, along with the regular townspeople. La Ronge was a jump-off spot for the northern wilderness.

Saskatchewan Government Airways (SGA), Athabaska Airways and upstart La Ronge Aviation were abuzz with airplanes flying from sunrise to sunset. I saw Vic in his office and I asked him if I could work for him for a few weeks until the work on the geological lab got underway.

"You could not have come at a better time," he said with a smile. "I'm supposed to send one of my guys to Southend to help out your dad for a couple of weeks. He just received his tractor train shipment and he doesn't have an assistant. But we're just too busy here and I can't afford to let any of my guys go. Would you mind going there for a couple of weeks?" he asked.

"I would love to go if nobody minds my working for my father," I replied.

Vic said, "Let me call Head Office. It's against our policy for family members to be working with each other, but since it's only for a temporary period, I don't think anyone will mind."

I left Vic's office so he could make his phone call in confidence. About five minutes later Vic poked his head out from his office and waved for me to come back in. The smile on his face signalled good news.

"No problem," Vic grinned. "You need to be on the plane tomorrow. Where are you staying?" he asked.

I told him I had just arrived in La Ronge that day and had no place to stay.

"Give me two minutes," he said, and then turned to his phone and dialed a number.

I could tell he was calling a hotel for a room. He hung up and dialed another number. He was now talking to an airline. Again he hung up, swivelled his chair to face me, and advised I was booked for the night at the La Ronge Motor Hotel. He said I could also charge my meal and breakfast to the room and he would look after it, and that I was to be at SGA, also known as Saskair at the time, tomorrow morning for departure at nine.

I wanted to kiss him but settled for shaking his hand and thanking him profusely.

The next morning I was on the Saskatchewan Government Airways scheduled flight into the north. It was a single Otter painted a dark yellow and trimmed in red. Weekly with mail, freight and passengers, it flew the circuit from La Ronge to Stanley Mission, Southend, Brochet, Wollaston and back. It was piloted by the shortest pilot I ever met—Sam McKnight—who was also its most experienced bush flier. His aircraft, typical of single Otters, always flew with the tail up and the nose down, supposedly so the height-challenged Sam could see out his aircraft windshield.

The plane landed on the ice at Southend and taxied to the area in front of the wharf, which was still frozen solid in about three or four feet of ice. I spotted Dad coming down the hill with a mailbag slung over his shoulder. The engine of the plane shut down and Sam jumped down, walked to the midsection of the aircraft, and opened the door. I saw Dad again and as this was well before the time of telephones in the north, I knew he had no idea that I was on the aircraft. I made my way out the door, jumped down, threw my arms out, and announced to Dad, "Tada—I'm your new clerk!"

Dad was pleasantly surprised, but puzzled, until I told him Vic sent me from La Ronge and I was to assist him for the next few weeks.

Over the next three weeks I reorganized Dad's grocery warehouse, re-piling the flour, sugar, lard and marking every case with the outfit year, 294, the cost in code and the retail price. The outfit year signified the number of years the Hudson's Bay Company had been operating since its founding in 1670. Hence, in 1964, it was 294 years in business.

In the dry and hard goods warehouse, we opened every case and marked every single item with a tag; either sticky, pinned, or string tags run through a marking machine, noting outfit, cost and selling price. It was tedious work but I did not want to leave my dad with any of this when it was time for me to go. I worked late into the night every evening to ensure I would finish. As the end of my three-week stint was drawing near, Dad received a wired message from the office. Bob Millard, the District Manager, would be arriving in two weeks and he wanted me to stay until he could meet with me.

What followed was an offer from the company for a full-time position as a manager-trainee, starting at $175.00 per month, board and room included. I was also informed I could remain in Southend for the next little while and train for the position under my father. I accepted.

It was a wonderful experience working with Dad and it was a great opportunity for me to reconnect with both my mother and father as my school years and the vast distances involved had separated us for long periods of time.

Normally, Dad was a man of few words; however, in the store working at whatever, he was in his element. When the store was quiet with no customers and we were keeping busy with mundane tasks such as cleaning or replenishing stock on the shelves, we spent many hours just talking as we worked.

Summertime had arrived in Southend and with the change in season, most of the community packed up and moved to their summer camps spread out over the vast lake. The people were hunters and trappers in the fall, winter and early spring. In the summertime they were all commercial fishermen supplying whitefish, pickerel, pike and lake trout to the Co-op Fisheries at Co-op Point also and more formally known as Kinoosao, Saskatchewan.

Some of the men chose to work as guides at one of the several fishing lodges on the lake catering to American tourists. A number of families moved for the summer to Co-op Point where the women and girls would find work in the fish plant cleaning and filleting. The only people who remained in Southend for the summer were the pensioners and they numbered no more than ten or twelve.

We were hard pressed to keep busy. Dad showed me how to prepare whitewash and I ended up whitewashing the fence, the stones lining the pathways, and the flagpole. I was to later find out these were essential skills for all trainees as these tasks were performed every summer without fail at all Hudson's Bay Company trading posts across the country. It became somewhat of a standing joke: if it didn't move, paint it white. We also raised the company flag every morning when the store opened and took it down every evening at store closing.

It was two summers prior that Dad had purchased the building used by Rose Valley Construction as the cook house when the Southend school was built. It was a wood frame building about 20 feet by 40 feet in size. It had to be moved approximately 120 yards from its original location onto the company property next to an existing warehouse.

I recalled how two years ago that cook shack had become a summer project for me and my brothers. We spent every day for the next two or three weeks hauling gravel from a pit across the lake about two miles away. There was no choice as there was no gravel to be found elsewhere. They used our canoe and several washtubs for hauling to our dock and then carried the gravel with buckets up our embankment to the project site. Dad and I had dug the shallow foundation and built the forms for the concrete. Once we had enough gravel, the concrete was mixed by hand in a wheelbarrow and poured.

The next task was moving the building by hand as there was no equipment and the added challenge was overcoming the moderate incline leading to the proposed new site. We had heavy wire cable and two building jacks that we borrowed from the Whitesand Control Dam.

We reinforced the four corners of the building with two by fours and wrapped the cable around. The building was jacked up, braced on log beams, and then lowered back down onto more logs for rolling. Dad built what he called a "dead man winch," a large upright log anchored in a hole and buttressed by additional woodwork.

The upright log had a hole drilled into it large enough to fit a long strong pole, one end of which was inserted into the hole. The winch-log was reinforced with a heavy rope, tightly wrapped around the opening to ensure it would not split. The cable was attached to the winch and then the brothers pushed the pole, around and around, in a circle, slowly pulling the building along.

Frank, Jim, Don, and sometimes Brian were soon bored and began hee-hawing or mooing in protest as they trudged around and around, but there could be no stopping. Their only short break came when I had to move the rolling logs from the back to the front of the building. We measured our progress in inches, but nevertheless, the building was actually moving. And I thought my Dad was insane when he said we would do this by hand.

We had to relocate the "dead man" several times but we managed to drag that building uphill, a distance of about 120 yards in about ten days and then a few more days to position it exactly on its new concrete foundation.

My brother Harold and I travelled to Reindeer Lake in 2013 to do some lake trout fishing. We stopped at the Northern store for some provisions and that warehouse is still standing on its concrete foundation some 50 years later. It is a lesson well learned from my father. I've never hesitated to tackle seemingly impossible tasks since then.

Summertimes in Southend afforded us extra time once most of the people left for their summer camps on the lake. Dad taught me the basics of bookkeeping and I went further and delved into the details of the operating statements and spreadsheet (form NS232 as it was known in the company) until I had a full understanding of what made the company tick.

We had to do an inventory of our goods that summer and I took the time to refer to a previous inventory and manually extend and calculate our rate of gross margin. I showed Dad our result, which was quite acceptable. We then packaged the approximately two hundred pages and shipped it off to our Head Office for our accountants to extend and calculate our return. The result came by mail two or three weeks later and Dad, now staring at me, could not believe it was exactly as I had calculated.

He then related to me the story of the "separate" pile of flour that all fur traders carried in their warehouses but never counted for inventory purposes. He told me that in days past when the trade was much simpler, inventory pages only numbered about a half dozen or so. It was very easy to calculate the return and if their return was a little low, they simply added a number of bags of flour from their "separate" pile to achieve the required or expected return. If their return was somewhat higher than expected, they reduced their inventory by deducting a number of bags of flour and adding them instead to their "separate" uncounted pile. Those wily old fur traders!

In Southend, Dad was somewhat reluctant to change so we still served all our customers from behind the counters. Customers would request an item and we would fetch it for them from our shelves. Dad's store in Southend was similar to the one he had in Duck Lake except now he had better equipment.

The oil drum stove was replaced by an Ashley wood heater. He now had a cash register, albeit operated with a crank, and a modern weigh scale. The weigh scale, the best they had in the 1960s, was still a fairly large piece of equipment with the weight dial set at eye level. Dad had just a bit of a problem trying to read the small print and as the print was at eye level, Dad had to tilt his head upward so he could focus with his bi-focals. His customers would laugh at him and make wry remarks in Cree.

"Look at Horace. He puts our goods on the scale, then looks up at the ceiling, guesses at the weight and charges us whatever he wants!" they joked.

The only customers we had for the summer were a handful of the old people, none of whom spoke English. It was a great opportunity to relearn my mother tongue language that I had lost when I was sent away for my education. The elders did not attempt to speak any English whatsoever.

The ladies depicted ca 1960 are Elders Caroline Bird and Lydia Jobb of Southend, Sask., with Len's brother Brian.

They had their own descriptive words for items that did not easily translate. Dad assisted by translating for me whenever I was stuck, and later we often shared laughs when he provided the literal translation for me. For example, a Cree elder wanting peanut butter would ask for "Alikochas Mayee," for which the literal translation is "squirrel shit." Squirrel Peanut Butter, of course, depicted a squirrel on their label. Honey was "Amoo Mayee," bee shit. Barley was "Eskwesis," little girls. Sausages were "Chugkasees," little penises. Bacon was "Coogoos," simply, "pig." Corned beef was "Moostew Weeass," cow meat.

"Iskochisa," the Cree name for batteries, literally translated means "little lightnings."

I have forgotten the word they applied to bologna. The literal translation was "something that just lays there." The elders had no idea what kind of animal constituted bologna, hence the descriptive name. No one can say they were without a sense of humour.

One day I was busy doing a monthly stock check in the ladies department, as sparse as it was. I had to count each and every item, every size and every colour and note the count in our stockbook. This enabled us to reorder whatever was selling. I was checking ladies bloomers and the size tag happened to be inside the garment. As I was busy opening up the ladies bloomers in search of the size tags, Sarah Thomas, a senior then in her 80s, observed my seemingly keen interest in ladies underwear. She hobbled up to the service counter, caught Dad's attention and loudly remarked in the Cree language, to much laughter from the customers milling about in the store, "Horace. There is something very odd about your boy. You better have a talk with him. He is much too interested in women's underwear."

Sarah Thomas was typical of the seniors in Southend. She wore a black beret, a dark cotton blouse most likely homemade, topped by a woolen cardigan, either dark wine, green or navy in colour. Like most women her age she wore a tartan skirt that hung down to her ankles. The women sewed their own skirts and the Black Watch tartan pattern was the bestseller of all our fabrics.

On her feet were moosehide moccasins, intricately patterned with beadwork, and worn with moccasin rubbers to cushion her feet from stones and protect her leather footwear from moisture. She also wore wire-rimmed glasses, often slightly askew on her weather-worn face, to aid her failing eyesight. She walked with a tilted limp, aided by a home-carved cane of dried poplar.

Sarah lived in a single-room log home. The logs were grey with age and chinked with moss and the floor constructed from locally sawn boards. The boards were cut at the small community portable sawmill. The roof was constructed of the same boards as the flooring and then covered with asphalt rolls of roofing material, black in colour. There was no ceiling; no insulation. Scrubbing, sweeping and foot traffic on the floorboards over the years wore the original rough hewn appearance down to an almost smoothly polished surface.

Sarah had her wooden bed, built by one of her sons, in one corner of the room, neatly covered with homemade feather pillows and patchwork quilts. A brightly checkered red and white oilcloth covered the wooden table that sat under a window. On the table was a sardine can ashtray, placed next to a tin of Player's Tobacco and a package of Zig-Zag rolling papers.

To one side of the table was a set of open cupboards made simply by stacking several wooden crates, one on top the other. On the other side of the table was a wooden stand on which sat her wash basin and a dishpan. Squeezed in between was her water pail that was freshly filled from the lake every morning by one of her granddaughters.

The cupboards held her tin dishes, mugs and cutlery, and her sparse assortment of pots and pans in the topmost sections. The middle and bottom sections held her meagre grocery supply of flour, sugar, lard, baking powder, tea and canned milk. A cardboard box under the bed stored her supply of dried moose meat.

A tin stove sat in the middle of the room and on the stove was an ever-present kettle of tea. Under her bed, next to the moose jerky, was her prized possession: an RCA wind-up gramophone that she would occasionally take out to entertain her friends. She would proudly wind the small crank located on the back of her machine, load the head with a new needle, and then gently set a 78 RPM record onto the turntable. The plaintive wailings of Kitty Wells and Hank Williams soon wafted in the air of her cabin.

On a shelf on the back wall sat a coal oil (kerosene) lamp. The lamp, along with a candle precariously leaning upright in a small tin dish, provided her light. On "poker nights," a neighbour often brought her Coleman gas lamp to augment the dim lighting.

Several nights per week Sarah would host card games in her house. She would spread a blanket on her floor and her visitors would sit forming a small circle on the floor. The games were mostly a form of gin rummy or stud poker. She and her friends loved gambling and they often gambled late into the night. I would occasionally accompany my mother to these games and I was always invited to play with the group. I suspect my popularity as a card player was due to my consistent losses.

The gradual changing colours of the leaves on deciduous trees and the restless flights of ducks, geese, loons and swans were the initial signs for the people to start thinking about wending their way back to Southend. The fishermen needed to start pulling up their fishing nets, closing up their summer cabins or dismantling their tents.

Those serious fishermen who planned on staying for the fall fishery would bring their families back so the children could start school. The men would then return on their own to their fishing camps and fish late into the fall season until the weather became too turbulent and cold.

In the summer and fall seasons, boat travel on Reindeer Lake was always dependent upon the wind factor. Although the huge size of the lake is broken up by thousands of islands, there were still a number of unavoidable wide open stretches that one had to traverse.

I had gained some experience in steering a watercraft through the six- and occasionally eight-foot waves that were quickly whipped up by the wind on the open expanses. It was never pleasant. As a rule of thumb, during the summer months the wind would often blow throughout the day and then calm down in the evenings. Most people travelled at night during this period. The fall months from late August on saw a reversal of the pattern. One could travel the relatively calm days but it was always prudent to be off the water before nightfall when the wind inevitably began to howl.

By the end of September, all the fishermen were safely home and preparations began for their annual fall treks to their trapping grounds. They needed to be at their trap lines before the snowfall and freeze-up to prepare their cabins for winter. While the rivers and creeks were still open they wanted to be able to reconnoiter their territory by canoe, and at the same time hunt for moose.

After making arrangements with Dad for trapping debt, they purchased their necessary supplies and left sufficient room on their accounts for their families to use. Those trappers with school-aged children could no longer take their families with them on the trap lines because the children needed to attend school. The trappers would load their supplies into their canoes—including their sleds and dogs—as they would not return until the lakes and rivers froze sufficiently to enable safe travel. Most did not return until close to Christmas.

It was early October that Adolph Cook invited me to accompany him on a weekend moose hunt down the Reindeer River and into Harriet Lake. The leaves had fallen off the trees and shrubs, making it easier to spot our game.

The fall air was crisp, so I packed my sleeping bag that Mom had made for me. Throughout the summer and fall, Mom had saved all the down feathers from the ducks that I and my brothers shot. Once she had the required quantity she sewed them into a material she called "ticking." Ticking is a tightly woven cotton material that prevented feathers from poking out. The ticking, stuffed with down feathers, was then layered with a flannelette sheet and totally enclosed in canoe duck, a light but tightly woven canvas.

The canoe duck had previously been painted with linseed oil several weeks before to waterproof it. Mom then closed the sleeping bag with leather lace and there was extra material at the head that could propped into a canopy for extra protection.

Adolph and I spent a comfortable night under the stars at Harriet Lake but we had no luck in spotting any moose. The next morning a chilly ominous wind began blowing from the north and Adolph thought it wise we turn around now and start making our way back home. The Harriet River is small and winding and heavily lined on both shores with willows fronting dark and deep forests. It was only when we reached the much larger Reindeer River that we realized the wind was blowing with gale force.

We quickly put on our rain gear before turning onto the bigger river. Our freighter canoe was propelled by a 10-horsepower Johnson Outboard and within a half-hour we were at Whitesand Dam. This was the water flow control dam for Island Falls Power that provided all the electricity for the town of Flin Flon and its iron and nickel mine. We struggled with the canoe, motor and our gear which were covered with ice. The spray that was created as we motored through the water quickly turned into a coat of ice as the temperature continued to drop. We finally managed to manhandle our craft and gear over and around the dam.

We now eyed Marchand Lake, a small lake at the top of the dam separating us from the continuance of the Reindeer River which would safely take us home. The rivers had been relatively easy to traverse but we were now sizing up the choppy waves on the small lake. We had a choice: camp here for the rest of the day and certainly for the night and hope that tomorrow would be better for travel, or continue our trip. We decided to take our chances on the lake and continue our run for home.

At this time of year we both knew that the weather could worsen and not let up for a number of days. We also knew an early freeze was possible and that would certainly add to the difficulty in which we found ourselves. We launched onto the lake and began fighting for the far shore about two or three miles away.

Every spray of water from the bow of the canoe as it cut its way through the waves covered us, our gear, and our canoe, and almost instantly turned into ice in the frigid temperature. There was no water pooling in the canoe that could be bailed out. It was turning into a thin coat of ice instantly and each spray of water added another coat of ice. The sheath of ice forming on our canoe, inside and out, was becoming thicker and thicker and our progress was noticeably slowing as our boat and gear became heavier.

Could the situation become any worse? Yes! It began snowing and with the gale winds driving the snow into our faces, it now became almost impossible to see. The snow was adding to the numbing weight of the ice and I was fearful that we were slowly sinking. My pounding heart was now in my throat and I never felt more helpless. I turned back to look at Adolph and he gave me a grimace which was not reassuring as he struggled to steer the canoe through the pounding waves. Suddenly, through the driving snow and spraying water, the dark shadow of the far shore came into view. Adolph immediately made for shore and I jumped to the bow with a paddle to guide us through any rocks.

We pulled the heavy ice-encrusted canoe onto shore and secured it. Adolph and I then tramped up and down the shore looking for a suitable spot where we could overturn the canoe and use it for the night's shelter. Not finding a suitable spot we turned our attention to the rocky shore. We climbed a treed rock prominence alee from the wind, not too far from our canoe, and found a mossy enclave that would protect us from the storm. It was now late afternoon or early evening. Under our rain gear we were dry but we needed to get warmth. It was too wet, windy and miserable to attempt making a fire so we decided instead to bed down for the night and seek comfort in our sleeping bags.

We used our paddles to shovel the snow out of our chosen area and then chopped down sufficient spruce boughs to form a thick springy mattress. Adolph had a large tarp which he spread out over the boughs on which we were to lay our sleeping bags. My sleeping bag that Mom made for me was enclosed in a waterproofed canvas so I advised Adolph to use the entire tarp to wrap around his sleeping bag. We stripped out of our rain gear and heavy parkas and crawled into our bags. The warmth soon chased the chill out of our bones and eventually we fell into exhausted sleep.

We awoke the next morning, I aroused by a shout of laughter from Adolph, and I poked my head out of the bag to about two feet of soft fluffy snow all around us. The wind was calm and the air, still cold but not as bone chilling as yesterday, promised a better day.

Southend is located on a large island. The night before we did not know whether we were on the mainland or the island. Before falling asleep I had thoughts of trudging overland through the deep forest before stumbling into the community. Worse yet, I also thought of finding ourselves on the mainland side where we would have had to cross two streams before finding ourselves across the river from our community.

Out of our cosy rock enclave, we could see that we were indeed on our island, about five miles from the community. We rolled our bags and tarp and loaded our canoe after we had spent considerable time banging and chipping as much ice as possible off the craft. We eventually made it home and I gave my mom an extra kiss and hug for the gift of her lifesaving sleeping bag.

6

FUR TRADE REDUX

TRICKS OF THE TRADE

In preparation for the fur buying that would occur throughout late November to early May, Dad led me through the instructional and fur-buying books. Once he had enough fur samples on hand he would go over each individual piece and explain how to measure, what to examine closely for quality, how to make allowances for damages, and finally, how to apply the pricing tariff and arrive at a value for the skin.

Horace explained all the tricks of the trade, and there were many—used by canny trappers to pull fast ones—over the buyers. The most common were improper stretches. Buyers determined the size of beaver skins by measuring the length and then the width. Beaver pelts should be perfectly oval; however, some trappers brought in pelts elongated and pulled out on the sides in an attempt to take advantage of standard measuring procedures. If the pelt of an otter, marten or mink was long and skinny, then it was probably overstretched as these skins were measured mainly for length. Many unwary or unseasoned buyers never bothered to check for the minimum width.

If the same skins were dried fur out instead of pelt or skin out, then you could be sure the trappers were hiding some damages. If the fur was unusually dark, mostly desirable in some species, we had to check to ensure shoe polish hadn't been applied. Foxes, wolves, coyote, wolverines and the like were sold with the fur out. Great care had to be taken as it was difficult to spot damages. Imperfections were usually discovered by feel.

Lastly, Dad explained all the differentiating signs that would identify a dog skin from a wolf. Yes, more than one unsuspecting buyer has been left holding the bag on a worthless dog hide. Dad explained that all it took was one error like that to forever spoil your reputation as a buyer.

He explained the wolf is a large animal. Size is always the first indicator. If the trapper tells you he has a small wolf, then you better double check all the features. Wolves have small rounded ears, fully furred inside and out. Their legs are generally longer and their feet larger. Their heads are larger and their muzzles longer. The wolves' fur is also distinctive with thick under fur and long guard hairs, especially at the shoulders.

Len Flett carrying lynx pelts from the trading post in Southend, Sask. to hang in a warehouse.

Coyotes look similar to wolves but are much smaller; generally, they are about half the size of a wolf. The coyote's large pointed ears and sharp, thin muzzles are also distinctive features.

When Dad started getting too busy with fur buying, he directed some of the trappers to me. There was reluctance of course as they wanted to deal with Okemow (Boss), not Okemasis (Little Boss). He reassured them that if they were not happy with my price, then he would take over.

They agreed, and very seriously I worked my way through the first batch of fur. I carefully measured, shook and fluffed the fur, examined the colour in the light, nodded my head in a positive manner as I handled a fine fur, and then scratched notes onto my work pad. I noted my offer surreptitiously on a piece of paper that I left in a specific spot under the counter as prearranged by Dad.

My father had taught me well because my pricing was always close to what he had estimated. However, when I made my offer to the trapper, his first reaction was always a negative one and he would request Horace take over. We needed to make the trappers comfortable with my buying. Dad would come over, repeat the same procedure with the fur as I had done, peek at my price hidden under the counter, and then make an offer which was usually five to ten dollars less than mine. It was not too long before the trappers became confident with me buying their furs.

The days leading up to Christmas were busy ones. The trappers were now all in and the wives assisted with the final preparation of the furs, neatly sewing any holes, brushing and combing out the furs. Bill Reese, Sooniyow Okemow (Money Boss), as the Indian Agent was called in Cree, made his community visit so he could prepare any orders, school supplies and housing supplies requiring delivery by tractor train.

Muskegee Okemow (Medicine Boss), the doctor, usually accompanied by Muskegee Eskweeyoo (Medicine Woman) a nurse, shared an aircraft with the Indian Agent to hold a day clinic at the school. Amigewmow (Prayer Boss), the local priest, made his home visits encouraging everyone to attend his Christmas services. My own

Christmas that year was very special as it was the first one I was able to share with my parents in 15 years.

The Boss is not always right...But he is always the Boss

Ile-à-la-Crosse? Where is that? I reread the letter from our Head Office advising my transfer to Ila-à-la-Crosse, Saskatchewan. As I read the travel arrangements that had been made for me, my excitement became mixed with a slight fear of the unknown.

I caught the Saskair scheduled flight into La Ronge and then bussed to Prince Albert where I spent a night. The next day I was on another bus operated by Saskatchewan Government Transport heading for Meadow Lake. Meadow Lake at that time was a bustling little "cow town" driven by farmers and ranchers. I was to catch a Waite's Fishery transport truck hauling freight into the North.

I found Waite's warehouse and learned I had about an hour before departure time. I went for a walk down the main street of a typical small town and slipped into a typical Chinese cafe for a quick lunch.

An hour later I was seated in the dusty cab of a semi, rattling down a winding, dusty road. We made brief stops in Green Lake, Canoe Narrows, and Beauval and dropped off freight at the local stores. Almost three hours later, we rolled into the community of Ile-à-la-Crosse.

I liked what I saw. The homes were mostly framed houses, neatly painted, and fronted by picket fences. The community was connected by gravelled roadways plied by a number of vehicles. It was very much different from the rustic and isolated nature of Southend. As we approached the Hudson's Bay Company store, the first thing I noticed was that the store did not have a flagpole with the company flag flying. I thought, "How strange."

Ile-à-la-Crosse was the home of Louis Riel Sr., born here in 1817. He was employed by the Hudson's Bay Company in 1837 until he moved to the Red River Colony in 1843. The following year he met and married Julie Lagimodière and together they had 11 children, including the eldest son Louis Riel, he of the Red River Uprising and Northwest Rebellion fame.

The semi pulled into the driveway of the local Hudson's Bay Company store and backed up to the rear door to deliver its freight. I hopped out, went into the store, and was met by the store manager, a wiry, red-headed, and freckled Roy Simpson. He introduced me to my fellow clerk, Ross McBean, and immediately put me to work unloading the truck and then sweeping out his warehouse.

At store closing, I followed Ross to our staff quarters which was just a half block away. It was a comfortably furnished three bedroom home located on a large lot. The building was known locally as the Bay House and we were the Bay Boys.

We had the option of cooking for ourselves at home or eating at Burnoff's Restaurant where we simply charged our meals to the company. Our home meals were rather spartan as our fridge usually contained only a hock of smoked ham, a loaf of bread, butter and mustard. Bottles of beer occupied the rest of the space.

Next door was the RCMP quarters that housed the commanding corporal, Bert Pless, and his family, and a separate quarters for one or two constables that included Hugh Daykins. Most of us simply called Hugh "Humphrey" because of his large size and friendly nature.

Down the road was the hospital supervised by Dr. Hoffman and assisted by some five or six nurses and technicians and probably about 20 local employees who did the cooking, laundry, cleaning and maintenance. Nearby was the school staffed by about a dozen teachers, including good friends Georgette de Laforest, Helen Schile, Darlia Ryan and Beach Boy-crazy Jacquie Grimard. When Jacquie wasn't teaching she was dancing non-stop to the Beach Boys. Cliff and Kathy Samoleski, Larry Chrispen and Norrie and Sharon Edwards rounded out the teachers whose names I remember. A large Roman Catholic Mission anchored the community.

The community of Ile-à-la-Crosse was founded in 1779 by French fur traders associated with the North West Company from Montreal. The Hudson's Bay Company attempted to establish themselves here 20 years later in 1799; however, they became embroiled in intensive competition and never gained a foothold until the amalgamation of 1821.

In 1846, Fathers Taché and Lafleche of the Oblate Order founded the Roman Catholic Mission and in 1860, Grey Nuns arrived and set up the hospital and school.

Most of the people were Métis, descendants of the French fur traders that plied the northern waterways and who married Cree women. I, hailing from a different part of the country, found it somewhat a curiosity, and most interesting, when I realized many of the elders could speak French, but not English, and that their Cree was actually a mixture of Cree and French.

"Keepaha la porte," I heard a woman admonishing her child as they entered the store. "Keepaha" is Cree meaning "close the door." "La porte" is French for "the door." I have since learned that Michif is the term for this particular language mix. Michif is the language of many Métis communities, especially those found throughout Manitoba and Saskatchewan.

There was a high number of mink ranchers in the Ile-à-la-Crosse and Buffalo Narrows area. It was a major industry for the region and when they came into the store to shop, they were unmistakable because they reeked of the pungent smell of wild mink musk and urine. The scent was so strong, the odour hung heavily in the store air for several hours after they left, despite the open windows and doorways that we hoped would clear the air.

I had worked for a short period with one part-time mink rancher in Southend. He was trying to get a young male to mate with an older female who, even though she was much smaller than the male, was ferocious enough to keep the young inexperienced male at bay. The rancher pulled on his heavy leather gloves, reached into the cage, and safely grabbed the female. He pulled her out and rapped her head sharply on the outside edge of the cage. The rancher then threw her back into the cage, whereupon the young male was able to grab the dazed female by the neck and have his way with her.

I did not stay for very long. It was difficult working with caged animals. The same clothes had to be worn every day when working around the cages. The mink had to become used to your scent, otherwise they would become agitated whenever you neared their vicinity. Mink are finicky animals, and when extremely excited, agitated or startled, they have been known to eat their young.

One early evening, I and the rancher were on our way to the wired cages to check on the mink when we noticed a black bear lurking in the woods. The bears often scavenged the food droppings under the cages and in doing so, sometime accidently upset and damaged the fragile cages, freeing the valuable little animals.

The rancher kept a rifle in a shed near the cages. He quietly retrieved the rifle, loaded it, and shot at the bear. The bear, sitting on its haunches in the dark shade of shrubs and trees, was bowled over backward by the shot, and disappeared into the thick woods. The rancher reloaded the rifle, handed it to me, and told me to go check for the bear while he inspected the damage to several of the cages.

I walked cautiously to the spot where we last saw the bear. There was no bear, but I spotted blood and I could see the general direction in which it had run. I decided to follow the track. The brush was thick and the daylight was dimming with the sinking sun. I had not gone for more than a few yards when the bear unexpectedly and noisily attacked with a loud guttural and angry roar, crashing through the shrubs. I wheeled and dashed in between and behind some nearby trees, where I now turned to face the attacking bear, raising and firing my rifle all in one motion. The bear dropped a few feet in front of me. My breathing was laboured, my knees wobbled, and my heart pounded.

Ross was the senior trainee so he was made responsible for the non-foods side of the store plus the office. I was put in charge of the grocery department and the warehousing. Two local employees assisted me with the operation of the grocery section. Geordie Belanger was a large man, a six footer about 240 pounds. Pat Ratt was the opposite, five foot seven and about 130 pounds.

It was like working with Mutt and Jeff. Geordie was a mature man in his late thirties or early forties and it was always a chore getting him to accept my direction. He would often give me a puzzled look, and then mutter under his breath, just loud enough for me to hear, "The boss is not always right, but he is always the boss." Over time, I earned his respect and we became close friends.

Geordie's brother, Leo Belanger, had been in the armed forces and after the war he became a bush pilot. He flew all over the north in that part of the country, including Buffalo Narrows, Dillon, Portage la Loche, Patuanak, transporting fish, trappers and prospectors. Three marriages bore him a total of 27 children, including Buckley Belanger, a cabinet minister in the NDP provincial government.

Leo's exploits as a bush pilot as told by him would fill another book. My favourite story that he told me is the incident on a small frozen lake somewhere around Portage la Loche where he had been told to pick up some fish. He landed on the small lake with no problem but he knew he was in trouble once the plane was loaded with several tubs of frozen fish. He eyed the very short space he had for the take-off before running out of lake. He also eyed the height of the spruce trees at the end of the lake that he had to clear.

Leo took out rope that he always carried in his plane for tying down cargo. He tied one end to his rear ski and wrapped the other end of the rope around the stoutest tree nearest the shore. He advised the fisherman that he was going to rev the engine up to full power and when he gave the signal with a wave of his arm, the fisherman was to cut the line with his axe.

This they did and the plane suddenly shot forward, pushing Leo back into his seat. The fully loaded aircraft had just enough speed, power and lift to clear the trees. Leo said when he landed the plane at Buffalo Narrows, he swore he had spruce bough branches stuck in his skis.

Leo told another story of picking up a load of fish from a lake out-side of Buffalo Narrows. He had spent several hours on a frigid day, first loading the half dozen or so tubs of fish into the aircraft, and then having a leisurely lunch and visit with the fisherman. When it was time to leave, his small aircraft would not start. He set his throttle, left the ignition in the "on" position, and climbed out the airplane. Standing out front, he grabbed a propeller blade and spun it with all his might.

The aircraft engine suddenly came to life with a roar and the airplane leaped into motion. Leo had just enough time to jump away from the front of the aircraft and hop onto one of the skis as the plane moved past him, frantically holding onto the wing strut for balance. He explained that perhaps he had accidently brushed his throttle too far forward when he was getting out of the plane. Reaching for his door, Leo then realized that the wind stream from the propeller plus the aircraft bouncing over the snowbanks on the frozen lake prevented him from fully opening his door. As he struggled to gain entry, he looked up and realized the aircraft was headed toward shore and certain disaster.

Leo grabbed onto the wing strut with both arms, jumped off the ski, and dug his heels into the snow. Slowly he managed to turn the aircraft and steer it away from the shoreline. It was less bumpy travelling in the snow in the other direction, and Leo was finally able to open his door, climb in, and regain control of his airplane. Leo gave me a big grin and then left me wondering whether he had once again pulled my leg.

The day I had arrived in Ile-à-la-Crosse, I was unpacking and chatting with my roommate, Ross, when he noticed me pull a moosehide jacket from one of my bags. It was plain, no beads, and simply adorned with fringes. Ross's eyes lit up. He hurried to his room and returned with his moosehide jacket that looked exactly like mine, right down to the sateen wine-coloured lining. His jacket had been made by a Dene woman in Portage la Loche. My jacket was made by my mother in Southend. Thereafter, we never went anywhere together without our moosehide jackets, making us easily recognizable as the "Bay Boys."

One Friday evening Ross and I attended a party at the teachers' compound and we overdid it—not leaving until sunrise. We walked home, albeit with a slight stagger, and finally got to bed by about 5:00. Our alarms rang much too soon as we had to be at work by eight. We struggled to our feet, no need to dress as we had slept in our clothes, and splashed cold water on our faces. We gulped down our coffee with several aspirins and hustled off to work. Roy met us at the back door of the store, took one look at our bleary-eyed faces, and muttered, "Jesus! Jesus!" (his favourite expression when irked, surprised or generally not happy). "You can't serve customers in that condition."

I was banished to the basement where Roy made me clean the sprouts from the large supply of potatoes that we stored in bins in the basement. The company had a large property next to the RCMP, and every spring and summer the RCMP kept their prisoners busy working our large garden plot.

Potatoes were planted, then weeded, watered and hoed throughout the summer and harvested in the fall. So indeed, we had tons of potatoes and I had to pick up and clean each and every single one, sitting in the gloom of the dank basement, with my head aching and my stomach heaving every so often.

Ross was banished to the marking room where he exchanged positions with the marking staff who were put on the floor to serve customers in his place. The marking room duties included cranking out hundreds of price tickets and affixing them to merchandise. Yawn!

The end of that work day could not have come soon enough, and with store closing at 6:00, we couldn't wait to get home and go straight to bed. However, Mr. Simpson had other plans as he handed me and Ross the store keys. Sternly, he told us that not only did he want us to balance and close the books for the day, but he also wanted the cash balanced for the week before we left. We finished around eight. Roy had no pity for us and in fact, that day, he purposely went out of his way to stretch our work day into a twelve-hour one. Another lesson well learned.

Later that fall, Ross and I decided to visit our fellow Bay Boys at Buffalo Narrows, a community about an hour north of Ile-à-la-Crosse and Portage La Loche, a further hour beyond Buffalo on the same road.

At Buffalo Narrows we met Ken Finnbogason, one of the three Bay Boys who, it was rumoured, had attempted to trim the shag rug in their living room with a lawn mower at a party the week before.

At Portage la Loche, we met Alister MacGregor, again one of three Bay Boys, whom we could barely understand because of his thick Scottish brogue. He had recently arrived from Scotland and as the junior Bay Boy, his naivety was taken advantage of by the other clerks in the house.

Alister was told it was his responsibility to round up the half dozen or so cows that wandered the property and bring them to the vicinity of the Bay House every morning before work. This he did religiously for several mornings before the local priest approached him and asked what he was doing. Alister explained his responsibility and the priest laughingly straightened the situation, explaining those were his cows and the property belonged to the church.

"Fook!" exclaimed Alister, his favourite expression, once the priest was out of earshot.

We spent the night in the Bay House at La Loche and I found there was a dearth of chairs in the house. I sat on the floor nursing a beer and finally asked, "How come no chairs?"

Alister said they had a cool evening a few nights before and no wood had been cut for the heater in the living room. They thought it good sport to burn their old wooden chairs. Since sobering up, no one yet had the courage or a likely enough story to tell Dave Houle, their manager.

After the weekend trip of visiting our neighbouring company locations, Ross and I developed an appreciation for the tidiness and comfort of our home.

Shamaganis (long knives) is the Cree name for the RCMP and all police, for that matter. Interestingly, the name has its historical roots in the sabers and lances carried by the US Calvary and often used when chasing down Indians during the American Indian wars.

In spite of the history, RCMP Constable Daykins and I became good friends. He was just next door, so quite often we shared a beer and steak together after our workday. Every so often he would find himself the lone policeman in town when Corporal Pless and the other constable would be busy in neighbouring communities that were part of their jurisdiction. He often responded to calls during the daytime on his own, but after sundown he thought it prudent his back be covered.

He would come get me at all hours of the night, often waking me from my sleep, to act as his backup when he had to respond to a domestic problem. All I had to do was sit in the police vehicle and call for real backup if any problems got out of hand. Fortunately, Hugh always managed to get these emotionally wrought, and often alcohol driven, domestic quarrels under control on his own.

Back at the store, whenever the workday slowed, I would chat with eight-year-old Debbie, Roy and Marge's daughter. She always came to the store after school as Marge, a nurse, was often still on duty.

If I had little else to do, I would often wander over to the other side of the store to flirt with the girls. In Women's Wear I would find Evange at her desk. I would walk over and lean on her desk leering at her. To her question, always asked in an irritated tone, "What do you want?" I always had the same answer: "You know what I want."

"Mr. Simpson!" she would call for the boss.

"Flett. You get back to work. Jesus! Jesus!" Roy often responded without even looking up from his paperwork.

The in-store banter always brought forth a hearty laugh from everyone, including Evange. Today, one has to be rightly more cautious about behavior that might be viewed, with a jaundiced eye, as harassment.

Florence Durocher was in charge of Ladies and Children's Wear. She was an older, cheerful lady with a ready smile and an easy laugh for everyone. One winter morning she came rushing into the staffroom just barely on time for work. She took off her coat and was in the process of hanging it up when the staff sharing coffee before work burst into laughter.

"Florence, where's your skirt?" asked Rose with a giggle.

Florence looked down at her slip and burst into a laugh. She quickly put her coat back on and rushed home for her skirt.

That same winter, I received a letter from Dad advising that he was being transferred to Cumberland House, Saskatchewan. It was fitting that Dad was being placed in a historic location for his retirement years. His life was changing, and mine was also about to take a change.

A few days before that Christmas, Florence invited me to her home for tea and a visit. Her niece, Josephine, was visiting from Saskatoon and she wanted me to meet her. I immediately fell in love with one of the most beautiful women that I ever met, one who would become the mother of Lynda-Gale, Geraldine, and Amber.

Okemow – "Boss"

Once again I found myself in a small aircraft winging my way over dark spruce, muskeg, blue-green lakes and countless streams. This time I was on my way for a six-week management job in northern Ontario so that the manager could go on a well-deserved vacation. After an hour of flying, a fairly sizable lake came into view. I scanned the shoreline and located the tiny community of Fort Hope.

In preparation for the landing I put my book away and checked to ensure my seatbelt was secure. I looked up again and wondered why the aircraft was not yet descending. We flew past the community, continued over the lake and then the plane nosed down and slowly began its landing procedure. I quickly looked around and spotted the lonely red and white buildings of the Hudson's Bay Company located about five miles from the community at the far end of the lake. As the pontooned Cessna 180 splashed down on Eabamet lake, I wondered what was in store for me.

A few days before, Roy had approached me and told me to go home and pack my bags because I was leaving. My heart dropped. What did I do? Was I fired?

"Flett, if I was going to fire you I would have done so the first day you showed up on my doorstep," Roy assured me.

We pulled each other's leg so often I still wasn't sure whether Roy was serious or not. Finally he showed me the telegram he had received, requesting me to report to Hudson's Bay House in Winnipeg as I was being transferred to Fort Hope, Ontario. The telegram also contained the details of my travel arrangements to Winnipeg and thence to Fort Hope. I was to depart tomorrow.

This was all too sudden. It was early July and I had just proposed to Josephine a few days before. We had discussed a marriage date for mid-October but that was as far as we got. We would have to complete our wedding plans by mail.

Two days later, the aircraft taxied to the small dock where we were met by the manager, Dave Collie, and his local assistant, Danny Slipperjack. Danny lived in the village and he commuted to work every morning by canoe in summer and snowmobile in winter. As Danny was standing closest to me as I got out of the plane, I extended my hand in greeting. I think he expected me to bypass him to shake Dave's hand first, and I also guess he never before saw a company manager that looked like him.

As we walked up the embankment toward the white building, I realized it was very similar to Duck Lake and Southend in that it was a combined dwelling and store. The front lower part was the store. The second floor housed the two bedrooms, and the lower rear section was the kitchen and living room of the dwelling. What caught my eye was the Hudson's Bay Company sign over the storefront. It was written in old English printing style, which was a hint to its age and condition.

I walked into the store and felt, after Ile-à-la-Crosse, that I had stepped back in time. It was dark and musty. I was not impressed. The business had the appearance of an old trading post of days gone by. I checked the business records and lo and behold; it was a trading post! My initial impression and feelings were about to change. The store's total annual purchase of furs exceeded its merchandise sales for the year. A twinge of excitement and familiarity came over me. My father had instilled in me a love for fur buying. I realized I was only there for six weeks; however, I had a feeling I might enjoy my stay.

The following day was busy in the store with people coming and going all day. People smoked in public places then and it was not long before a cloud of blue smoke hung in the confined air of the store. Upstairs, each bedroom had an open metal grill on the floor to circulate the air and heat when required. On busy days in the store, the same clouds of smoke drifted up and billowed into the bedrooms. When our baby, Lynda-Gale arrived, Josephine had to block the grates with pieces of plywood that I had cut for this purpose. In the store, I made my way through the people to the doorway as I had to retrieve some flour from the warehouse. At the doorway, I noticed a child in a tikinagan propped up in a ten-gallon drum that we used as a garbage can.

"How ingenious! No one is going to accidentally knock that baby over in this crowded store," I thought to myself.

At the end of the day, Dave was rather puzzled by our paltry sales in spite of the day-long traffic. With a hint of a smile, I thought to myself, the people here of the Ojibway Nation were just as interested in me as I was of them. They were Anishinabe and I was of the Muskegowuk, First Nations terms for the Ojibway and Cree respectively.

The Cree and Ojibway are closely related as we both belong to the Algonkian linguistic group along with the Naskapi, Montagnais, Mi'kmaw and several other nations. (See Linguistic Table in Appendix.) The languages are similar in that many words have the same root. It is possible for fluent speakers to be able to communicate within the same family group and at least understand the gist of the communication.

For the record, there are nine major First Nations linguistic groups in Canada encompassing a total of 63 tribes, all with their own distinct language, customs, culture and territory. The Beothuk comprised the tenth language group and the 64th tribe; however, they were hunted to extinction by the colonizing peoples of Newfoundland. By population, according to 2011 Census, there are a total of about 1.4 million Aboriginal people in Canada; 850,000 are First Nations, 450,000 Métis, and 60,000 Inuit.

The common thread woven through all tribes and binding us together as a people is our belief in the Great Spirit and his embodiment in all things created by his hand. The concept of animism has been described in a previous chapter.

In later years, as an executive of the company, I had the opportunity to visit many, if not most, First Nations communities across the country. I was always amazed and in awe of the diversity amongst our people. I attended many meetings of First Nations people where the opening prayer and welcoming statements were always conducted in the language of the hosting Nation. The fact that most often I could not recognize a single similar word never failed to astound me. I may as well have been in Outer Mongolia. In spite of that diversity, the Canadian white majority still attempts to treat us as one nation, one people.

An interesting fact is that we do not consider the Inuit as falling under the same family of First Nations. The differentiation is in spiritual beliefs. The traditional Inuit spirituality is based in shamanism, a belief that a Shaman could act as an intermediary between the natural and supernatural worlds. The Shaman could also control spirit forces for the purposes of curing illnesses and looking into the past and future. The Shaman was a powerful individual who could communicate with spirits, both good and bad. He acted as a healer, counsellor and spiritual leader for his people.

The end of August and the end of my six-week stint was fast approaching and yet I had not heard a word from Head Office. I was starting to feel a bit uncomfortable and anxious. I sent a telegram to the office asking when I would be advised of my travel plans back to Ile-à-la-Crosse. Several days later a telegram arrived over my two-way radio advising that Dave Collie was being transferred to Sandy Lake and that the replacement manager intended for Fort Hope had resigned. I was asked to be patient while they searched for a suitable replacement manager.

Not good news. I knew that a single planned move could trigger a chain reaction of potential moves that the company always tried to avoid. Prepare for the worst case scenario—I'm stuck for a time.

One business day the store was fairly busy when an unexpected summer storm struck. Thunder and lightning storms anywhere in the Precambrian Shield are always spectacular and Fort Hope was no exception. A wind storm that accompanied the thunder and lightning whipped the lake into a frothy brew of wild waves and white caps. It was closing time but the six people still in the store who canoed over from the village were stuck until the storm blew over.

The people chatted in Ojibway, which I did not understand, and then to my surprise two of the men picked up brooms and started sweeping the floor. The four women meanwhile started working on the shelves, folding and neatly rearranging all my merchandise. They laughed and chatted as they worked and my heart warmed to these people.

That evening I picked up pen and paper and wrote a letter to C.H.J. Winter, the District Manager for the area. (He was simply known in our company circles as "C.H.J."). I advised him that I enjoyed Fort Hope and in the event he could not find a suitable replacement for Mr. Collie, I was more than willing to take on the role as Store Manager. I just needed the time to return to Ile-à-la-Crosse to get married.

About a week later, our company de Havilland Beaver aircraft landed on the lake in front of the store and taxied toward our dock. Leaving Danny in charge, I went down to meet the aircraft. As the pilot was securing the Beaver to the dock, a pipe-smoking, ascot-wearing English gentleman stepped from the plane. When he was not puffing on a pipe, he was chain-smoking cigarettes. C.H.J. Winter was, however, the perfectly-mannered English gentleman.

That evening, Mr. Winter told me about his Arctic experience in Gjoa Haven (or a similar location). The Hudson's Bay Company stores were unheated and in their homes they depended upon shipments of coal brought in by their annual sealifts. One year, the supply ship never arrived because the shifting ice floes and ice packs made sea travel in that particular area impossible. This was the same general area where the Franklin expedition met its demise over a century before. C.H.J. told me how he had to take stock of his food supplies. That wasn't the biggest concern because he could go hunting with the Inuit as he had done many times before.

The biggest concern was a source of heat for cooking and comfort. The "comfort" he knew he had to sacrifice. That fall and winter he had had to search for and gather swamp grass. He dug through the snow and pulled enough swamp grass to tie into clumps for burning. On one of his regular searches for swamp grass along the seashore, he happened upon an old sea wreck. He not only was able to salvage some wood for burning but he also stumbled upon a supply of coal that the ship had carried—probably for fuel. He survived that winter after much deprivation. My respect for Mr. Winter increased several fold. He had paid his dues to attain his level of management.

The next morning we went through the store, the books, the warehouses and I knew he was impressed, especially when he noticed the freshly white-washed pole fence, flag pole and rocks lining the pathways. I silently and facetiously thanked my dad for his training in what was important to the Hudson's Bay Company. And I also light-heartedly thought to myself, "I told you so, Roy. Flag poles are important."

Before he left the next morning, Mr. Winter confirmed the management job was mine, and that he would immediately arrange for a relief manager. I needed a temporary replacement so that I could take a week to return to Ile-à-la-Crosse to get married. In the meanwhile, I received a letter from Dad telling me that my grandfather, Alexander Flett, had retired from this very same location. It was then I felt that my being in this community was somehow meant to be.

Woody Magnusson, my stand-in best man, lifted a glass at the end of the table and wished me and Josephine well. Mrs. Pless and Marge Simpson had hurriedly arranged a bridal dinner in my old Bay House with about a dozen guests. Mr. Winter had given me travel dates which were earlier than the marriage date that Josephine and I had planned. I telegraphed Ross McBean, my intended best man, at Rossville, Manitoba that dates had changed. We received a telegram back from store manager, Dave Brears, advising that Ross had already left Rossville for his vacation.

Ross arrived the day after the wedding just as Josephine and I were preparing to leave. I offered to have him come on our short honeymoon to Winnipeg which was enroute to Fort Hope, but he laughed and reminded me he had friends in Ile-à-la-Crosse other than just me. He wished to stay and visit for a few days.

Josephine and I made it back to Fort Hope ahead of the freeze-up. Tom Pollock, my relief manager, was on his way to Bearskin Lake to assume management of that location. Cal Russell, a Scot whose own countrymen I'm sure never understood him because of his extremely thick brogue, was my nearest neighbour in Lansdowne House. On one visit to Lansdowne, I spent the evening smiling and nodding my head at Cal. I had no idea what he was talking about as I had tired of asking him to repeat what he had just said.

There were a number of Scots managing stores all around me. One day a helicopter landed in front of our store. The occupants were conducting some sort of survey or aerial prospecting. One of the men came into the store and asked me, "Where is the store manager?"

"I am the store manager," I announced proudly.

Without skipping a beat, he asked: "How come you don't speak with a Scottish accent?"

We conducted our business after we had stopped laughing at each other.

One late October or early November evening, Josephine and I went to the village by boat to have dinner with friends. That evening I had stepped outside after dinner to check on the weather and I noticed that the temperature had plummeted within a few hours. I took a quick walk down to the water and one could see the ice crystals forming and spreading rapidly outward from the shoreline on the quiet lake. I hurried back to our friends' house, got Josephine and told her we had to get going immediately. The lake was freezing up.

It was a frigid ride back across the calm lake and when we got to within two or three hundred yards of our destination, we ran into solid ice. The ice was thick enough that I worried we might damage the flimsy canvas covering on our canoe. I shut the outboard motor off, gingerly stepped out of the front of our canoe and onto the ice. I desperately held onto the canoe while I tested whether the ice could hold my weight. It did and I dragged the canoe with Josephine in it the rest of the way to our shoreline.

For the next two or three weeks we saw no one. I had a store but no customers. Finally a young man walked across the ice for a few supplies. A week later the first customer to brave the thin ice with his snowmobile was John Yesno. He was actually one of my competitors; Brian Booth, a former Hudson's Bay Company man was the other. John was semi-retired, but still sold a few goods now and then, especially during freeze-up and breakup when the Hudson's Bay Company was isolated from the village. He had been doing so well during the freeze-up that his store was running short of supplies. He needed some of my goods, which I was only too pleased to supply.

John remembered my widower grandfather and the two daughters that he had with him in Fort Hope. He also remembered my uncle, Albert "Toots" McIvor, who managed the store in Fort Hope from 1957 to 1962. Toots was also a career Hudson's Bay man who often travelled with his cousin, my dad, when they were on vacation-leave together from the company. John told me that at 60 years old, "Toots" was still a powerful man. He is remembered in Fort Hope as being able to lift a full 45-gallon drum of gas, a total weight of close to 400 pounds.

I helped John load his snowmobile and noticed he had a long rope dragging from the rear of his machine. I asked about the rope and John laughed and said, "that's for someone to pull me out of the water if I go through the ice."

Our kitchen was equipped with a hand pump over the kitchen sink. This was our water supply. I suppose I should have crawled under the house in the fall and ensured our pipe to the well was properly insulated. Of course, I didn't and of course, our water supply froze solid.

I found an ice chisel and an axe and trudged through the snow to the lake. I walked out about a hundred feet from the shoreline and started chiselling through the ice. It was mid-December and the weather was frigid. I chopped through almost two feet of ice before hitting ground. Ground? Obviously I was too close to shore. I walked out another hundred feet and started chiselling again. This time I hit water, but it was muddy water. It was again obvious that I still was not far out enough.

I looked back and to the left where the dock was now frozen in next to the creek that ran alongside our property. I realized that where the canoes came to shore along the dock, the creek had cut a channel. Away from the channel, the shoreline was shallow for some distance. I decided to walk an extra one hundred feet or so out, and this time I hit deep clear water.

I got my snowmobile and sled and tied a wash tub to the sled. At the waterhole I filled the tub and then covered it with a plastic tablecloth and lashed the cover tightly with cord. I proudly hauled my water to the house but soon found, in spite of the plastic cover, that I had lost most of my load. There was maybe a pail or two of water in the tub. I made several trips but only managed to fill our water drum about one quarter full.

The next day when Danny arrived for work, I told him about my problem hauling water and he laughed. We found another 45-gallon drum and he showed me how to lash the drum to the sled. Then, when we had filled the drum from the water hole, instead of covering the drum, Danny floated a clean board on the water. We hauled the drum of water successfully up the embankment and to the house with barely any loss of water. The board prevented the water from slopping around in the drum. Danny also kicked snow into my waterhole for insulation so that next time I had to get water, I only had a little bit of chopping to do. I was slowly learning.

That same weekend Josephine and I decided to visit the community by Skidoo. We were about halfway to the village when Josephine told me her legs were freezing. I made my way to shore and the tiny log house occupied by Mr. Ooshag and his wife, Maria, Danny's grandparents. I knocked on the door and when the wizened old man opened his door, I said in Cree, "Tugkawyow." He understood we were cold and needed to warm up. He directed us to his little cast iron stove in the middle of his cosy home.

Mrs. Ooshag pulled up Josephine's pant leg to see what she was wearing and then directed a stream of Ojibway at me that I did not understand. She made it known that she was not happy with me and then she gave me a blanket to wrap around Josephine for the rest of our short trip. We were still learning.

One evening after sunset, I and several friends, including Charlie Okeese and Andy Yesno, decided to take a Skidoo ride on a trail which led to Miminiska Lake, about 50 miles west of Fort Hope. Miminiska was a rich trapping area for several families and these families spent their entire winter hunting, trapping and living off the bounty of the land. As we turned a tight corner on the trail, I noticed a sled to one side of the trail and as I slowed I was startled by several men standing alongside the trail, ghostly lit by the moonlight.

Josephine, who was riding behind me on my Skidoo, looked up to see why we were stopping, and shrieked in fright at the sight of the strangely attired men, standing apparition-like in the woods. These were trappers from Miminiska trekking by foot to Fort Hope and pulling their furs and supplies on small toboggans behind them.

For added protection from the wind and cold the men wrapped their heads and upper bodies with flannelette sheets folded like giant scarves and knotted at their chests over their parkas. A flannelette sheet was torn into strips and the strips were wrapped around their wrists to prevent the cold from entering their sleeves. On their feet, they wore outer, over-sized moccasins stuffed with straw, giving them an overall otherworldly appearance. Strange, but very effective for their harsh environment.

They had heard the roar of our Skidoo engines approaching and knowing we would not see them immediately in the dark, they prudently stepped off the trail and waited for us to pass by. They smiled and apologized for frightening our women, explaining they were on their way to Fort Hope to pick up supplies. They had walked non-stop all that day and into the evening, and would continue walking non-stop throughout the night until they reached the destination of their home village in the early morning hours.

Early the same winter I met the affable Andy Waboose who spoke excellent English. He learned the language from his days as a miner at Pickle Lake. We entered into a simple business arrangement whereby he turned a portion of his home on the reserve into a convenience store. I supplied him with all the goods, did all the accounting, and paid him a straight commission of ten percent of sales.

One Sunday afternoon he was at my store with his Skidoo and sled to pick up supplies for his business. He was carrying a case of Carnation canned milk on his shoulders out to his sled when he slipped off the stairway entrance to the store. The case of milk weighing close to 50 pounds dropped on his leg, which had twisted to a vulnerable angle. His leg snapped and when I reached him after hearing his call for help, I knew it was not good news when I found his foot twisted at a strange angle from his leg. The nursing station for Fort Hope was still at least a year away from being built.

I straightened his foot as best as I could and with Josephine's help affixed a splint. We laid Andy on a toboggan and hauled him into our house where we laid him on a cot we had assembled in our living room for this purpose. We administered the strongest painkiller we found in our company medicine chest. I sat up with him throughout the night and fed him codiene tablets whenever he complained of the pain.

Finally that Monday morning, I was able to connect with Kenora by our two-way radio, and ordered an aircraft to evacuate Andy for proper medical care. Andy's last word before being lifted into the air ambulance was to get his brother Walter to take over his business.

On Sundays when our store was closed, I enjoyed putting on my snowshoes and walking through the still and quiet of the forest. With my shotgun on my shoulder, I headed toward an area that had several small clearings. On finding a clearing, I would cock my shotgun and slowly, silently, walk forward until suddenly a ptarmigan would explode from its snow cover. No matter how mentally prepared you were for that burst from the snow, it was still very startling to have the peace and quiet of the forest shattered from almost under your feet. If you were able to compose yourself sufficiently to get a shot off, it was like skeet shooting. You only had a few seconds to get the bird before it reached the cover of the thick forest.

The ptarmigan in winter is a beautiful snow-white bird of the grouse family that ranges from the northern forests to the barren lands of the Arctic. In early evenings, ptarmigan like to burrow shallowly into the snow for the night. Overnight, the crust of snow covering the ptarmigan hardens just enough that the bird has to thrust itself, wings beating madly, to break through the snow cover. It literally explodes out of the snow.

On March 13, 1968, our daughter Lynda-Gale was born in Sioux Lookout, Ontario. She was a beautiful baby with a full head of thick black hair. Josephine and I, proud parents, fawned over the baby. Every quiet moment I had in the store, I slipped into the house to admire our baby. About two weeks after the baby was home, Josephine called me in a panic. The baby's belly button had fallen off. I also panicked. What do we do?

Ellen Neshinabe was in the store. She was the community medicine dispenser. I asked her to come into the house to see our baby and tell us what needed to be done. She laughed when she realized our concern and assured us that everything was normal. Such is life in a isolated area where one has no access to telephones or friends and family nearby to turn to for advice.

Ellen told us it was the custom for the people to place the baby's umbilicus in a moose- or deer-hide pouch and then hang it in a tree. That way the baby always knows where its home is.

Shortly thereafter, Josephine and I decided to visit the village and our friends to show off our new baby. I now had a sled with a box that I could tow behind my Skidoo. I bundled Josephine and the baby into the box wrapped with blankets, and the baby double-wrapped just to be on the safe side, topped with a windproof tarp.

It was a 30- to 45-minute ride to the village by the time we pulled up to the teachers' house where our friends resided. I pulled the tarp and blanket off Josephine and then we unwrapped our baby. We were aghast at the sight of our baby drenched in sweat and gasping for air.

Caroline Slipperjack, Danny's wife, then showed us the proper way to wrap and travel with a baby in winter. It is a wonder Lynda-Gale survived her parents' learning curve on adapting to life with a baby in the wilderness.

Our home and store was powered by a 32-volt electrical system. There was a small shed in the backyard housing a small Onan gas generator and two rows of wet cell batteries. The two-volt wet cells were hooked to each other in series, 16 in all, generating 32 volts of electricity. The electrical system was very basic, driving a light bulb in each room and powering a two-way radio that we used for our communication with the outside world.

The generator was used to charge the batteries. I would run the generator until the batteries were bubbling and the indicators in the batteries signalled the cells were fully charged. The electricity stored in the batteries was sufficient to light our home for a number of days. A gradual dimming of the light bulbs signalled time to start the generator and recharge the batteries.

Simple, yes. Problem free, no. All machinery is subject to breakdowns and I still curse the many hours I spent in the dark and cold of that power shed trying to get the generator to start. It was not long before I became expert in dismantling and reconstructing the Onan generator in the dim illumination of a flashlight.

That winter, tractor trains arrived not only with goods for our store but also with building materials for our new store planned for construction in the rapidly developing village.

It was an exciting day when the chug chug of diesel engines broke the still of the early winter morning. A lone Caterpiller tractor, puffs of smoke streaming upward from its exhaust pipe, was clearing its way up the embankment from the lake pushing snow out of its way with a blade out front. Following close behind were several tractors each pulling two or three large sleds behind laden with goods for the store.

I had intentionally ordered more goods than our store and warehouses could hold. I converted one of our two bedrooms into a temporary warehouse and blocked off one half of our living room for storing canned milk, which was freezable. I appreciated the tolerance of my wife as my business invaded the sanctity of our home.

Spring finally arrived and the beauty of our historic, isolated location was breathtaking. Our upstairs bedroom faced the east and it was always a pleasurable experience to be greeted every morning by the rays of the early rising sun.

One spring morning, Josephine and I looked out our bedroom window as we were rising and we noticed several small rabbits friskily gamboling about and nibbling at the fresh grass on our front lawn.

We decided to see if we could catch one of the bunnies and we ran downstairs and out the door; I in my underwear and Josephine in her nightgown. The tiny rabbits, just recently born, were still very agile and easily eluded us as we ran back and forth in bent-over positions until we both collapsed on the grass laughing.

Another spring visitor to our home was a black bear. Our garbage pit was located in the woods just behind our house. While we attempted to burn most of our refuse, there were probably enough morsels left to make the pit a regular fast food stop for the bear. The bear then made a habit of entering our yard and we had to bang pots and pans to drive him away. Unfortunately, I eventually had to shoot the animal because Josephine and I would often return from the village in the dark, always with our baby in arms, and we could never be sure if the bear was around.

The morning I shot the bear I told our first customers that entered the store where the carcass could be found. They borrowed some rope from me and were quite pleased to tow the animal and load it into their canoe. They asked if I would like some of the meat. I politely declined. It was some years later that I found I was of the bear clan and learned from elders that we do not eat our clan totems.

Meanwhile, development in the new village was burgeoning. A sawmill had been operational for two years and now piles of two by fours and boards were drying and curing. They would be required for the construction of many more homes that would be needed to house the people moving in from their traditional grounds. The migration to this centre was necessary so that their children could attend school.

The people of Fort Hope were undergoing a radical change in their lifestyles. They were moving in from their traditional hunting, fishing, trapping, and gathering grounds. What was different was that after millenia of nomadic ways, they were now moving into a village-style life on a permanent basis.

The village featured a new school, a few new homes with many more to come. Two churches were under construction: one Roman Catholic for Father Ouimet, and the other Anglican for Reverend Gerald Kaye. A nursing station was in the planning. There was a diesel station, generating power for the school and community. Water and sewer lines were being installed and roadways and streets being laid out. It was a model village; planned, designed, and constructed for the people by the Department of Indian Affairs under the auspices of the Indian Agent responsible for Fort Hope. Too bad the people were never consulted about what they needed or wanted.

The people were moving from a life of self-sufficiency to one of dependence upon the government—not the kind of dependence envisioned by our elders and leaders when the Treaties were signed, one that would be akin to the dependence of a landlord upon his tenants —but one that sucked the pride and sense-of-being out of many of the people.

Where was the economy to replace the independence of hunting, trapping, fishing and gathering enjoyed by our people for millennia? The next few years would be fine as there was much construction work to be done that would require many loggers, carpenters and labourers. But what of the long term once enough houses were built to accommodate the people moving in from their traditional lands?

This was 1968, only a year away from when Neil Armstrong and Buzz Aldrin would step onto the moon; when Neil would utter those unforgettable words: "One small step for man, one giant leap for mankind."

Somehow, those words rang hollow for our people. Somehow, instead of a giant leap forward, we were taking a giant leap backwards.

In The New Village

Our new store and home was under construction on the reserve. Ray and his Icelandic crew from Riverton, Manitoba were on site immediately after the spring thaw. First up within a few days was the metal-clad warehouse. This enabled Ray and his crew to move from the tight, damp confines of the tent to the spacious and dry accommodations offered by the warehouse.

It was not long before the foundation of the combined house and store was in place and the skeleton of the building started taking shape. By mid-July, the carpenters had the building enclosed and were now busy with the interior work. The store was mostly completed by early August and when I was reviewing the plans with Ray, I asked when he was going to start the fixturing work for the store. He looked at me and said that was my responsibility.

For the next week or so I boated to the village after store closing and worked until about midnight, setting up counters, shelves, and equipment. Later at the official store opening, C.H.J. Winter flew in from Winnipeg to assist me. He looked around the new store and made a comment about the excellent job Ray had done with the fixturing. I advised C.H.J. that I had done the fixturing because Ray told me it was my responsibility. C.H.J. gave me a quizzical look and advised that company building crews always did the fixturing. It was part of their contracts.

Ray pulled a fast one on me but I must say it was good experience for me. I was also left without sewer service as there was no dry location on the property on which to install a septic field. We did, however, manage to find a relatively dry spot on which we built an outhouse. We even had a problem trying to install poles for a clothesline but again eventually located a dry spot where we could dig the necessary holes.

The property on which our store and house was built was sharply inclined. The front of the building was built at ground level but the back end of the building was constructed on six foot posts. The ground was boggy and wherever we dug, the hole would immediately fill with water. I hired a couple of the local men to trench the property along our property line to drain the moisture. By the following year the property was sufficiently dry for me to install a septic field.

Installation of the septic field required gravel and the gravel pit was several miles down the lakeshore. That winter, gravel was hauled by snowmobile and sled by the tubful. To get at the gravel, the men had to build a large fire on the pit to melt the snow and ice. It was painfully laborious work but within a few weeks we had a sufficient quantity.

A pump and pressure tank had been installed, with a line to the lake. The line of course froze as soon as the cold weather set in. I set up a water drum and hauled water from the lake by Skidoo as needed. Chiselling ice for a water hole was hard work. As I hauled water only once per week the water hole would be frozen tight by the time I needed to use it again. I noticed that all my immediate neighbors were sharing my waterhole so I decided to leave my ice chisel by the water hole, hoping that my neighbours would keep the hole open.

Immediately after I chiselled the water hole open, my neighbours were happily walking down with their water buckets. Within two to three days they were scooping water from the shrinking hole with a large pot to fill their bucket. By the weekend, the hole had shrunk to a size where they needed a small dipper to fill their bucket. They were very pleased when the weekend rolled around and I had to chisel the hole back to a size that would accommodate a bucket.

It was some time later I asked one of my neighbours why he waited for me to widen the water hole. The simple answer was that the ice chisel belonged to me and they were not about to touch my equipment. The water hole was also mine but I could not lay claim to the water itself. In the end, amusingly, it was not about the industriousness of the people which I had begun to suspect—it was simply about respect.

The following spring I set out to correct and complete what had been left undone by our building crew. I had never before installed a septic field but I did have the blueprints that Ray had left behind. I carefully followed the plan and when completed, I was pleasantly surprised that everything worked. I then hired some men and had them dig a well. Fortunately we hit good clean water at about 12 feet. I installed an insulated waterline buried a minimum of six feet deep to the well. Problem solved.

Next I replaced the wood kitchen stove with a propane one and also installed a propane water tank. We were now set comfortably in our home for the next three years.

The business in the new store boomed. The company sent me a trainee, Allen Wheaton, to assist. He transferred out after a short stay and was replaced by Bill Moore, newly arrived from Ireland. Bill enjoyed his privacy and shut the door to his bedroom every night. Unfortunately, that deprived his room of any heat during the wintry nights and every morning his blankets were frozen tightly to the walls. He just shook his head in disbelief at the sight of his frosty blankets.

That fall and early winter, the store was so busy that our grocery supplies were rapidly depleting. Toward the end of the freeze-up period our grocery shelves were almost like Mother Hubbard's cupboards. The only goods we had left in any quantity were rolled oats, canned meatballs and Kraft Dinner. The last week of freeze-up, our daily menu remained unchanged. Porridge for breakfast and Kraft Dinner with meatballs for lunch and dinner.

Josephine was pregnant with our second child and the due date was somewhat touch and go with the freeze-up period. I had wanted her to go to Geraldton, our nearest hospital, before freeze-up; however, Josephine decided that was just too long a stay to be away from me and Lynda-Gale. She would leave on the first plane after freeze-up.

The first plane after the freeze arrived around the first week of December carrying our mail and parcels that had accumulated over the five or six week period. Mail days were very exciting then, as letters from friends and loved ones kept us in touch with the outside world. Josephine was too excited to leave. She promised that she would leave on the next plane.

A few days later the weather turned for the worse. A blizzard blew in from the north, the temperatures plunged, and the winds began howling. There were days when one could not see beyond two or three feet. Josephine chose this time to go into labour.

Josephine's contractions were well spaced so there was so immediate emergency. I contacted our air service provider, Austin Airways, in Nakina and they advised they would remain in communication and on standby for the weather to break.

I walked to Ellen Neshinabe's house and she came over to see Josephine. Ellen confirmed the baby was still some time away from arriving. She said she would go alert Patta Moonias, an elder very experienced as a midwife, to ensure she would be available if needed to deliver the baby.

The next morning, there was a slight improvement in the weather. The high winds had dropped and the snowfall was beginning to ease. I called Austin Air on my two-way radio. They were still on standby. They advised they had received several truck loads of grocery supplies for the store that they were now preparing for airlift. Their weather was improving slowly and they would call me to advise as soon as they were able to fly.

By mid-afternoon I was becoming anxious. I expressed my concern to Austin Airways about Josephine's condition. I knew they shared my concern because Josephine, without hesitation, had cooked and looked after their pilots whenever they were grounded in our area by weather. They said there was a further break in the weather at their end and that they would attempt a flight.

The pilot of the Norseman aircraft called me as soon as he was in the air. I gave him our weather conditions, which were not the best, but we hoped that there would be further improvements in the hour he would take to arrive in our vicinity. I was never more relieved to hear the roar of the Norseman engine as the aircraft flew over our building in its landing approach. The visibility was still not the greatest but the pilot, Archie MacDougall, was their most experienced.

Some time ago, Archie had had to spend a night with us because of inclement weather. Over a glass of scotch, he related how he had dropped off a couple of grizzled prospectors on a small lake about 60 miles northwest of Fort Hope. It was sometime in early October that Archie had dropped them off and arrangements had been made to pick them up at the end of the month.

Archie told me it had been a cold month and when he flew over the small lake in his Norseman, the lake was enclosed in ice. It was too early for the freeze-up so he knew the ice on the small lake was an anomaly. Fort Hope's Eabamet Lake was still ice free. Archie made several passes over the lake, just touching the ice with his pontoons with enough force to crack it up. He said he then flew back to Fort Hope, waited a few hours, then flew back to the small lake.

Sure enough, the wind had pushed the cracked ice sufficiently that Archie now had room to land his aircraft and pick up the men. The prospectors were clearly relieved to be rescued as they were not equipped or supplied to wait out a freeze-up period lasting five to six weeks. I looked at Archie and accepted his story with a grain of salt. It was a great tale. I was too polite to tell him his story was a real stretch.

Archie McDougall was not only a great storyteller, he was also a great pilot. As the chief pilot for Austin Air in Nakina, he undertook the challenge of this flight himself. He expertly landed his aircraft on the ice in front of our village and taxied toward shore.

The plane was quickly unloaded and Josephine and I boarded. I had arranged for Margaret Yesno to babysit Lynda-Gale, and I left the store in the hands of Bill. The aircraft flew us directly to Geraldton and when we landed, Austin Air had arranged a vehicle to drive us directly to the hospital.

Josephine, now safely ensconced in her hospital room, told me to go the hotel and get some sleep. She knew I had not slept for two days. The nurses assured me that as soon as the baby was to arrive, the hospital would call me at the hotel. I wanted to be present for the birth of my baby as I had not been present for Sandra or Lynda-Gale.

I was awakened from a deep sleep by the hospital calling me the very early morning of December 11, 1969 to advise I was the proud father of a baby girl. And sorry, they did not have time to call me because when the baby decided it was coming, there was no stopping her.

I got to the hospital as quickly as I could. I was somewhat hesitant about walking into the hospital room and seeing Josephine. I had expected to see someone who had just given birth to be bedraggled, beat up and the worse for wear. Instead, there was Josephine sitting up on her bed, hair brushed and looking fresh. She jumped out of bed, took my hand and led me to the nursery window where she happily pointed out our baby.

Once home, Geraldine Kaye was a quiet, happy, contented baby. I would awaken in the early morning and listen for her cry, which never came. A nagging fear would force me to get up to check and ensure she was still breathing. Sure enough, without fail, every morning she would be happily playing with her toes, blanket or rattle. I would pick her up and she would gaze at me with her huge, charcoal-dark eyes, smile, and my heart would melt.

A small aircraft from Superior Airways out of Armstrong, Ontario landed in the village and dropped off some passengers. I and a few friends had ridden down to the airplane on our snowmobiles, curious about the unfamiliar aircraft. We chatted with the pilot and he told us about the hundreds of moose tracks he saw on a small lake about 20 miles to the west. He noted that he could see the trail to Miminiska and that the small lake was not that far off the trail.

We knew that moose never tracked up an open lake like the pilot described so we suspected it was a herd of woodland caribou. It was early afternoon so we decided to take our rifles and go check out this lake. Both Andy Yesno and Charlie Okeese said they had a good idea which lake the pilot had been talking about. We fueled up our machines and struck out on the hunt.

We crossed a small creek which ran across our Skidoo trail and surmised that it flowed into the lake we were looking for. We dismounted and as quietly as possible, we made our way on foot toward the lake. There were no tracks but we kept pushing through the deep snow, hoping we would soon come across some evidence of the caribou. We began to regret that we did not bring snowshoes as the lake was a little further from our snowmobile trail than we had initially figured.

We finally arrived at the lake and looked around at the empty landscape. The were no caribou—not even tracks. Obviously we were not in the right location. The sun was rapidly sinking toward the horizon and the temperature was noticeably dropping. We decided to turn around and return home.

Back in the village, Andy and Charlie came over to my house that evening and we pored over some maps that I had of the area. We realized we had been short of our target and had we proceeded about another five miles further, we would have been in the right area. We decided we would give it another try in the morning.

The next morning we proceeded on our hunt much better equipped. We each towed sleds behind our snow machines and carried snowshoes, axes, thermoses of hot coffee and sandwiches for lunch. The day was crisp and snappy cold. Our breath hung in clouds of ice crystals as we spoke and made plans for the day. Frost rimmed our eyebrows and eyelashes.

We had calculated an extra five miles of travel from the point where had stopped the previous day. Once we reached that particular point, we carefully timed ourselves and stopped once we thought we were in the correct vicinity. We put on our snowshoes and proceeded in the direction of where we thought the lake lay. It was not long before we ran into tracks everywhere. It was obvious the herd had been here for some time.

We started inching our way, being extra careful not to make any noise. The wind was in the right direction, blowing into our faces. Once we could make out the clearing that was the lake, we spotted the small herd feeding on moss hanging from the dead trees along the shore.

Andy went left, Charlie proceeded straight ahead and I went right. Andy would take the first shot because he would be at the bottom end of the small bay where the caribou were milling about feeding. Charlie would take the next shot from his position and I would take the final shots before the small herd broke out of the bay and onto the open lake.

I got into a comfortable laying position behind a fallen tree, cocked my rifle and waited. A shot rang out, a caribou dropped and the herd bolted. Another two shots rang out and two more caribou dropped. The herd was thundering past me as I chose my target and pulled the trigger. Another caribou dropped. By the time I was able to reload another cartridge, the herd was just far enough away that I was not able to get a good target within my sights.

We gutted the animals and then conferred about the best way to get our kill out. We could skin, quarter, and then carry our meat out on our backs. Or we could make our way back for our machines and sleds and cut a trail through the bush to the lake. It was extremely cold so we decided to cut and pack a trail. We would save the butchering for the warmth of a shed back home.

Cutting and packing down a trail to the lake was a little harder and took longer than we thought. We struggled with the machines and loaded sleds in the bush, pushing and pulling through the deep snow. Finally we were all out of the bush and on the trail for home. The sun had set and a bright moon was rising in its place. It was brutally cold and the fact we had worked ourselves into a sweat hauling the game out of the deep bush did not help matters. We should have made a fire to warm and dry ourselves before hitting the trail for home.

We put our heads down and just drove, trying to escape the freezing wind by huddling behind our tiny windshields. I could see Charlie ahead of me but neither of us turned our heads to look behind us because of the frigid cold. We pulled into the community and only then did we realize that Andy was not with us. As I had a bigger machine, I told Charlie to go home and that if Andy did not show up within the hour, I would go and look for him.

After I had warmed sufficiently, I fueled up and went back in search of Andy. I was almost all the way back to where we had shot our caribou before I spotted Andy out in the middle of one of the larger lakes that we had to cross. His snowmobile had broken down in the middle of the lake. He realized that he would probably freeze to death if he attempted to walk to shore where he would have been able to make a proper fire and await rescue.

Instead, he removed the hood of his snowmobile and had it propped up as a windbreak. Within this small shelter, he had a fire going in a tea pail made by ripping the foam padding out of his snowmobile seat, soaking the foam in oil and gasoline, and lighting it afire. He did this a number of times throughout the evening. This action probably saved his life. He was shivering cold—hypothermia was obviously setting in.

I picked him up and got him behind me on the Skidoo and we headed for shore immediately. I got a roaring fire going and within ten or fifteen minutes a smile from him indicated he was going to be all right.

We decided to abandon his snowmobile and sled for the night. We overturned the sled with the caribou carcasses and covered it with as much snow as possible with the hope of hiding as much of the scent as possible from the wolves. We would need to return with two machines tomorrow; one to tow Andy's snowmobile and the other to tow the sled and caribou. We arrived back to the village and I dropped him off at his house around midnight. I fell into an exhausted sleep that night.

"Let's go visit Father Oiumet," someone suggested.

The tractor trains had come and gone already that winter and we were anxious to see what new snow machine Father Oiumet would be driving. Father Oiumet was related to the Bombardier family in Quebec and every year, the Bombardier company would send Father their newest and biggest model of the Skidoo snowmobile. Father Oiumet, a small wiry man in his 40s, loved to travel by Skidoo.

Father Oiumet lived in Lansdowne House, which was located about 75 miles north of Fort Hope. He was responsible for the Roman Catholic parishes of both Lansdowne and Fort Hope. In winter he made at least weekly trips to Fort Hope by snowmobile. One weekend he arrived on his Skidoo from Lansdowne sporting a bandage from his lip to his cheek and when he smiled, he was missing two or three teeth.

"What happened to you, Father Oiumet?" we asked.

"I ran into a clothesline while I was speeding through town on my Skidoo. Luckly, I wasn't beheaded!" he explained with a tooth-less smile.

Andy Yesno, Charlie Okeese, Bill Moore and I ran a final check on our machines, fuel, and essential spare parts like an extra engine belt, spark plugs, gas line, gas filter, rope, axe and basic tools. We filled empty one-quart oil containers with gasoline and stored them in tight crevasses wherever we found them in and around our Skidoos.

The trip was a three- to five-hour one depending upon the condition of the trails. The day was bright and sunny with little wind but the thermometer was hovering around minus forty Celcius. Or Fahrenheit. It didn't matter which because the temperature of minus 40 is the same on both scales. It was bloody cold!

Our small caravan of four snowmobiles pulled out of my yard and we hadn't even reached the lake when one of Bill's skis fell off his machine. He took one look and said, "I'm out."

Andy, Charlie and I proceeded without Bill and before we were even off Eabamet Lake, about five miles from the community, Andy's machine began coughing and sputtering. We halted, checked Andy's fuel filter and found it frost or ice covered. We shook and cleaned the ice and frost off and lowered it back into his gas tank. We had to repeat this procedure two or three times throughout the trip.

The third time we had to stop for Andy to clean his filter, disaster befell us. While Andy was cleaning the filter, suddenly it just snapped off the fuel line, taking about three or four inches of the fuel line with it. The frigid cold had eventually made the plastic fuel line brittle. Andy's machine was a large heavy Polaris model. The gas line ran from the engine in front, through the driver's seat to the tank located at the rear. The gas line was now too short to reach the fuel in the tank.

We were at about the halfway mark of our trip to Lansdowne and seriously thinking about turning back. We finally thought of a makeshift repair which consisted of punching a hole in the cap of a quart container of spare gasoline. We had extra gas line that we ran from the container directly to the carburetor of Andy's engine. Andy pulled the starter and the engine came alive. Holding the quart container between his knees while driving, we were able to cover good distances between refills.

We were happy to finally pull into the community of Lansdowne House where Father Oiumet welcomed our visit. He proudly showed us his newest wide track Nordic model Skidoo that he received from Bombardier.

It was not long after the start of the first spring melt that flights of ducks and geese could be seen winging their way north. The days were warm and as the snow melted, little streamlets of water wended their way toward the still frozen lake. Someone suggested a hunting trip at Devil's Rapids. Devil's Rapids is on the Eabamet River south of Fort Hope. The ever-present open water here always attracted the first of the northward migrating ducks and geese.

There was no trouble with our snowmobile trip over the lake because it was solidly and uniformly still frozen. However, once we reached the river, we had to proceed with caution because river ice varies in thickness depending upon river currents. As we neared Devil Rapids, the Skidoo trail took us off the river and we proceeded overland through the bush the rest of the way to the rapids.

Temius Nate, Walter Waboose, Andy Yesno, Charlie Okeese and I comprised the hunting party. A short distance from the rapids we got off our Skidoos and walked the rest of the way so we wouldn't spook any ducks. As we approached the rapids we carefully spread out and then crouch crawled the final few yards to the water's edge. The ever cautious and suspicious birds must have heard us as most had swum to the opposite shore.

My dog was a runner and we made sure that she was able to keep up with us for this trip. We needed her for the hunt. The plan was to get her running back and forth on the shoreline in front of us. The ducks, ever curious about dogs, would gradually swim over to investigate. We had sandwiches with us and we tore off pieces to throw onto the shore in front of us. The dog was soon running back and forth eating the pieces of sandwiches that we were throwing out for her.

Sure enough, the curious ducks started to cautiously swim over in our direction. Soon there were dozens of ducks within shotgun range milling about on the river. We waited for Temius to fire the first shot as planned. "Boom" his shotgun echoed across the water.

We all fired in unison as the ducks attempted to take wing. Ducks and feathers dropped everywhere. We got up from our hiding spots and did a rough count of the dead ducks floating about. There were at least 30. We started retrieving our ducks from the water and finally got the last one with the help of a long pole.

We made a fire and boiled some tea while we ate the rest of our sandwiches. It was late afternoon and the sun had been beating down warmly all day. We got on our snowmobiles and started for home.

We broke out of the forest trail and eyed the river ice, which was now a dark shade. It had been a white colour when we passed over it that morning. We got off our Skidoos and walked onto the ice to test. It felt strong enough but no one felt confident about the colour. One option was to spend the night and leave in the early morning when we knew the ice would be safe to travel on.

The other option was to send the smallest and lightest Skidoo over the ice to see if it would hold. We all turned and looked at Charlie. He had the smallest Skidoo plus he was the youngest of us. We were thinking young and foolhardy. He laughed and said, "Okay. I'll go."

Charlie got on his Skidoo, started his engine, and then took a run at the ice. Lake and river ice always thawed first from the shoreline and outward, therefore the first few feet were always the most dangerous. As Charlie sped onto the ice, we knew he was in trouble as soon as his tracks started breaking through the ice about ten feet from shore. He slowed and appeared prepared to jump off before he disappeared into the water with his Skidoo.

He came up almost immediately, sputtering and swearing as we reached out to him with a long pole that we had kept nearby for just this emergency. We pulled him in and he stripped his wet clothes and put on wind pants and sweaters that some of us took off and handed to him. We had a roaring fire going in no time and soon we had his clothes stretched out and drying by the fire.

We threw poles onto the ice and walked on or stayed close to them as we surveyed the hole where the Skidoo had dropped. We could see the Skidoo in the shallow water. We removed the metal passenger backrest from one of the Skidoos and tied a rope tightly to it. It had a natural bend to it like a big fish hook.

We lowered it into the water and hooked the back end of Charlie's machine. We then cut a channel in the ice toward shore with an axe and pulled the sunken Skidoo along this cut. Once close enough to shore, we cut more of the ice until we were able to fully retrieve the machine.

Thankfully the engines were simply made and it wasn't long before we had it apart, dried, and then reassembled. A few pulls of the starter and the engine coughed to life.

Around the fire it was constant laughter with Charlie swearing at and laughing with us. The temperature had dropped very quickly once the sun had started to set. Around three o'clock that morning we could see that the ice had whitened and we knew it was then safe to travel on.

The lake ice in front of the village seemed to be a favourite stopping place for flights of geese winging their way to the north. They would land to rest on the ice about one-half mile away—well out of shotgun range.

The local hunters did have an ingenious method for approaching near enough to bag one or two geese. They used light sleds about six feet in length and the front of the sled supported a piece of white cloth about three feet by three feet affixed like a sail. The purpose was to hide the sled and hunter and blend in with the ice and snow still on the lake.

The hunter would lie on the sled with his shotgun at the ready. He would slowly propel himself along the ice with his hands and once near enough would rise and fire off a shot or two, downing at least one goose.

Geese often landed on the small bays along the shoreline of Eabamet Lake. I tried sneaking up on them many times without any success. They were just too wary. A local hunter then told me that next time I went hunting to take my dog.

He advised that you can walk toward the flock with your dog on a leash and as soon as you see that the geese are becoming wary and agitated, drop to your hands and knees beside your dog. Continue to crawl toward the geese on your hands and knees keeping your dog next to you at all times holding tight to his leash. The geese will honk and hiss and all will have their necks outstretched looking at you but they will not take flight until it is too late.

I decided to take his advice and I finally bagged my first spring goose.

The traditional way of hunting always took place at the south end of the lake where in several bays, long grassy reeds grew tall, offering excellent cover. Hiding in the reeds in the late afternoon and facing north with the sun setting in the west, one could spot the flights of geese from a distance coming in for their evening landing. On a good day one could bring home as many geese as he could carry.

The many hunting trips I participated in with my friends from Fort Hope afforded some time for storytelling. Andy Yesno and Charlie Okeese related several stories about their residential school experiences in Sault Ste. Marie. Most of the stories were heart-wrenchingly sad as they recalled their constant gnawing hunger and the loneliness for their families which at times drove them into periods of despondency. Other stories were light-hearted—like the time they were walking through a public park and came upon ducks that fearlessly walked up to them looking for handouts. They quickly looked about and they were alone. They grabbed a duck, wrung its neck, tucked it under Andy's jacket, and coolly strolled out of the park. They continued walking until they came upon a wooded area on the edge of town where they were able to build a fire and feast upon roasted duck.

The most amusing of their tales was the snuff incident. The First Nations boys loved Copenhagen Snuff and it was the tradition of the boys in school to share their snuff when they were lucky enough to receive some in parcels from home. Snuff was a prohibited substance in school. They could not let the supervisors know when they had some in their possession.

The boys would wait for evening for the "lights out" signal, once the supervisors had completed their rounds. This was the safe time to pull out the snuff they had received and to share with their roommates.

The only problem was that, with so many boys in the same dormitory, the small tin of snuff would not last for very long.

The boys therefore worked out a practice for sharing that ensured their treasured snuff would last at least a few nights. Shortly after the supervisors made their final inspection visits for the night, the lights would be turned off and the supervisors would retire to their own quarters for the evening. Whoever had snuff would then take it out in the darkness, open the lid, call out "snuff!" and then count to ten. There would be a rush of boys vying for a pinch of snuff. At the count of ten, the owner of the snuff would snap the lid back onto the tin of snuff. If you didn't get a pinch of snuff, then you were out of luck until the next sharing night.

One day, Charlie and Andy were strolling in the woods near their school when they noticed dried rabbit turds on the ground. They got the bright idea of collecting the turds until they enough to break up into the consistency of snuff. They then each filled an empty snuff container, stashed the tins in their pockets and eagerly waited for nightfall.

That night after the supervisors' rounds and the signal for "lights out," Andy and Charlie opened their snuff cans, yelled out "snuff!" and began counting to ten. They deliberately counted slowly to ensure everyone got a pinch.

They were both beaten by their roommates that night; however, they laughingly recalled how the memory was so worth the trouncing they had received.

The third year in Fort Hope was busy. However, I did not know just how much busier it was about to get. Brian Booth was my competitor and his store was right next door to mine.

Early one morning I heard a pounding on my door and someone yelling "Fire! Fire!."

I jumped out of bed and opened our bedroom door. I saw a flickering red reflection of a fire on my walls. Startled, my immediate thought was that our home was on fire. I turned and yelled to Josephine to wake up and get the babies out. I grabbed my pants from the floor and went hopping out to the kitchen trying to get my feet into my pant leg. I lost my balance and fell face first onto the kitchen floor.

"Len! Len!" yelled Danny from the door. "Brian's store is on fire!"

I had almost knocked myself out when I hit the floor, but as I sat up dazed, I looked out the kitchen window and I could see that Brian's store was ablaze. I gathered my senses, looked at my pants and realized they were Josephine's slim jeans. No wonder I couldn't get my big feet into them.

Meanwhile, Josephine came rushing out of the bedroom, Lynda-Gale under one arm and Geraldine under the other. I told her we were okay, and that it was the store next door that was on fire. We looked out the window and could see that there was no hope of saving Brian's store. It was enveloped in flames.

I told Josephine to get dressed and to dress the girls in case we had to evacuate. Danny and I got some gunny sacks out of the store and wetted them down thoroughly. Sparks were flying from the burning building and we needed to ensure nothing caught fire on our property. Danny patrolled the yard and I climbed up on the roof and swatted any live sparks that landed. Neighbours came to assist to ensure we were safe.

The business kept booming in Fort Hope. Every year more people were moving into the community. I did everything I could to maximize our sales. Most of our goods were delivered by tractor trains on an annual basis. It seemed if I had the warehousing capacity, I could sell whatever I brought in. Fort Hope was a very new community; therefore, there were no old or extra buildings that I could rent for warehousing.

The back end of our building, which was built into an inclining property, was six feet off the ground and skirted in. All that was needed was a little excavation and I had extra warehousing under the house. That fall I also ordered the largest tent that was available and hired some men to construct a tent frame complete with flooring. Here I was able to store a good quantity of furniture delivered on the tractor trains.

The spring and summer period was a hubbub of activity. Airplanes on floats were constantly flying into the community picking up men for prospecting, line-cutting, guiding and tree planting. Tree planting was the biggest summer seasonal employment activity for the men of the community, followed closely by forest fire fighting.

I would make a mental note of the number of men picked up by the Department of Natural Resources for tree planting and then ensure I had a good stock of canoes, boats and motors on hand or on the way. When the men arrived home from their seasonal work with cheques in hand, all the big ticket items were the first to go.

Tourism and fishing lodges on the lakes and rivers were also hives of activity. Float planes were constantly buzzing in from Nakina and Armstrong flying American fishermen in and out of the camps. One summer day a lightning and thunderstorm typical of the Precambrian shield suddenly struck. This was followed by several days of strong winds and rain.

When the weather finally cleared, the radio waves were crackling with all the fishing lodges calling for aircraft to pick up their stranded guests. Airplanes were busy flying about and I could hear the fishing lodges angrily calling for service.

An aircraft landed at my dock and I advised the pilot, who was also the base manager from Armstrong, that the fishing lodges with stranded guests were screaming for his air services to get them out. "Nope. Can't do it," he matter-of-factly stated. "I've got people lined up on my dock wanting to be flown out. I can't please everybody."

His priority was flying out all the newly arrived tourists and fishermen in Armstrong because, he said, the stranded ones in the bush were already mad at him. Why upset the new arrivals by also making them wait. That way, he rationalized, only half of his customers were mad at him. I shook my head and smiled at his reasoning.

The idyllic summer evenings and weekends were occupied by games of baseball and volleyball. If we weren't playing baseball or volleyball, we were out fishing. In winter the outdoor rink was always alive with games of hockey. If we weren't playing hockey, we were always occupied in our free time with our snowmobiles and hunting. It was a pleasant life. There was little alcohol and certainly no drugs. Many of the people were still involved with trapping and every one fished to augment their sustenance. The summer months were busy with seasonal work.

I was now going into my fourth year as store manager at Fort Hope and I had taken notice that a number of my Hudson's Bay Company colleagues in the area had already been transferred to larger stores. I began to wonder if I was being taken for granted, so I wrote a terse letter to our office asking for an explanation.

I was advised to be patient as C.H.J. Winter had retired and a new District Manager had just been appointed. Dave Brears was scheduled to make a tour of his new district shortly, and I was advised I could discuss my concern with him.

When Dave Brears arrived shortly thereafter for his inspection, he was impressed by what I had done. He asked if I would stay one more year to enable him to get a full handle on his position. He promised I would get a good promotion. I agreed as I realized I was now part of the decision making process, and that my career path was not totally in the hands of others. It was a case of negotiating: "I will do my best for you and you will do likewise for me."

That summer, Josephine and I took our vacation and George Scott came in as my relief manager. George became an old friend and our paths would cross, not only mine and also Bill Moore's, several times in the future. That summer, Fort Hope was trenching the community for water and sewer, and power lines were being strung as electricity was to be provided by diesel plants.

A six-foot deep trench ran alongside our road in front of our store. George had been invited to visit Temius and Josephine Nate for a drink one evening. George walked out into the dark (there were still no street lights) and completely forgot about the trench, into which he fell headlong, thankfully without injury.

George was disoriented when he got back up on his feet after the fall, and he couldn't tell left from right inside the dark trench. The

236 Flett From the Barren Lands

trench was too steep and deep to crawl out. He felt his way along the wall hoping to reach the end of the trench, not too far from where he had fallen in. Instead, he headed in the wrong direction, and it was several blocks of blindly feeling his way. Finally, he was able to walk out of the trench.

When we returned from our vacation, we started packing for our transfer to Oxford House, Manitoba. After five years, I had grown to love the community of Fort Hope. I was going to miss the many friends we had made and especially the elders. I have always maintained a special place in my heart for the elders who had treated us as family.

My wood cutter, Daniel Waboose, always ensured we had a supply of dry wood, cut, piled and neatly stored from year to year. The year the new store was built, we looked at our new wood furnace, which was huge. It had a fire-box which measured six feet so I told Daniel to cut our wood in five-foot lengths. I was tired of constantly stoking our wood stoves and heaters. Here, finally, was a firebox that could be filled with enough wood to not have to worry about re-stoking until the next morning.

When winter set in I found myself struggling with the weight of the five-foot lengths. When I had to ask Josephine to assist me in carrying these pieces up our steps and into the furnace room, I had had enough. The next day, Daniel was out there cutting our wood lengths in half.

Daniel spoke little English but usually understood enough to understand what I needed. One day he finished doing some work for me and we were just chatting in our backyard. There was an old tree stump near his foot that he kicked at, and when the stump partly fell apart, he smiled and told me the stump was "rusty." I also took a kick at the stump and pieces went flying. "Yes. Very rusty," I said with a smile.

I was not about to contradict or correct an elder who was pleased with being able to communicate with me in his limited English.

I loved the improvised English of the elders when they did not know or could not remember the correct word. A nurse was asking John Yesno about the symptoms of a young girl that had fallen ill. John stated that she "fall down, sleep and forget." We had to think a moment before we realized, he was telling us that she had fainted.

One of my final goodbyes was to elder Andrew Nate who expressed serious concern when I told him I was leaving the community.

He asked, "Who will look after us?"

I had developed a good system of managing debt accounts with elders. Every time they came into the store for purchases on their account, I took the time to explain how much they had spent to date. I then advised how much credit room they still had, and how much cash they would get when they paid off their account at the end of the month.

I always kept simple notes on their accounts because occasionally someone would forget a conversation. I would then remind them on such and such a date, they had made specific requests and here was the note.

When Andrew expressed his concern because I was soon leaving the community, I was flattered and my heart was warmed by his words.

I assured him that Arnold Shields, who was taking over for me, would look after him and everyone else in the community.

Arnold and Rita were married just before coming to Fort Hope. They told us of their wedding night at the Fort Garry hotel in Winnipeg. Rita, the blushing bride, went into the bathroom to change for the evening and to her horror and absolute embarrassment found herself locked in. Arnold had to call the front desk and explain their predicament. The management sent up two carpenters to remove the bathroom door and finally free Arnold's new bride. Rita was, indeed, a very blushing bride.

7

LEARNING TO BE MORE THAN JUST A BOSS

OXFORD HOUSE

It was June 1972 when Josephine and I, with our children Lynda-Gale and Geraldine in tow, arrived in Oxford House, Manitoba. Oxford House is an old historic community, established in 1798 as a trading post of the Hudson's Bay Company. The post is situated on Oxford Lake, which is the source of the Hayes River. York Factory, at one time the heart of the fur trade in the new world, lies near the mouth of the Hayes River, which empties into Hudson Bay.

Oxford House lies on a historic canoe route; therefore every summer saw paddlers passing through on their way to York Factory and Churchill. They would stop at our store for their last opportunity to pick up supplies. Most canoers were fairly young and adventuresome. One pair that stopped for supplies were older and I could tell by the supplies they purchased that they were also experienced woodsmen.

I invited them to my house for coffee and a chat. They advised that not only were they making this canoe trip for pleasure, they told me they were also prospectors and would be checking out the territory on the way to Hudson Bay. They related a story about a prospecting trip that they had been on a few years past in northern Ontario. They had a close call to being stranded by ice and as they described their rescue, it began to sound familiar. Here were the same men that had been rescued by Archie McDougall and his Norseman. They confirmed that, yes indeed, the pilot did break the thin ice cover on the lake with his pontoons.

Since then, I have always been in wonder of the fact that, in spite of the vastness of the Canadian north, how small it actually seems whenever one runs into people of like kind.

1972 was also significant in that a charter aircraft carrying nine high school students back to Oxford House from Winnipeg at the end of that school year tragically crashed, killing all the occupants. It was a somber introduction to the community. Knowing how difficult it had been for me to attain high school just one decade before, it impressed upon me the full extent of that tragic loss. Today, the 1972 Memorial High School in Oxford House is so named in memory of those students.

As I was introduced to the local staff at the Oxford House store, I was struck by the fact that many carried the names of old Scottish Hudson's Bay fur traders: Grieves, Bradburn, Hart, Sinclair, Wood, Whiteway. There is even a small private cemetery on the company's property that commemorates some of those same names among others.

As I inspected the buildings on my arrival, my attention was caught by an old fur press covered in dust and sitting long forgotten in a corner of a warehouse. The fur press was used to compress the fur to manageable 90-pound packs for the freight canoes and York boats. They were then transported to York Factory where they would be loaded onto ships destined for the London market. This was certainly a reminder of the ties of this location to the heydays of the early fur trade.

The company sat on a beautiful piece of property overlooking the lake and the entrance to the historic Hayes River. This was part of the legacy of the Royal Charter of 1670. The early traders claimed the choicest locations for their trading posts and as time evolved, communities gradually built up around them.

That fall, it was an impressive sight to watch large rafts of wood, tied to canoes, being floated to the community. The local people were laying up large supplies of wood for the coming winter. I had not seen this done to the same extent in other First Nations communities.

Another outstanding characteristic of this community was the unbelievable amount of Copenhagen snuff being consumed. Even women and girls were prone to chewing this obnoxious substance. It was rather disconcerting to be speaking to a pretty girl or an attractive woman when suddenly, "Phhht!" a stream of tobacco juice would come flying out of the side of her mouth. This was a community addicted to these tiny cans of chewing tobacco. I ran out of snuff in the store once. Once was all I needed to learn my lesson. I had to quell a near uprising on my hands by chartering an aircraft with some supplies which included as much snuff as could be found in the shops of nearby Thompson.

The store was bustling. The weekly sked plane had arrived with the mail and perishable freight: fresh meat, bread, dairy, fruit and produce. We operated the post office located at the rear of our store. The store was packed with lineups in front of the post office, lineups at all the check outs, and even lineups at the dairy and produce coolers as people waited for the goods to be brought out.

I checked the back room and two people were busy packing boxes with fresh goods from lists tacked to a wall. They explained these were standing orders from the teachers of the community. I immediately realized my staff were being diverted at a time they were most needed on the floor, handling the crush of our local customers.

The people from outside the community had the resources to purchase in bulk from Winnipeg and ship in on the winter roads or fly all their non-perishable groceries in on the weekly flights. Ordering perishables from Winnipeg was sort of touch and go as many times their perishables arrived spoiled. Hence their desire for this long-time practice of weekly standing orders from our store.

After some consideration, I advised the teachers we were no longer able to provide that special service. I surmised I could probably just hire someone extra for that specific purpose; however, I needed to get

242 From the Barren Lands · Flett

across to my staff who our most important customers were and they were not the people from outside the community. A few noses were out of joint but they quickly got over it. We just ensured we had enough perishables for everyone and most of the teachers got into the practice of shopping for perishables the day after the initial rush.

At the end of the day, the staff were sweeping and shovelling the mud, dust, paper, and debris from the mayhem of the day. As I went around assisting the staff with straightening and covering the shelves with drop cloths before sweeping, I noticed a number of empty liquor bottles strewn on the shelves.

One of my management trainees, Murray Giesbriecht, informed me that was an on-going problem every mail day. Liquor ordered from the Liquor Commission would arrive in the mail and some of the men would stand in the rear aisles with their parcels and secretly drink in the store. The store was so crowded and busy that people seldom noticed these shenanigans.

The following week on mail day, I kept a discreet eye on a group of men until I spotted them passing an open bottle of liquor amongst themselves. I immediately confronted them, advised them this was a public place, and to take their liquor elsewhere. They looked at each other; I expected trouble but I held my ground, and then one turned to leave and the rest followed.

Several days later, one of the men came to speak to me in my office. He apologized and told me he did not mean any disrespect. He also told me I had the respect of all the men involved because I had confronted them personally and did not resort to threats of calling the police.

The men no longer drank in the store but that did not stop them from drinking. They would pick up their liquor parcels from the post office and then go sit in the wooded area behind our warehouses just off our property. This led to another issue with one of my local staff. Zach (not his real name), was one of my grocery shelf fillers and on mail days he was kept busy lugging flour, sugar and lard from the main warehouse.

His friends drinking in the area behind the warehouse would call him over and he would have a nip out of their bottle during the course of his work. Toward mid-afternoon and after several visits to his drinking friends, he was literally staggering under his loads. I would call him into my office, thoroughly ream him out, and advise him to go home as he was not allowed to work under those conditions.

Zach, it seemed, could not resist the temptation offered to him by his drinking friends and after a number of times I advised him that I had had enough and that this was his final warning. I told him next time he took a drink while on the job, he was to go straight home as he would be fired.

Not long afterward, one Sunday Zach was out and about in the village drinking with his friends when he noticed my truck parked at a friend's home that I was visiting. He came over to the house and belligerently banged on the door. He told John, the school principal, that he wanted to talk to me. John called me to the door and Zach started his drunken tirade about me being the worst manager he ever had to work for.

"If you want to fire me, then fire me!" he shouted at me.

He then took a swing at me that I was able to sidestep.

"All right, you're fired!" I replied, as I punched him in the eye.

The punch quickly ended the confrontation. His friends picked him up on his wobbly legs and escorted him away.

The next day after the store opened, Murray came to my office and said Zach was back at work. I went to check and there was Zach, his black eye hidden behind sunglasses, as busy as could be hustling to and from the warehouse with goods for the store. I decided to let him be as our confrontation had happened outside of work hours.

I thought, just maybe, Zach had learned his lesson, but it was not to be. He was the perfect employee for over a month. Then one mail day, Murray came to my office and said Zach was at it again. I went to check and sure enough, he was again drinking on the job. I told him I wanted to see him in my office.

He came into my office and he spoke for me.

"I know, Mr. Flett. This was my last warning. I'm sorry," he offered the apology.

He then stuck out his hand and I took it and we shook. He also stated that I had always treated him fairly and with that he walked out of my office.

It seemed every month there was a telegram from George Reese, one of our company accountants, advising that Oxford House Band cheques had been returned to the company in a NSF (non-sufficient funds) position. He would further advise to discontinue cashing any more cheques from the Band until the present batch were cleared by the Band's bank.

This created an irksome problem for the Band and awkward business relations for myself. The chief at the time, Gilbert North, asked if there was anything that could be done to resolve this ongoing problem. It was very difficult for the chief as he would be hounded personally by those band members stuck with cheques they could not cash.

I advised Gilbert it was a cash flow problem. The Band and Indian Affairs were always a month or two behind their accounting. What was required was knowledge of the Band's present cash position and the cash flow accounting system they were using did not seem to be working. I told Gilbert that I was confident that we could arrive at a beginning cash position that I could work with. Our company was by far the biggest dealer in the Band's cheques. Armed with information regarding all the Band's cheques cashed and remitted by our company, Gilbert and I flew into Thompson.

Gilbert advised the Band's banker to provide me full access to their account. It wasn't very long before we arrived at an approximate present cash position for the Band. With that information, Gilbert advised his financial managers that I was to be provided with a copy of all deposits to their accounts and information on any large cheque amounts, if any, that were to be cashed elsewhere other than at my store.

Band cheques were kept on separate remittances, and daily, the amount of the cheques cashed were deducted from the band's running cash balance. As the funds started to deplete, I would warn the

Band and they would curtail spending until a deposit to their account was received. In dire situations when requested by the chief, I would sometimes sit on a batch of cheques until I knew there were sufficient funds in their accounts to clear.

NSF notifications from our Head Office ceased. Month to month our businesses ran uninterrupted. The Band began receiving larger amounts for special projects. Business boomed and my store became the first store in an isolated fly-in community to break one million dollars in sales. It was a significant milestone.

It was customary for our stores' offices to be managed by senior management trainees. Two of my more loyal and efficient trainees that I had the pleasure of working with in Oxford House were Gareth Mills and Tom Gallivan. The only problem was that trainees were constantly being transferred and when I would lose my office manager, I would find myself running the office while I was training someone new for the position.

Matilda Wood was an extraordinary local employee who assisted me in the office. I spent extra time with her training and gave her more and more responsibilities. Finally I asked if she would like to become our Office Manager and assume full responsibility for all our office functions. She accepted after I assured her I had full confidence in her ability to do the job. Arguably, she was one of the first local employees throughout our chain of stores to assume that position.

Our management trainees were overly involved in the freighting functions mainly because few local people had driving licenses. Even I, in fact, did not have a driver's license. Murray Giesbrecht, my trainee who hailed from a farming background in Steinbach, taught me how to drive our truck.

One local employee that I had hired for freighting purposes in fact was Matilda's husband, Johnson. He had a half-ton truck that we sometime had to hire to assist the one-ton truck we had. When he worked for us, he did an excellent job; however, he was worth much more than we could afford to pay him. Not wanting to lose his services,

I decided to sell him our truck and assist him in establishing a local freighting business.

I sat down with him and Matilda one evening and worked out a freight business plan and cash flow for him. It involved him buying our truck with a bank loan to be secured by a freighting contract with our company. All the cards fell into place and he took over our freighting responsibilities. One less problem for me to worry about as he provided excellent and dependable service.

That summer I had to supplement our winter road shipments with a number of DC-3 aircraft charters to ensure we had enough inventory to carry us over to the next winter road season. I remembered a pilot friend from Nakina who had to drive his Volkswagen Beetle to Geraldton with a DC-3 wheel to replace one that had gone flat. The DC-3 crew were appreciative that they would soon be airborne and homeward bound. They decided to fly my friend and his vehicle back to Nakina with them after they had measured their cargo doors to ensure the car fitted. It did.

Murray wrote his father and enclosed my cheque for four hundred dollars so his father could buy us a used Volkswagen and ship by CN to Thompson care of our DC-3 charter company. About a week later we offloaded the Beetle from the aircraft onto the back of our truck. We drove the truck and backed onto a gravel pile nearby and drove the Beetle off onto the gravel pile and thence onto the road.

As I proudly drove the little vehicle through the village, I could see the people standing and staring at the strange sight. I just smiled and waved at them as I drove by. Children laughed and chased after me, running alongside and behind the little car. I had to slow down to ensure I didn't run over anyone. It was a fun vehicle; a frivolous purchase strictly for our own pleasure.

A few days later I received a letter from one of our accountants at Head Office who had been checking waybills attached to billings for the aircraft charters. He wrote there was a unbelievably large error on one the waybills listing an automobile along with our grocery goods and yet I had signed off on the bill. Surely there must be an explanation.

I assured him the billing was correct and that I indeed had flown a VW Beetle into the community. I also referred him to an entry in the store's journals where I had charged my personal account for the cost of the freight.

At that time, Eaton's Catalogue Service sold basic automobile parts for a few car models that included the Volkswagen Beetle. The availability of parts through a catalogue was one of the reasons for me making this whimsical purchase.

One day I was leaving a friend's house when I heard an aircraft taking off from the airstrip. I was driving the Beetle so I decided to check the strip on my way back to the store. The was a small shipment of two or three hundred pounds of candy for our company that the aircraft had simply unloaded and left on the tarmac in front of our small airport building.

I threw the candy into the back seat of the car and drove back to the store. On arrival at the store I hopped out of the vehicle and I instructed one of my employees to unload the candy from the car. A minute later that employee came running into the store to tell me my car was on fire. I grabbed an extinguisher from a wall and ran out to the car. Sure enough, there was smoke floating up from the back seat area.

We quickly emptied the vehicle of the candy and traced the source of the smoke to the back seat itself. I pulled out the back seat and found the padding underneath smoldering away. We extinguished the hot spot before it burst into flames. The battery for the vehicle is located under the back seat. The weight of the candy pushed the seat down sufficiently for the wire springs under the seat to make contact with battery terminals and cause a short circuit of sparks whenever we drove over a bump.

During the early winter we would take the bug onto the ice and zip up and down on the lake alongside the community, doing donuts to the great amusement of the townspeople. The summer of 1975, before leaving the community, I sold it for $600, which covered all my costs.

The fall of 1974, sometime around the end of September, Chief Gilbert North asked if I wanted to go moose hunting with him over a weekend. We decided we would simply load the canoe, along with all our camping and hunting equipment, into my aluminum boat. The trip to the south end of the lake was about an hour with my boat fully loaded. We left late Friday afternoon around four o'clock, leaving work a little early.

We arrived at our destination with enough daylight time to comfortably set up our camp and prepare our evening meal. The tent was quickly set up in a small clearing just off the sandy shore where we beached our boat. Dry wood was lying about and in a short time we had a small fire blazing in front of our tent.

The air was turning crisp but not yet uncomfortably cold. The yellowed leaves on the trees were dropping and flights of ducks and geese were now wending their way south. As we sat at our campfire chatting and sipping tea after we had eaten, the sun slipped below the horizon and coloured the skies in hues of pink, yellow and red. We turned in early and bedded ourselves down comfortably in our sleeping bags.

We arose early the next morning, washing in the sparkling clear but icy waters of the lake. The aroma of bacon and eggs wafted in the air and our campfire coffee percolated loudly in an aluminum pot. The sunrise was spectacular with colour but we also knew that "red skies in the morning, sailors take warning."

After breakfast and coffee, we loaded our rifles into our canoe and pushed off the beach into the water. We paddled toward the point of land only about fifty yards and as we rounded the point we heard the splish splash of something walking in the water of the small bay about five hundred yards away.

The bay was still dark as another point of land directly across from where we were sitting in our canoe hid the rising sun. We could just make out glints of white on the beast's legs indicating a mature animal. Then we saw the white glint of antlers. It was a bull moose. We waited until it reached the opposite point of land and quietly watched as the moose disappeared into the dark cover of the woods.

Gilbert and I swiftly and silently paddled across the mouth of the bay, headed for the point of land directly in front of us. As we neared the point Gilbert whispered to me to put down my paddle and get my rifle ready. He would handle the canoe alone the rest of the way. We listened and we could hear the moose making its way through the dense bush, coming right in our direction. Gilbert expertly and silently paddled and steered the canoe into position where he thought the moose would show itself.

Suddenly the willow bushes waved and parted in front of us as the huge bull muscled his way to the lake shore. His head was down as he used his antlers like a plow, clearing his way through the brush. When he came into full view and lifted his head, I pulled the trigger and shot him squarely in the chest. He turned and started running as I fired another shot into his side. I was reloading when Gilbert said, "No. It's okay. We got him."

The moose had run a short distance through the willow and turned for the water where he went down with a tremendous splash. I wished I had brought my 30-06 rifle which would have dropped him immediately with the first shot. However, the 30-30 Winchester, a light rifle, is excellent for hunting in brushy areas.

We pulled the canoe onto shore and prepared for the heavy work. We tugged and pulled the moose as close onto shore as we possibly could, but we knew we would have to skin, clean and quarter the eight-hundred-pound beast in the water. We worked as quickly as we could in the water as the clouds darkened and a light rain began to fall. Within an hour we had the moose cleaned and quartered and the pieces loaded into the canoe.

Gilbert and I paddled back to our camp which was only about fifteen or twenty minutes away. We laughed and marvelled at how fortunate we had been with our moose hunt. We broke camp and loaded everything into our speed boat and in a little over an hour we were back home.

I backed our truck to our dock area where we had parked our boat loaded down with the moose and camping equipment. We loaded the truck and I drove Gilbert to his house, unloaded his gear and his share of the moose including the head and antlers. Before we drove off for Gilbert's house I made the mistake of stopping at my house first where Lynda-Gale and Geraldine spotted the moose head laying in the back of our truck. The moose head, with its glassy eyes still open, appeared to be staring haplessly at the girls with its tongue lolling out of one side of its mouth. The girls screamed and cried and accused me of extreme cruelty. To this day they refuse to eat moose meat. Such is life with a family of sensitive girls, who would scream and cry and accuse me of mass murder whenever I accidently ran over a rabbit or squirrel or hit a bird with my car. When I went hunting, I would have to pluck and clean my duck or goose in the bush and then announce as I carried the carcass into the house, "Chicken for dinner."

Back in the house, Josephine and I carefully cut up our moose, wrapping, packaging and labelling each piece. I thought there should be enough to last us the winter. Then there was a knock at the door. It was Ruth with a big smile on her face. She heard I had shot a moose. I gave her a large package. Another knock, another visitor, another package of moose meat gone. By the end of the day I made sure I kept enough meat for at least a few meals.

Of course, throughout my ten years in Fort Hope and Oxford House, the people always shared their hunt with me. They would bring choice cuts for me and I would offer pork chops, beef or chicken from our freezer in exchange. As I was not normally a hunter, I knew I would never be able to return their gesture of sharing otherwise.

The winter of 1972-73 was the first time the community received its annual shipment of freight by trucks rather than tractor trains operated by Sigfusson's Transport. Sigfusson's land use permits that enabled them to build bush roads and operate tractor trains was not renewed by the government in 1971. That winter was the last of the tractor trains in Manitoba.

The following year, Northland Petroleum headed by Phil and Richard Lazerenko and Gardewine North headed by General Manager

George Friesen combined resources to pioneer trucking over temporary winter roads into northern Manitoba. While the roads cut through the bush were very rough on the equipment, the ice roads plowed over open rivers and lakes were the most dangerous. A number of rigs over the years have crashed through the ice.

A winter road trucking season can also be very short depending upon a number of factors. The freeze-up period from November to early January is crucial. Very cold weather is required to freeze the ice on rivers and lakes to minimum thickness of two-and-a-half feet or more. Snow acts as an insulator therefore the less snowfall in the early winter, the faster ice is made. Heavy snowfalls, on the other hand, slow the natural ice making process, which in turn shortens the delivery season. The warming of the weather that arrives sometime in March signals the end of the freighting season.

Truckers look for 29 inches of pure blue ice before they risk their rigs and loads with a combined total weight of 80,000 pounds. Depending upon the weather, the average winter trucking season lasts about eight weeks beginning in mid January and running to mid March.

Road construction delays and mild weather hampered the initial winter trucking season in 1972-73. When the trucks started arriving in Oxford House we needed to offload and turn them around as quickly as possible. I hired local men for the unloading as all the freight handling was done by hand. The trucks would arrive at all hours and whenever they arrived we started offloading, no matter the time.

For about two weeks with one or more trucks arriving almost every day with goods and building materials, I and my management trainees did not get much sleep. We needed about six men for every truck and one day we were unloading four trucks at the same time. Phil Lazerenko and George Friesen happened to choose that morning to fly into the community to check on the progress of the winter road shipments.

They saw three trucks backed into various warehouses and the store being offloaded while I was studying the waybills of a fourth truck that had just pulled in. I invited them into our house for a coffee and they were impressed to see Josephine pouring coffee, cooking and serving breakfast for the truckers.

George made a point of letting Hudson's Bay Company senior management in Winnipeg know how well we had been handling the winter truck freighting challenges and how we went above and beyond the normal call in treating their drivers.

The District Manager to whom I reported was Wally Buhr, who was very much a gentleman. Like C.H.J. Winter, he spent some time in the Arctic as a fur trader. Wally described one particular trip he had to make overland from either Cape Dorset or Lake Harbour (now Kimmirut) to Frobisher Bay (now Iqualuit).

What was supposed to be simple trip by dog sled of a few days stretched to over a week because of weather. He related how he quickly ran out of food for himself and his dogs and how the weather became bitterly cold. By the time he finally arrived in Frobisher Bay, his cheeks had been frozen solid. As his face slowly thawed, his cheeks split and over several days he had fluids, including blood, oozing from his open wounds.

He also related a trip to Scotland on a tour and while there he thought to visit some relatives in a village that he located by way of letters. Wally laughed as he described the dirt floor of his relatives' home and the chickens running afoot within.

After two-and-a-half years in Oxford House, I expressed to Mr. Buhr my desire to move on to larger challenges. He readily agreed and advised he would certainly keep me in mind as opportunities became available.

In 1975, my youngest daughter Amber was born. Josephine had flown out to Thompson and was cared for by our friends, John and Linda Bagacki, until her due date. Ruth Hart babysat my girls, Lynda-Gale and Geraldine, who were now seven and five. We eagerly awaited this newest member to our family.

On May 29, I received a radio-phone call from John advising the arrival of our beautiful baby girl. I remember John saying he had never before seen a newborn baby with such thick flowing black hair.

Two months later, we were transferred to Winnipeg where I was to begin receiving training and experience in executive management.

It was about ten years later, I received a phone call on a separate matter from Tommy Weenusk, who was now the chief of Oxford House. Tommy had been one of my employees when I was a store manager in their community a decade before. There had been a recent rash of suicide attempts by teens in his community and he was concerned and not sure where to turn.

As we discussed the issue I became more interested and volunteered to assist. I discussed the community issue with Marvin Tiller, our then President and CEO, and he gave me the okay to proceed.

On arrival in Oxford House, Tommy and I planned a course of action involving a series of community meetings. It was our hope the community members would identify the issues, take ownership, and provide some possible resolutions.

We first held a general community meeting, followed by a meeting of the elders. We then called for a meeting of the youth as suggested by the previous meetings of the community and elders. It was there that the more outspoken of the youth asked for sports programming which was noted by the teachers in attendance. They also requested a local radio station so they could play their own music and have something to listen to in the evenings. I checked out the cost and had our company subsidize the radio station at a cost of about $5,000.

After that meeting, the local constable, John Chubb, who I was to find out was very well respected in the community, approached me and Tommy. He advised that the youth that attended the meeting that evening were the healthy youth. Not one of the "at risk" youth that John dealt with every other night or so were at the meeting.

John provided us with a list of approximately 20 youth who he identified as being "at risk." Tommy and I quickly realized that John was the key player in this community crisis. John agreed he would meet with these youth in groups and get them to discuss their issues with him. The youth knew what was going on in the community and they openly discussed their problems with John.

The main issue with the youth were the parents who drank excessively and created a chaotic and unstable home life. The youth would leave their homes when the parents started drinking and just wander about aimlessly the entire night. If the weather turned for the worse, they would break into buildings to temporarily get out of the cold or intemperate weather. Vandalism was simply a pastime, often conducted out of a silent rage at their parents.

The conclusion was that these youth needed a safe house. They would not integrate into the general community and they preferred to remain distant and amongst themselves only. They appeared to trust only one man and that was John Chubb, ironically, the local policeman.

In the end, one of Tommy's band councillors donated a house that he was no longer using. Band members donated their time to repair the house, and the house was furnished with the assistance of some band funding. Cots were put into the home along with blankets. The pantry and refrigerator were kept filled with food. I donated stereo equipment and a box of records on behalf of the company. Others collected books and magazines for the home.

John laid down the ground rules for the safe house with the kids. All they had to do was clean up after themselves and they were welcome to use the home whenever they needed. The house would never be locked. John advised the youth that he, and only he, would drop in occasionally to check on them.

I followed up with Chief Tommy about a year later and he advised there were no further suicide attempts in his community. The long term solution to issues of this type are stabilized home lives. In its absence, this was an effective temporary fix.

On The Move

The first year I spent in Winnipeg was routine and uneventful. I did not have many responsibilities and it was probably a good thing as I had many adjustments to make to fit into city life. My training that year consisted of me filling in for the district managers who were out of the office travelling to their stores. I would answer their phones and do my best to resolve their issues. If the issue was serious or complicated, I would pass the call on to another district manager or up to the regional manager if need be. I also reviewed their files and attempted to resolve the issues or fulfill requests for advice from junior store managers. The district managers appreciated me attending to their more mundane tasks and it was great experience for me.

I also booked myself into a driving school and a month later bought my first city vehicle—a 1972 used Ford Maverick. I purchased our first TV and immediately traumatized my girls, Lynda-Gale and Geraldine, with a showing of *The Wizard of Oz*. They ran out of the living room screaming and watched the rest of the movie by poking their heads around the doorway. To this day, even as grown women with their own children, they still shiver and tremble with anxiety whenever they see the Wicked Witch of the West.

The girls were enamoured with their baby sister. Whenever baby Amber cried in her crib for attention, the girls would run over and standing on their tiptoes would try to console her. When they couldn't, they would themselves begin crying along in sympathy.

The following year we transferred to Lac La Ronge at the end of June. It was a pleasant idyllic summer broken only by the fleet of float planes roaring over our house as they took off from the lake on their flights starting at six in the morning.

Saskair, La Ronge Aviation and Athabaska Airways provided important links to the North with their float planes. Many communities were just in the process of developing airstrips and more and more wheeled aircraft were becoming common sights.

This was the first store I had to manage since leaving Oxford House and it was an entirely different experience. The La Ronge store was clean and spacious, the staff well trained and experienced, but the business was much slower paced and very customer-oriented.

There were a number of other retail outlets including Robertson's Trading and the Co-op store that were the main competitors. In Oxford House we were the only store and the priority was always to have enough stock on hand.

In La Ronge, the challenge was the struggle for customer support. I noticed that both Robertson's Trading and the Co-op store had the support of the First Nations community which represented about 70 percent of the population. I focused my attention on this potential market but just did not have the time as we were, once again, on the move.

In September we transferred again, this time to the bustling mining community of Lynn Lake. The manager, Bob Henderson, was in dire need of an assistant and the Head Office thought it would also be a good opportunity for me to sharpen my merchandising skills. I took charge of Furniture, Electronics, Sporting Goods and Hardware.

Although Lynn Lake was first and foremost a mining town, I noticed a large number of First Nations people from Brochet, Lac Brochet, Co-op Point, Pukatawagan, and even some from Southend, my old home, came into town to shop. I knew some of the people that passed through so I told them to bring their furs to me that winter and also to spread the word that I, an experienced buyer, would be paying top dollars for their furs. Some of the people knew me but, more importantly, most of them knew and trusted my father. I became the beneficiary of his solid reputation.

Lynn Lake in previous years purchased no furs. The last week prior to Christmas, the staff were amazed to see the long lines of trappers with their bundles of furs. They waited patiently as I worked my way through their winter catches of beaver, mink, otter, lynx, foxes, wolves and other species. In a matter of a few weeks I managed to purchase over $100,000 worth of furs.

I was also responsible for Furniture and Electronic sales. We ran a January sales event that promoted televisions and it was quite successful. We sold a number of television sets including one to an Asian customer. He was somewhat taken with the service I provided him and after we had concluded the transaction, he wanted to engage in social small talk. It was near the end of the work day and as he was one of only a few customers left, I had the time for him. He was interested in who and what I was so it was natural that he ask the question, "What is your nationality?"

I informed him that I was an Indian. This was in the mid-70s and as a people, we had not yet set our own identifying definitions. This would not occur until discussions began over the patriation of the Constitution Act of 1982. The English and the French had been identified as the Founding Nations in the various discussions leading to the Constitution without mention of our people. That upset our leadership and collectively we began identifying ourselves as First Nations to impress the fact that we were here first. The Constitution Act refers to us as Aboriginal people, which included the Métis and Inuit, and this identifying term over time also came into acceptable use.

"I am an Indian," I proudly informed him.

"Oh," he said in a surprised tone. "When did you come over?" he continued to probe.

I laughed and told him, "No, you misunderstand. I am a Canadian Indian."

"Oh," he said in a tone that now suggested confusion. "When did your parents come over?"

Apparently he had a clear idea in his mind who Aboriginal people were, but evidently, I did not fit that picture.

There were some Native people in Lynn Lake, many gainfully employed like myself; however, there was a also a group of Aboriginal people encamped in tents or makeshift shelters on the outskirts of the town. Most of this group were impoverished, some troubled and some involved with alcohol. Racist rumours abounded in the town about these people absconding with the town pets to casually roast while lounging around their campfires.

I was asked by a friend, Sonny Ballantyne, to assist a local group of activists in the running of the Native Friendship Centre. I thought about the many extremely condescending rumours about Native people circulating about the town. I did not hesitate and quickly agreed to join their board. That was the start of my life-long commitment to activism within the Aboriginal community.

Pukatawagan

Early that spring we received a phone call from Head Office. The store manager in Pukatawagan had fallen ill with jaundice and they asked if I could commute and manage the store there until the manager was back on his feet. I was to spend the work week in Pukatawagan and then fly back to Lynn Lake for the weekends so I could be with my family.

Pukatawagan, a Cree First Nations community, lies between Lynn Lake and The Pas. It is serviced by air from The Pas and Lynn Lake and by a railway which runs between The Pas and Lynn Lake. The rail line upon which the community is dependent for the haulage of all its supplies is approximately ten miles east of the community. A winter road in season rounds out the transportation options.

Pukatawagan is a picturesque community but it is plagued by a relatively large population with few economic opportunities. Land contamination issues caused by diesel oil spills continue not to be adequately addressed by the federal government which ultimately has fiscal responsibility for the community. This has hampered the housing program with the inevitable result of overcrowding issues.

Squirrel, the store manager of Pukatawagan, had previously worked for me in Fort Hope. He met me at the airport. He was not bedridden; simply quarantined from working in the store until he was once again well. Jaundice is not contagious; however it might be passed through the handling of food which is inescapable in a grocery store.

The store ran efficiently and the young office manager, Shirley Castel, had full control of credit issues. In later years I encouraged her to try store management; however she opted for political leadership of her community. She became the Chief of her Band for a number of years, which is not an easy task.

One weekend after work, Squirrel, our two trainees and I were invited to the nursing station for dinner and a movie. Gail Cadillac, the nursing supervisor was in the community checking on the nursing station. Our paths kept crossing in the North, first in Fort Hope where she was one of the first nurses in the community. I was then surprised when she arrived in Oxford House to run the nursing station there for about a year. And now we bumped into each other again, this time in Pukatawagan.

We had just finished an enjoyable dinner when there was a knock at the door. One of the nurses answered the door and then called Squirrel, telling him it was his freight hauler. I could hear raised voices at the door. It was obvious that Big Louie (not his real name), the freight hauler, had had a few drinks. It was also obvious that they had no love for each other.

Finally, Squirrel came back and asked his trainees if they could take his truck, which he had just newly purchased for his own personal use, and go back to open the store so that Big Louie could unload his truck. He had just picked up this unexpected freight from the airport and Big Louie insisted he be offloaded immediately. The nurses told the boys they would hold off on the movie until their return.

After a half hour had passed we began to wonder what was the holding the guys up. We tried calling the store but no one was answering. The store was about a half mile away but we decided we better walk back and check. Squirrel and I were about halfway there when we noticed the two trainees walking our way. We immediately assumed they had a mechanical problem with Squirrel's truck.

"Bad news, Squirrel," said one of the trainees. "Big Louie smashed your truck up."

"What!!??" asked Squirrel. He couldn't believe what he was hearing.

The trainee explained further, "After we had unloaded Big Louie's truck, he got back into his vehicle. He then noticed your truck parked nearby and he intentionally ran into it. Then he backed up and smashed into it again and again."

"I'll kill that bastard!" screamed Squirrel as he took off running down the road.

I got more details from the trainee. Big Louie drove a one-ton truck with a massive grill in front that made short work of Squirrel's half-ton. The trainee told me that when they left the store, Big Louie was passed out inside his truck. I sensed more trouble to come so I started running in an attempt to catch up to Squirrel.

I arrived at the store and ran around to the back. There was Squirrel's demolished truck and Louie's vehicle nearby still running. I could see Louie's slouched form asleep in the cab of the truck. I wondered where Squirrel was but I kept walking toward the staff house. I was already in the verandah when the back door was suddenly flung open and Squirrel came running out, wild eyed, with a rifle in his hand.

I stepped in his way to stop him and grabbed him by the shoulders. I attempted to talk some sense into him but he wouldn't listen. I now had my hands on his rifle and when he started to struggle with me, I put a choke hold on him until he went limp. I took the rifle from him, looked at him and asked if he was all right. He nodded his head in affirmation that he had calmed down. I led him back into the house, put the rifle away, and then explained to Squirrel that I was going to call the RCMP to report the incident.

I guess my ruckus with Squirrel must have awakened Big Louie because he was now pounding and screaming incoherently at the back door. I told Squirrel to stay calm, that I would step outside and deal with Louie. Squirrel nodded yes, but he still wasn't speaking with me. I stepped to the back door and glanced over my shoulder toward Squirrel to ensure myself that he was indeed in control of his wits. I then unlocked the door, slipped out to deal with Louie, and closed the door behind me.

The first thing that ran through my mind was a sizing-up of Big Louie. I was lean and strong, but he was a large, barrel-chested, muscular man. I would have to stay out of his reach if matters turned for the worse. I tried talking to him in a calm manner while he kept cursing about Squirrel and threatening to kill him. As he grew more and more agitated, I thought it would be prudent if I just slipped back into the house. The door was behind me as I talked to Big Louie so I felt for the doorknob behind me, found it, and to my horror found it was locked.

I quickly looked around for a weapon but saw only a wet mop standing in a corner. "Big help that would be," I thought to myself.

I was now contemplating on throwing the first punch when I heard the front door slam. To my absolute surprise and dismay, I saw Squirrel striding purposefully toward Big Louie's truck, high-powered rifle in hand.

"Bang! Bang! Bang! " Squirrel fired three shots into the radiator of the truck.

Big Louie tore out of the verandah, ran toward the wooded area behind our staff house, hopped the fence and disappeared into the woods.

I stared, stunned, at Squirrel. He walked toward me in a non-aggressive manner, the rifle now simply cradled in his arm. He handed me the rifle and we walked back together into the house. I told him I would have to report this to the RCMP and to our Head Office. He nodded his head in agreement as he entered his bedroom and closed the door behind him.

The sun had set and it was now dark. I called the RCMP in Lynn Lake and they advised they would fly in immediately. They had a police vehicle which they parked in our yard when they were out of the community. They also entrusted their keys to us. They asked if I could meet and pick them up at the airport with their vehicle to which I readily agreed.

About an hour and a half later, we were driving back to the community from the airport where the RCMP Twin Otter had landed and parked for the night. The two constables and the pilot planned on spending the night at their local detachment which consisted of a front office, their three-bedroom living quarters and a holding cell for unruly prisoners. We stopped at the detachment which was almost next door to the store and parked the vehicle.

As I and the two officers approached our staff house on foot, a voice suddenly barked out from the darkness, "Stop or I'll shoot!"

"Squirrel???" I called out as I had recognized his voice.

"Squirrel. It's me, Len. I'm here with the RCMP. Everything is going to be all right," I implored.

"Don't anybody move!" Squirrel yelled back at us.

I could now see in the darkness that Squirrel had barricade himself under the verandah. He had overturned a Skidoo and pulled it in beside a wheelbarrow to block himself under the porch.

The RCMP officers, who personally knew Squirrel, now stepped in and advised me to stay back as they would handle the situation.

They talked to Squirrel and convinced him to come out and give up his rifle. He crawled out from under his hiding place and then tried to explain to the RCMP that he had been afraid Big Louie would return to the staff house for vengeance. Squirrel was quite indignant when the officers locked him up for the night in their holding cell to cool off.

The next day I called our office and after explaining what had taken place, agreed that Squirrel should be allowed to take some holidays to recuperate. He took the next available flight out and I was stuck with the management of Pukatawagan for a few more weeks. Squirrel went on to a successful career in retail.

I was overjoyed to finally rejoin my family in Lynn Lake after two weeks and I returned with a number of the well-known "Puk U" sweatshirts for everyone.

It was not long after my Pukatawagan experience that I received a phone call from Dave Brears of our Head Office offering me a District Management position in Winnipeg. Dave, who had been my district manager in my last year at Fort Hope, had recently been promoted to Divisional Management of Central Region and he was doing some reorganizing. I accepted.

8

MOVING ON UP

KITCHI-OKEMOW – "BIG BOSS"

District Manager of Northern Ontario II! This appointment of July 1, 1977 fulfilled what I thought was a lofty goal I had set for myself 13 years before when I first started with HBC. I had boasted to my First Nations friends in Southend that one day I would be back as Kitchi-Okemow (big boss).

Alaster Gillespie was the district manager of the other half of northern Ontario. We each had about a dozen stores for which we were responsible. Travel in northern Ontario was still mainly by float plane. The province was gradually shifting to air strips in its larger remote locations but it would still be some time yet before the company could dispense of its De Havilland Beaver aircraft. This aircraft was equipped with pontoons for the summer and wheel/skis for the winter.

Management of a district of stores had its own particular challenges, especially in smaller stores operated by junior managers. Most newly-appointed managers knew the basics of store management—sales, accounting, merchandising, etc. A trait more difficult to assess was the ability of young managers to cope with isolation and operating not only a business but also a household in a difficult environment. One could not simply pick up a phone to repair a furnace or fix the plumbing.

There was nothing more disheartening than to arrive in a location where the well and septic field had been allowed to freeze and inadequate adjustments had been made to make the home life livable. I enjoyed the challenges of improving sales and merchandising techniques—but, fixing frozen water pipes, furnaces and power generators, and cleaning house for a bachelor—not so much!

Back at the office, Alaster and I would wrap up the work week by meeting at the bar of the Fort Garry Hotel for one of the hotel's famed double martinis. We would spend a good hour and laugh and commiserate each other about our previous week on the road.

It was some time after I had assumed control of the district of Northern Ontario II that Head Office reorganized the alignment of some stores. The result was that Fort Severn, a lonely post on the shore of Hudson's Bay at the mouth of the Severn River, was added to my district. I took an immediate interest in this location as it was the home of my maternal grandmother, Nellie Bluecoat, who I met as a child but could not remember.

I made arrangements to visit the community as soon as possible and found myself winging eastward in the dead of winter over a vast tract of frozen muskeg. On trips of this nature, flying endlessly over the vast expanse that is Canada, I often studied the terrain below me out of boredom and wondered to myself, "If our plane went down, could I survive here while awaiting rescue?"

I would look for a source of water and shelter; lakes, rivers, streams, trees. If the terrain was particularly harsh and uninviting, I would eye my fellow passengers and morbidly ask myself, " If I had to resort to cannibalism, who would I eat first?"

Luckily, in my 41-year career covering vast distances by air, I never experienced any mishaps. Close calls, yes. On one flight out of Lac La Ronge shortly after we had taken off from the airport in a Cessna 180, a small aircraft, the windscreen suddenly turned black.

The oil cap had popped off the engine and a stream of oil obliterated our view. The pilot instinctively turned the aircraft around and semi-glided back to a safe landing.

On another flight in northern Ontario, again in a small aircraft, we ran into foul weather and we were forced to lower our flight path to one just barely over the treetops. I was sitting in the passenger seat next the pilot. He was struggling with the visibility as an unrelenting rain pelted our windscreen. The pilot handed me a map and asked me to assist him with the visual navigation.

We would find ourselves over a lake and we would have to identify where we were on the map. Once we verified our location the pilot would continue on to the next lake targeted on the map. The pilot was in search of a lake located at the end of a roadway running from Pickle Lake, our final intended destination.

The wind and the rain were tossing our little aircraft about, making for a very rough and frightening ride. We finally spied the lake the pilot was searching for and he quickly landed and taxied to shore. He called his base on the aircraft radio, advised our whereabouts, and then we sat and waited until we were picked up by a van about 45 minutes later.

The tiny settlement of Fort Severn finally came into view as our plane steadily droned forward. As we circled the community prior to landing, I was able to pick out the red roofs of our store and dwelling. Our pilot was busy covering the cowling of the aircraft with an insulated canvas blanket when several yellow and black Skidoos arrived to meet us. The store manager, Chris Burke, introduced himself and extended his hand in greeting.

A bone chilling ten minute ride to the store through a blustery minus 50 degree semi-arctic air could not have ended sooner. I was not adequately dressed for a snowmobile ride and my legs were now numbed from the cold. We quickly went through the store meeting all the local staff. I understood the Cree of the people as they commented to each other after we had passed. They confirmed to each other that I, indeed, was the Kitchi-Okimow.

Chris then invited me to his house for coffee, where his wife, a Cree woman from the community, had the table all neatly set. Chris laughingly told me about how he had replied to an ad in London, England, that was looking for recruits seeking adventure in the Canadian north with the Hudson's Bay Company. He said he arrived in Fort Severn ten years ago, stepping off a pontooned Norseman aircraft, wearing a dark suit topped with a bowler hat and carrying a "brolly" tucked under his arm.

He was fortunate to have had an interesting manager, George Heller, who would, years later at the turn of the century, become President and Chief Executive Officer of the Hudson's Bay Company. Chris quickly adapted to the new country and its people, the Cree, learning their language, customs and ways. He developed a deep love for the country around Fort Severn and for years declined any opportunities to move within the company.

After Chris had provided me with his background, we were finishing up our coffee when I looked out the window and saw Chris's three-year-old son running around outside in the snow. He was in his bare feet wearing only underwear and a T-shirt!

"Chris!" I called him in somewhat of a panic. "Your boy is outside in his underwear and bare feet."

"Ah, we don't have to worry about him. He'll be in as soon as he turns blue," he told me with a chuckle.

I spent a pleasant two days with Chris and his family and when I told them I loved and missed our country foods, every evening after work became a feast of moose, caribou, ptarmigan and fish. As we ate, Chris regaled me with stories of the community and its people. Chris loved the area and the people and whenever he had spare time, went on hunting trips with his friends.

A few years earlier, Chris had been made aware by some of the local trappers that just over the border and into Manitoba were trapping areas that had not been touched for years. Chris talked with some men who had hunted and trapped the area and they agreed that it was probably rich with fur bearing animals.

Chris advised the men he would be willing to advance the cost of an aircraft charter plus stake the trappers with enough supplies to keep them working in the area until Christmas. A group of four men agreed to go. Chris arranged for the aircraft that fall and the trappers flew off in a Norseman to be dropped off on the Kaskattama River in Manitoba.

Near the mouth of the Kaskattama River where it drains into Hudson's Bay was an old airstrip built on a gravel bar. The trappers were organizing their equipment and tramping about in search of a location where they could set up their tent and gear for the fall and winter. They heard a large aircraft land and then take off after a short while. They surmised correctly that it had been a DC-3 aircraft. Puzzled, they decided to walk down to the shore where they knew the airstrip was located to investigate.

At that time of year and in that part of the country, the men knew well enough to always carry their rifles in case of a polar bear attack. It was late October and the bears would be wandering the shores of Hudson Bay waiting for the big freeze that would enable them to walk out onto the ice in search of seals.

The men broke through the cover of willows that lined the shore and to their surprise they spotted four polar bears wandering about the old air strip. They quickly lifted their rifles and brought down the four bears, all the while trying to calculate in their heads the value the hides would fetch.

Later as they were skinning the bears, the men noticed an unmistakable yellow "x" painted onto the rumps of each of the bears. Back at their camp, the men tried to remove the markings with some kerosene that they had for their lamp. The kerosene didn't work, however, they decided they would remove the markings with turpentine once they were home back in Fort Severn.

About a week later the men were back in the camp after having been up river for several days setting traps. Their ears perked at the droning sound of an approaching aircraft in the distance. They heard the aircraft, again a large multi-engine one, possibly a DC-3.

The aircraft landed and after a short stay, took off again. As the men had previously done, they decided to go investigate. And what do you know? More polar bears!

Back in Fort Severn, Chris was listening to the CBC Radio North evening news one night. The town of Churchill was describing their new Polar Bear Control experimental program. From mid-October to early November, the town had problems with polar bears gathering along the sea coast waiting for the ice to form on the bay. Once there was sufficient ice, the bears would venture out in pursuit of the favourite prey—seals. Until then, they often wandered into town presenting great danger to the populace. They were especially feared at Halloween when children were out and about trick or treating. Every vehicle, with headlights brightly abeam, was used to form a protective circle around the town as soon as the sun set. Polar bears are the only animals known that consider humans prey. They have absolutely no fear of man.

The program with which Churchill was experimenting involved live trapping the bears, marking their rumps with an "x" in paint, and flying them to the Kaskattama River region about one hundred and fifty miles south of Churchill. The town intended to shoot any marked bears that returned as these would obviously be the problem bears. As no marked bears ever showed up back in Churchill, they deemed their relocation program a huge success.

Imagine Chris's predicament when the trappers returned at Christmas after a tremendously successful trapping season. The men had eight polar bear skins, all indelibly marked with the telltale "x" on the rumps. Chris told them he could not buy the hides, explained why, and furthermore, he swore them all to total secrecy.

District Management in Northern Ontario was followed a year later, 1978, by a promotion to Saskatchewan District I. The work and challenges in the new district were similar, except now, I was working with more experienced management, with larger stores and better infrastructure. Most of the stores now in my charge were located on roads, so I would find myself every other week flying to Saskatoon or Thompson, and then renting vehicles.

One of the stores that fell under my responsibility was Cumberland House. This was home and for the next five years, as part of my job, I was able visit every few months and stay a few days with my proud parents.

In 1983, my career shifted from operational responsibilities to that of support functions. I assumed the position of Employment Manager in an effort to assist the company in developing more Aboriginal employees into management positions. I quickly found that I was somewhat deficient in personnel policy matters and procedures. After some discussions on long range goals for myself, I was promoted to Personnel Manager for Central Region for the purpose of acquiring crucial skills for my next challenge.

Personnel Management was excellent training for myself. However, the day to day responsibilities of hiring and firing, salary administration, long, involved disciplinary procedures, fielding queries on minute personal matters for staff, were smothering and, in the end, just not for me. I spent one year in this position until I had enough and requested and received a promotion in 1985 to a Head Office function called Manager, Native Affairs.

My position as Personnel Manager was somewhat groundbreaking as I hired a number of people of diversity including Aboriginal people for management training which was not the norm at the time. I also hired our first female management trainee, Joan Delaronde, who became the first female store manager in our Northern stores.

In my position as Manager of Native Affairs, I became more interested in developing training programs and creating opportunities for Aboriginal people, both within and outside our company.

The last few years appealed to a growing conviction within me that I had to start taking advantage of my position within this company. There was an ever-present need to assist our people in making changes to their appalling situation. Not only was I busy trying to climb the corporate ladder within our company, I was now fully involved and engaged within our Aboriginal community.

I worked with other early activists in Winnipeg; Bill Shead, Marion Meadmore, Don Marks, Mary Richard, Murray Sinclair, Eric Robinson, Barbara Bruce, Marileen McCormick, Wayne Helgason, Dan Highway, Phil Fontaine, Yvon Dumont, just to name a few.

I was invited to the Board of Directors of Me-dian Credit Union, an Aboriginal financial institution, in 1983 (Me-dian stands for Métis and Indian). A short time later Me-dian, along with about 20 other credit unions in Manitoba struggling with deficit positions, were slated for closure. I recognized the potential for Me-dian and had developed a simple business plan for a quick turnaround of its fortunes.

The Board of Directors voted me into the position of the Chair and I promptly called Phil Fontaine, then Vice-Chief of the Assembly of First Nations and Yvon Dumont, President of the Manitoba Métis Federation. Letters were sent and phone calls made to the province requesting a reprieve for Me-dian. The province relented under the political pressure and Me-dian was provided with a capital loan of $375,000 to be repaid over seven years.

Aboriginal people were beginning to stream into Winnipeg and they needed banking services. Our people were still mostly poor and they needed ready access to their cash on a month to month basis. This was before ATMs became popular. I discussed and Bill Shead agreed with me that we target more Aboriginal members and ensure we had adequate staff to look after their needs. We were about to become a store front, over-the-counter service provider. Where other credit unions had one or two tellers, we were operating with at least six. Our customers had a need, not for savings accounts, but for chequing accounts. Chequing accounts paid no interest. The cost of our money to operate the credit union was zero. We were making our money on transactional fees and we were busy. On paydays, the lineups stretched to the doors. The loan was repaid in three years and Me-dian became and remains the most profitable small credit union in the system.

Me-dian Credit Union also developed a very loyal clientele and this became most evident in an attempted robbery at its then Broadway location in Winnipeg. A lone robber walked into the Me-dian on a very busy day, and loudly shouted out, "This is a robbery. Everybody face down on the floor."

The robber had one hand in his jacket pocket poking outward and toward the customers on the floor in a threatening manner. With his free hand, he tossed a bag to the tellers behind the counter and ordered them to fill it with cash.

On the floor were the Chornaby brothers, who were in Winnipeg for business. They were rough and tough business men who owned and operated a freighting service back at their home in Island Lake. They looked at each other, and then both started to get up from the floor. The robber screamed at them to stay down.

"If that's a gun, then you better shoot now because we are going to kick your ass," coolly stated one of the brothers.

The robber made a dash for the door and out into the street with the Chornabys in hot pursuit. The brothers ran down their prey after several blocks and, yep, they kicked his ass before handing him over to the police.

By 1985, I was now a volunteer Board of Director on the Interprovincial Association of Native Employment, the Youth Business Learning and Development Centre, and Anishinabe Respect, an Aboriginal skills training program. I was Vice-Chair of the Indian Business Development Group, Deputy-Chair of Canadian Council for Native Business, Chair of the Kirkness Adult Learning Centre and Chair of Me-dian Credit Union.

I became a driven man on a mission and it would take a tremendous toll on my personal home life. My marriage to Josephine fell apart that year. I had spent far too much time on the road in my company positions. When I was back in Winnipeg, I spent far too much time at the office trying to keep up with my job plus handle my commitments to our community. Josephine disliked the loneliness of the city and my near constant absence did not help matters. She left and moved first to Cumberland House with my parents and then to La Ronge. We shared the responsibility of raising our girls.

A Manitoba Chapter of the Canadian Council for Native Business was set in Winnipeg and I became deeply involved. The organization was founded by Murray Koffler, who is best known as the founder of the Shoppers Drug Mart chain. The intent was for member mainstream businesses to provide professional and experienced mentorship to fledgling Aboriginal businesses.

The Canadian Council for Aboriginal Business later moved to providing internship positions within mainstream businesses for Aboriginal people. This became an excellent source for attaining business experience for our people.

I recruited Barbara Bruce to the Canadian Council for Aboriginal Business by convincing her it was necessary we start taking advantage of what mainstream businesses had to offer. As usual, Barbara did an exemplary job of working this position.

I also began accepting speaking engagements, talking about the social and economic potential of Aboriginal development. In addition, I added the St. Norbert Foundation to my list of directorships.

Around that period I received a call from Graham Dixon, the Executive Director of the Canadian Bankers Association. I, along with Barbara Bruce, Phil Fontaine and Yvon Dumont, were invited to a roundtable discussion with the Senior Vice-Presidents of the major banks in Winnipeg.

My experience with Me-dian Credit Union stood us in good stead as we advised the bankers their biggest problem was on being stuck with the need for a driver's licence as a piece of identification. We reminded them that many of our people were arriving in the city from remote locations where there were no roads, no vehicles, hence no driving licenses.

We said that for many of our people this was their first time in a city and the first time that many needed to use banking facilities. Bank employees were predominately white and it was just not a comforting situation for our people. A few Aboriginal employees would make their businesses more inviting.

Charles Coffey, Senior Vice-President for the Royal Bank took our words to heart. He took the lead in hiring and training Aboriginal employees and identification requirements for our people were changed. Cross cultural training programs were developed and implemented.

Toward the end of that year I met Rainey Jonasson. She was tall, statuesque, and striking. Rainey was employed by the Government of Manitoba in developing and delivering training programs. She was a volunteer director at Anishinabe Respect when we first met. Rainey was as deeply committed as I on Aboriginal issues, with a focus on cultural practices and the understanding and revival of old traditions.

We attended a number of traditional ceremonies and powwows and Amber developed an interest in dancing. Rainey made Amber a beautiful navy and white Jingle dress and taught her the basic dance steps. Amber also developed an interest in basketball, emulating Michelle, Rainey's six-one daughter who was a star with the University of Winnipeg's team. Amber also began attending ceremonies and she was bestowed with her spirit name, Petawbun Ekwai, (Woman of the Dawn).

In 1987, Ian Sutherland, an investor with a family background in the Hudson's Bay Company, gathered a number of investors for a buyout of the Northern Stores Department from the HBC for $180 million. Marvin Tiller remained in the top position as President and CEO after the change in ownership.

1990 continued to be a hectic year for me. I became involved with the Aboriginal Centre of Winnipeg, assisting Wayne Helgason, Mary Richard, Marileen McCormick, Bill Shead and others in pursuing the dream of consolidating Aboriginal services under one roof in a central location. Specifically, the CPR building at Higgins and Main was targeted for acquisition. The property had been listed for sale for a number of years. The historical building was successfully purchased, and the centre, with some seed money that I was able to leverage from The North West Company, became a reality in 1992.

I had previously been appointed by the province in 1988 to its Clean Environment Commission and in 1989 to its Skills Training

Advisory Committee. My commitment to the community and my own scrabbling to stay afloat within our company's upheavals and management changes again took its toll on my personal life. My relationship with Rainey fell apart.

Rainey went on to achieve a successful career in academia at the University of Manitoba, earning a doctorate degree along the way. I continued my painfully slow progress up the corporate ladder of our company.

Minister Without a Suitcase

Elijah Harper, born in Red Sucker Lake, Manitoba in 1949, was the first member of a First Nations in Manitoba to be elected to the provincial legislature in 1981. Prior to his election as a MLA, he was the chief of his small band. Jennifer Wood became his lifelong assistant and the invaluable person who kept him organized.

Elijah's tenure as chief is remembered for his purchasing the first community satellite dish in the far north. Dishes back then were about 12 to 15 feet in diameter. What was memorable was that every so often, two or three men had to run out from the band office and manually move the huge, heavy dish using a log as a lever, until a signal was restored.

Edward Kennedy and Len Flett negotiating with the Chief and Council of Nelson House, Manitoba.

In 1986, Premier Howard Pawley appointed Elijah to the Manitoba cabinet as Minister without Portfolio, responsible for Native Affairs. This was a groundbreaking event for the Aboriginal community and we celebrated with a large reception for Elijah at the Marlborough Hotel.

Elijah's welcoming speech drew much laughter as he related to us how he announced to his Oji-Cree speaking father, by phone, his appointment to cabinet. The closest translation for "Minister without Portfolio" into Oji-Cree was "Minister Without a Suitcase."

The "Mister Without a Suitcase" was to become a key player in bringing down the Meech Lake Accord of 1990.

Negotiated by then Prime Minister Brian Mulroney and the ten provincial premiers in 1987, the Meech Lake Accord proposed amendments to the Constitution of Canada. It was an attempt to bring the Province of Quebec into the constitutional family, as Quebec alone had refused to accept and sign the 1982 Constitutional Act. The Constitution was patriated by Prime Minister Pierre Trudeau, formally ending rule by Great Britain.

The Accord proposed devolution of powers to the provinces, "opting out" clauses for federal programs, plus it included the provision of special status to Quebec as a "Distinct Society."

The provincial and federal legislatures were given three years in which to approve and ratify the Accord.

Since the patriation of the constitution from Great Britain in 1982, Quebec remained reticent, refusing to accept and sign the Canada Constitution. The Supreme Court ruled that all provinces, including Quebec, fell under the new rules of the Constitution Act of 1982, whether they signed onto the agreement or not. Nevertheless, the issue of Quebec sovereignty hung palpably in the air.

The initial intent of the Meech Lake Accord was noble; however, it was driven by the ambitious Brian Mulroney and negotiated with the ten provincial premiers behind closed doors. "Eleven men in suits" became the derisive catchphrase describing the undemocratic process of developing the Accord. There was no public consultation or debate, and most glaringly, the Aboriginal leadership were entirely shut out of the process.

Support for the Accord gradually deteriorated over the three-year grace period, as Aboriginal organizations, led by Phil Fontaine and the Assembly of Manitoba Chiefs (AMC), hammered at the Accord. In desperation, Mulroney convened a First Ministers' conference, again behind closed doors, on June 3, 1990.

All ten premiers, including Frank McKenna and Clyde Wells, signed consent to this new eleventh-hour Accord, albeit with certain provisions which provided escape clauses. Only the First Nations stood firm at all times on the side of democracy.

Strategists for the Assembly of Manitoba Chiefs noticed that the Manitoba Legislature required the unanimous consent of its MLAs in order for the Meech Lake Accord to be adopted. Phil Fontaine and key chiefs within the AMC approached and lobbied the lone First Nations MLA in the provincial government, Elijah Harper. They convinced him to utter his simple but unforgettable "No," thereby rightfully bringing down the Meech Lake Accord.

9

THE CORPORATE LADDER

A NEW DIRECTION

In 1989, a management change at the top occurred. The investors in the new company, temporarily called the Hudson's Bay Northern Stores, grew tired of the inaction on our shares and replaced the President and CEO. Marvin Tiller was out and Ralph Trott was in. Ralph ruthlessly trimmed the "old boys club" and brought in fresh talent including Edward Kennedy.

I moved back into retail operations as Director of Native Business Development.

Edward Kennedy became Vice-President of Corporate Development in 1990 and he put together a team including myself and Jim Clarke. It was an exciting period as Ralph Trott steered the company away from its money-losing merchandising operations in non-native communities. He shifted the company focus toward the profitable Aboriginal communities and my value immediately gained ground. The same year the company was renamed The North West Company, launching an enterprise that was determined to shake off the dust of the Hudson's Bay Company and become a leading retailer in a new age, but at the same time retain a tie to the history of the country.

Prior to the purchase of the Northern Stores Department from the Hudson's Bay Company, The Bay had been using the Northern Stores as a cash cow for years to prop up its weak cash flow. Little money was reinvested back into the Northern Stores and as a consequence, the infrastructure of that department had slowly and gradually fallen apart.

Many stores, warehouses, and staff houses throughout the North were in dire need of replacement or major repairs. Environment Canada tightened its rules and the new company found itself with a large environmental problem in many of its locations. It would take a number of years and about fifteen million dollars to clean up the environmental issue.

The problem originated from years of selling gasoline from 45-gallon drums. From the late 60s the sale of gasoline literally exploded in the North with the advent of snowmobiles and higher powered outboard motors. Gasoline would be dispensed using wobble pumps to pour into one-, two- or five-gallon containers. Gasoline was invariably slopped and splashed accidentally onto the ground.

Once the wobble pumps reached the bottom of the drums, that was end of the pumping. The drum was then simply turned upside down to drain the last bit of remaining gas. Shipping companies handling the empty drums insisted they be returned completely empty for safety reasons.

In my last year at Oxford House, 1975, in addition to several 5,000-gallon bulk tanks, we still had several hundred drums of gasoline stacked around our gasoline shed.

By the 1980s and 1990s, bulk fuel tanks housed in compounds built to environmental standards replaced the 45-gallon drums.

In 1992, the company acquired the Alaska Commercial Corporation and Jim Clarke moved to Anchorage to assume the management of our new venture.

In 1993, Ralph Trott resigned to move on to new challenges. Ian Sutherland assumed the position of President and Edward Kennedy became the Chief Operating Officer.

The same year, with our focus on Aboriginal communities and my corporate title being Director, Native Business Development, I began having problems with middle management dumping their Aboriginal issues on my desk. Any time complaints or operating issues arose that involved our Aboriginal employees, customers, or communities, the complaint or issue was sent to me for my attention. It became overwhelming.

I discussed the issue with Edward and it did not take him long to understand that Aboriginal relations extended far beyond myself. This was a company focusing on Aboriginal business and as such, Aboriginal relations had to become the responsibility of everyone in the company. My corporate title was changed to Director, Stores Development, eliminating the "Aboriginal" designation. The change in the corporate culture was immediately perceptible once everyone became accountable not only for Aboriginal but also community relations.

To deal with our infrastructure and cash flow issues, Edward began to focus his attention on store leases. The grand plan was to bring in the First Nations as partners to our developments by having them finance, own and lease new buildings to our company. The First Nations would leverage the funding required for the projects from the banks backed by the strength of our long-term leases signed with the Bands.

There was steep learning curve for all involved—the First Nations, the banks, Edward and myself. Edward had come to the company with an MBA, B.Comm. and a law degree; he was what I called "hyper-educated," but he possessed little experience in dealing with First Nations. I did not have the education but I did possess years of experience working with the First Nations and their communities.

Edward and I spent many hours, oftentimes late into the evenings; he explaining leases and I explaining the distinctiveness of First Nations communities. He explained all the legalese involved in the wording of standard leasing documents until I had a full understanding. We also discussed the economics of various projects until I gained an understanding of returns on investments and other benchmarks that identified viability. In short, Edward provided me with the tools to negotiate and make the necessary decisions on the spot.

Two years later Edward was transferred to Alaska to take over the ailing operations from Jim Clarke who had been released from company service.

On one of my trips to Toronto in late 1990, I attended a Native Women's Symposium with a friend. A beautiful dark-haired woman attending the forum approached me, handed me her business card and asked, "What tribe are you?"

She immediately turned a deep red after asking the question, turned and hurried back to her seat without waiting for my answer. I glanced at the card and it read "Marguerite Letourneau." I carefully put the card into my pocket with a mental note to follow up on my next trip.

About a month later, I found myself in Toronto walking by Marguerite's workplace on my way back to my hotel. I decided to stop in and ask for a dinner date which she accepted. She regaled me with her stories and quick wit and we began a long distance relationship. Marguerite was divorced with two adult children: Harmony, at the time married to Rolph Van Dalen in the Netherlands, and Allison, just entering her university years. Marguerite also had Teddy, her Chocolate Lab dog. I fell in love with Marguerite and later that year I asked her to move to Winnipeg to be with me. A few years years later we wed.

Horace Flett, my father, died on June 10 of 1992 at the age of 85 from Alzheimer's disease. He retired at age 65, but then continued to work part time until he turned 70. The Cumberland House School was situated behind the store and every day at lunch time, when Dad was still in his mid 60s, his youngest sons Alex, Jerry and Ted would leave the school and eagerly wait outside the store entrance door. At 65, Dad was still lean, wiry and spry. The minute he stepped out the door, he would dash down the street with his laughing and screaming little boys in pursuit. He raced his children the two or three blocks home every day and that kept him young.

Dad also enjoyed gardening. He gardened all his life. No matter how far north he found himself as a fur trader, every spring he dug his garden plot and planted his seeds.

Cumberland House sits on an old floodplain and the soil is dark and rich. The garden behind his house occupied his entire backyard and in addition, he had the use of the priest's garden plot which was located behind the church, for growing potatoes. From dawn to dusk, Dad worked his gardens well into his late 70s. His fall harvest would fill his basement bins with potatoes and root vegetables which kept his entire family well fed all winter. Neither I nor any of my siblings, could leave home after a visit without a sack of potatoes and vegetables in our vehicles.

It was Dad's gardening that provided the first hint of a looming issue. He would poke his head into the house and ask Mom if he had had lunch. Mom used to laugh when she would tell us that if she was feeling lazy, she would reply to Dad, "Yes dear. You ate." However, she would soon begin to feel pangs of guilt. She would then prepare some lunch and call him in.

As the disease slowly ate away at his memory, Dad found it more and more difficult to speak English and reverted to speaking only Cree. The disease was relentless and within a few years he became no more than a vegetable himself. My heart would ache in deep sorrow as I tried to speak to him and he would stare at me with unseeing eyes.

We had thought about institutionalizing him and in fact Mom and I, with Dad in tow, inspected some facilities in Prince Albert. The only institutions available at the time for Alzheimer victims were facilities intended for the mentally insane. As we walked on guided tours through the facilities, Dad would stop and stare at the compulsive antics of some of the inmates. Finally, Mom turned to me and said, "No. We cannot put your father away."

Mom and my sister Linda cared for him at home; they changed, cleaned, and hand-fed him in his final years. I and my siblings visited often to assist in whatever way we could. On one such visit, Dad had a relapse and my brother Don, a large man, picked Dad up in his arms and ran with him in his arms all the way to the nursing station, which was several blocks away. The nurses successfully revived him.

It was a sad day when my father died. I and my siblings and our families immediately started to make our way home when Mom called.

282 From the Barren Lands · Flett

We met in Nipawin where we chose a casket for Dad and out of respect for Mom we planned a Christian funeral.

Once at home in Cumberland House, a wake was held for Dad. My daughter Amber sang an Aboriginal song of lament, accompanying herself with her hand drum, while I "smudged" the coffin. The heavy, sweet smell of burnt sweetgrass and cedar hung in the air. I placed an eagle feather in my father's hands and a tobacco offering in his casket.

Several months after Dad's death, my mother came to Winnipeg to visit Marguerite and me for a few weeks. Mom loved visiting her niece, the late reverend Phyllis Keeper. Phyllis was the daughter of Eleazer Beardy, Mom's older brother, and was a member of the Muskrat Dam First Nation. She became a minister of her church, like her father and her grandfather before her. Her brother, Gordon Beardy, even became a bishop of the Anglican institution.

Phyllis regaled us with her stories of home and residential school. She said the first time she ever ate Jell-O, she screamed in fright when she touched the brightly coloured dessert and the Jell-O quivered.

Phyllis is the mother of actresses, Joy and Tina Keeper. Tina, best known for her role as RCMP officer Michelle Kenidi in the CBC television series, *North of 60*, happened to be home when we were visiting. We were discussing family relations and explaining how we were related to each other through both sides of the family.

Tina's father, Joe Keeper, from the Norway House First Nation, and my father were first cousins as their mothers were sisters from Norway House. And, of course, my mother was Phyllis's aunt.

Tina puzzled over this for a while and then her face brightened and her eyes widened as she exclaimed, "Oh my Gawd! I am my own cousin!"

Four years later, it was Joe Keeper that came to our door in the middle of night to awaken us with the news that Mother had died. I was 54 years old but, suddenly, I felt like a child. An unexplainable dark blanket of emptiness draped over me. Losing your mother is, somehow, more traumatic than losing your father.

Many years later, I still feel the loss of my parents; however, I now realize that they and I are part of the same life-cycle. They led full lives, and left numerous offspring with many cherished memories as their legacy to this world.

Vice-President

In 1995, our Alaskan operations were experiencing serious problems and Edward Kennedy was sent to replace Jim Clarke. Edward would remain in Alaska for two years, returning in 1997 as the new President and CEO of The North West Company. Upon his arrival back in Winnipeg, he immediately purged the company of many of the senior management who had risen from the ranks of the Hudson's Bay Company. I survived.

Edward promoted me to Managing Director, Store Development and Public Affairs and the following year promoted me to Vice-President. In addition to my core responsibilities for Store Development and Public Affairs, I assumed responsibility for the Store Planning and Construction Department, Real Estate, Inuit Art Marketing Services, and Fur Marketing. My colleague Vice Presidents that first year were Gary Eggertson, Carl McKay, John Mcferran, Terry Sweeney, and Brad Vollrath.

The first decision I made when Real Estate fell into my portfolio of responsibilities was to place a moratorium on all land sales within the traditional territories of the First Nations. I had been asked several times in recent years to become involved in attempting to resolve land issues with First Nations.

The company had become embroiled in a dispute over land in Big Trout Lake a couple years prior when our store manager removed a sign posted by the First Nations within the boundaries of the company's property. The sign was an advertisement for the band-owned local store, encouraging the people to patronize their own store. Our company store manager tore the sign down and stated that the First Nations had no right to post signs on The North West Company's property. Bad move. Try explaining Terra Nullius, with a straight face, to that chief and his council, or to any chief and council in Canada for that matter.

The First Nations responded by demanding the company leave the community. They then barricaded the road to the store and forbade the use of their roads for access to the airport. They ordered their people to boycott the Northern Store and to patronize their own store. After a few weeks of futile meetings, the company ran out of options and was forced to close this operation. A senior officer of the company retorted that it would not be long before the Band would be requesting the company to return. Many years later the company is still waiting for that invitation. My advice—"Don't hold your breath."

In another instance, the company held title to some real estate located within the First Nation of Port Simpson, British Columbia, to which our Real Estate department had agreed to accept an offer to purchase made the previous year. The deal never closed as the First Nations immediately embroiled the company in lawsuits.

On top of those issues, a board director was making enquiries about unused properties for possible purchase and that did not smell right.

A number of factors were coming into play with the issues of the company's land ownership in the North. All of the locations had been chosen many years earlier when water routes were the only mode of transportation. The company held choice properties fronting the old fur trade waterways of centuries past. As airstrips were being built, the communities began to grow away from the company locations, leaving our stores mostly isolated.

The company over years had become somewhat arrogant in the their relationships with the First Nations because, sitting on their own privately held lands, they did not fall under the jurisdiction of the local First Nations governments.

In order for the company to continue prospering in the North, it was essential for the company to relocate to the centre of the communities where it could better serve the populace, better face the growing competition, and be seen to be an integral part of the communities. And also place themselves under the direct jurisdiction of the Chief and Council. A number of older managers of the old school saw this as a possibly disastrous move.

The company, after over 300 years of dictating to the Indigenous population, were now uncomfortable with the thought of the "shoe being on the other foot." The source of the "un-comfort" is jokingly best portrayed by First Nations comedian, Don Burnstick, who, with tongue-in-cheek, often stated that "White people have the Mafia; Indians have Chief and Council." Far too many of our non-Aboriginal managers took this for the literal truth.

Nevertheless, the company proceeded, under my direction in the area of Aboriginal relations, to reposition itself, and quite successfully so, on many reserves. There have been no major issues and subsequently, positive progress has been made under First Nations jurisdiction.

Another decision I immediately made as Vice-President was to review our Public Affairs donations. The bulk of our corporate giving was earmarked for the Winnipeg Symphony, Royal Winnipeg Ballet, the Winnipeg Art Gallery, etc. These were, and continue to be, very worthwhile projects; however, there was a very deliberate business intention tied to the decision to divert the bulk of our corporate donations to the Aboriginal communities in which we conducted trade. We needed to demonstrate to the people from whom we made our living, that we also had their best interests in mind.

Fundraising options in the Aboriginal communities are very limited. The contributions made by our company often formed the major and sometime the only portions of the communities fundraising efforts and over time this came to be fully appreciated by the people.

I was also handed responsibility for Inuit Art Marketing Services and Fur Marketing; both departments appealed to my sense of the traditional and historical aspects of the company. Bill Moore managed the Inuit Art Services and George Scott looked after the Fur Marketing. Both men had crossed my career path very early in, and continued throughout, our company lives.

At the time, Inuit Art Marketing Services was leasing space from the North American Fur Auctions located in the same building. Bill took me on a tour of the Fur Auction facility as it was preparing for a major auction and he laughed when he saw my reaction.

"It does look like they killed every animal in North America, doesn't it?" Bill offered when he noted my amazement at the seemingly endless racks and racks of hanging fur. The fact was that most of the fur was ranched and the wild furs, just a small percentage overall, was part of the annual trapping harvest. I also came to the realization that fur harvested by Indigenous people was just a tiny percentage of the overall production. Non-Aboriginal farmers do a lot of trapping in their off-season, especially for beaver and coyote, and fur ranchers are the overall largest producers of furs.

Jerry Whiteway had been my handyman in Oxford House. Any repairs or renovations to my buildings and sheds or any yard work requiring attention such as my septic fields, wells, water lines, etc. were looked after by Jerry. He was reliable, hard working and I depended on him.

I remember one cold, blustery Sunday morning in Oxford House, he was working for me putting snowmobiles together. We had a small garage next to one of warehouses for work of this type. I had some catch-up work to attend to in the store, so I left Jerry on his own. At one point I had to retrieve some items from the main warehouse. I found what I had been looking for and on my way out, locked the warehouse again.

An hour or so later, Jerry came to the house and said he heard someone, a child, crying in the warehouse. We ran to the warehouse, unlocked the door and found my six-year-old daughter, Lynda-Gale, half frozen and sobbing at the door. I had accidentally locked her in when she had followed me into the warehouse and began wandering about without my knowledge.

A number of years after I had left Oxford House, I ran into Jerry in Winnipeg. I was walking down the street dressed in a suit, white shirt and tie, topped by a scarf and overcoat, and carrying a briefcase. I was heading for an important meeting. Jerry decided to walk with me. We talked as we walked. He had become a street person, battling addictions, and living under bridges and in dark back streets. As we walked along, two street people stepped out from a lane, greeted Jerry and asked him who I was.

"This is my lawyer," said Jerry with a big grin.

The street people laughed at Jerry and then faded back into the anonymity of the city streets.

When Jerry asked me for two dollars I couldn't refuse because, somehow, I still felt indebted to him for possibly saving my daughter's life.

I ran into Jerry again sometime later just as I was leaving Gibralter House where I worked. Big mistake. Now he knew where I worked. Every time he was down and out, he would come to the office looking for me. He became a nuisance. I would give him his two dollars and tell him he could not disturb me at work. He promised he would not come to the office to bother me, but that did not stop him.

Finally I told my executive assistant, Janice Heinrichs, about my problem with Jerry. I told her to tell the receptionist that, whenever Jerry came looking for me, to simply tell him that I was out of town.

The next time Jerry came to the office and asked the front receptionist for me, she advised Jerry that I was out of town. At that moment, our President and CEO, Edward Kennedy, was passing by and he overheard the receptionist.

"No, he is not out of town," said Edward. "Len was just in my office a few minutes ago."

"Let me check with Janice," said the receptionist diplomatically as she picked up her phone.

She called Janice on the phone, then turned to Edward and Jerry and advised, "I'm sorry. Janice said Len just left out the back door for the airport."

"That is very odd," said Edward. "Len never said anything about having to go out of town."

He then turned to Jerry and said, "Maybe I can help. What did you need to see Len about?"

"I just need two dollars," replied Jerry.

"Wait a minute," offered Edward. He then returned to his office where he realized he did not have any change and that the smallest bill he had was a ten.

Edward returned to the entrance foyer and handed Jerry the bill. Jerry stared at the ten-dollar bill in his hands for a moment until he realized his windfall. Deliriously happy, he promptly grabbed his new-found friend, Edward, in a big bear hug and planted a sloppy wet kiss on his cheek.

The dire need for repairs, renovations, expansion and new developments throughout the company put a huge strain on our limited capital resources. In discussions with Edward Kennedy, I pointed out that the several Aboriginal economic development conferences that I had attended focused on partnerships and joint ventures between First Nations and mainstream businesses.

The First Nations were encouraging these ventures by stating there were advantages to tax exemptions with on-reserve businesses. Edward ruled out joint ventures as we could not work around the issues of asset ownership. However, this led to lease agreements as the vehicle for our expansion and redevelopment of our businesses with First Nations in many locations.

We would target a location and run several business models until our development team could all agree on the most efficient proposal. We had Store Planning draw out proposed floor layouts and estimated costs for the total financing that the First Nations would need to leverage for the project. We worked out the parameters within which I could safely negotiate. Impressive Power Point presentations were made and draft lease agreement proposals drawn up.

Armed with this information I would organize an initial meeting with the Chief and Council and they would arrange for their lawyers and advisors to attend. Where we had existing stores that needed to be redeveloped, I first had to convince the Chief and Council that we were serious about a partnership. Not only would the community have a new modernized store, greatly expanded and equipped with all the latest services, the Band would own the building and as landlords, lease the facility to the company.

I advised the Bands that if they had the need and the necessary resources, they could easily expand the store proposal into mall projects including motels, restaurants, offices, and other small businesses, all made possible by the fact that our company would be the anchor tenant.

A lot of excitement was created with each project, and not all the excitement was positive either. Every community and every proposal had its opposition, often citing recent or historical wrongs committed by our company. The story of the furs piled to the height of the gun barrel needed to purchase the firearm was invariably brought up. The accusation was that every year the company made their gun barrels longer and longer. Having made their point, they would then sit back and await my reply.

As a First Nations person myself, it was easy for me to say that my grandfather, Chief Samson, wasn't stupid enough to fall for such a ruse and that I was sure their grandfathers weren't either. I also explained that the company throughout its history was meticulous in its record keeping and that nowhere in the archives were to be found any mention of this practice. It was myth.

The opposers would then shift their attention to our company property and ask how we managed to get private title to property abutting their reserves. I would have to give a history lesson on the fur trade, Terra Nullius and the Royal Charter of 1670 giving all lands draining into Hudson Bay to the company.

This raised many eyebrows. I would simply continue and explain that this was all based on the English Law system, same as the Royal Proclamation of 1763, of which all First Nations were fully aware and depended upon for their rights and land claims.

I would advise the Bands they could not cherry pick their laws and that they would have to hold their noses and accept that this was part of the history. This was always the lead-in to my closing lines needed to seal my proposal.

I advised the Chief and Council that as an inducement to the agreement we were prepared to turn over the company lands to the ownership of the First Nations. I further stated that at the end of the lease, which usually averaged 20 years, the Band was in the seat of power. They, and only they, had the authority to renew the lease if they wanted to continue their relationship with our company.

I reminded them that the company had been around on First Nations territories on their own terms for over 300 years. This was now a time for the First Nations to take control and share in this economic opportunity. I advised we would lay out the terms of the agreement and ensure, through negotiations, that clauses such as management training for their people would be included. I reminded them again, that with local staff trained for management, the First Nations could then very easily determine not to continue the relationship with our company at the expiration of the lease, if they so desired.

These were scary words for our senior management; on the other hand, there was no better incentive for them to provide the best retail service possible.

The final result before I retired was that 50 First Nations communities entered into lease agreements with our company. At an average of about two million dollars per project, this put approximately one hundred million dollars worth of physical assets, totally owned by the First Nations, on reserves. The projects generated about 800 new jobs, and over time, stimulated new economic ventures such as malls, band offices, restaurants, motels and other retail outlets.

The number of Aboriginal management members within the company also rose significantly from about 20 plus when I started in the position to well over 200 by the time I retired.

Through these ventures, the North West Company greatly stretched its initial limited cash flow so that it was able to kick start and position itself, in a very short period of time, as the premier retailer of the North. Under the leadership of Edward Kennedy, the company has since developed into a plus-billion dollar Canadian corporation with retail operations throughout Canada, Alaska, the Caribbean, and the South Pacific.

The interesting and ironic part of all the negotiations that I was involved in was that I, a First Nations person, representing a large, white mainstream business, was always negotiating with a battery of white lawyers and advisors representing the Bands. I still see many First Nations organizations dependent upon non-Aboriginal consultants and lawyers and I wonder how long it will be before our people become comfortable with hiring professionals from within our own community.

My work, recognized by both our company and the First Nations as win-win situations, benefitting all parties involved, led to my nomination and recognition in 2002 by the National Aboriginal Achievement Foundation (now Indspire) for an achievement award in the category of Business and Commerce. I was further honoured with the Order of Canada in 2004, a Lifetime Achievement Award from the Aboriginal Chamber of Commerce in 2008, and the Order of Manitoba in 2012 along with the Queen's Jubilee medal the same year.

I am proud of the acknowledgements. However, I do look at my Queen's Jubilee medal with some reservations and wonder why I should be rewarded with a medal celebrating a woman who is the epitome of a class-structured society.

Len Flett and Dr. Gilles Pinette of Winnipeg are presented with National Aboriginal Achievement Awards in 2002.

CONCLUSION

RETIREMENT

Our cottage in Killarney was the pride and joy for Marguerite and me. For a number of years it was our summer home, raucously filled with the laughter and screams of grandchildren Dolph, James, Libby, Kathleen, Michelle and Sarah.

When I retired from The North West Company in 2005, Dan McConnell, with whom I worked a number of years, replaced me. Dan kept me busy for another year or two with contract work. Peggy Meiklejohn ensured we, the former Nor'westers, stayed in contact by Facebook. However, Marguerite and I soon found we were spending most of our time at the cottage, which we had winterized to extend our season. Whenever I was in Winnipeg, I could hardly wait to leave the din of the city and get back to the peace and quiet of our cottage.

The following year we sold our condo on the Assiniboine River, purchased our lake house in Killarney, and moved there permanently. Killarney, a scenic little farming community tucked away in the southwestern corner of the province, just 20 kilometers from the American border, sits on Killarney Lake. There is an Irish flavour to the town with its Erin Park, which also contains its own Blarney Stone, and Kerry Park, the racetrack dubbed the Irish Downs, and a number of Irish named businesses. Ironically, I have yet to meet an Irishman. The town and municipality of Turtle Mountain is populated mainly by people of Scottish, English, Mennonite and Hutterite heritage.

The lake is a draw for the community, attracting 1,500 campers and cottagers every summer. It is also a popular retirement community with many lake homes surrounding the tiny prairie lake. The community upgraded its airport runway to accommodate 15-minute jet ambulance service to Winnipeg. A first-rate hospital is headed by the thoroughly competent Dr. Anton Pio.

The home we purchased for our retirement was ideally suited to our needs. Everything was on one floor—no upstairs—no basement —no climbing stairs in our old age. It was situated on a beautifully treed acre of land with 150 feet of lake-frontage. I enjoyed the ample size of the property with its numerous trees and bushes. The raking, cleaning, trimming, shovelling kept me busy and physically active.

When we purchased our property, the previous owner advised that he had lost about 4 or 5 feet of lakefront from erosion. I spent the rest of that summer, and the next, digging out rocks from a local landfill, and hauling back to our property in our SUV. I then manually carried each and every rock on my back from our driveway to the lakefront to shore-up the property. It was truly yeoman's work, but one that I enjoyed immensely for the exercise. And it served the purpose for which it was intended.

Every warm summer day was spent water-skiing, tubing and swimming. When we were alone, Marguerite would pack a lunch and we would drift about in the middle of the lake, reading, chatting, and sipping on a glass of red wine feeling smugly adventurous as we kept an eye out for the RCMP patrol boat.

As the years quickly slipped by, on hot summer days when we went out on the lake to swim, we found it more and more difficult to climb out the water and back into our boat. We decided, instead, to add a pool to our property and with assistance of grandson James, we extended our deck around the pool area. It was a beautiful and welcome addition to our home.

The year we purchased our property, the deer population appeared to be at its peak. The municipality had counted over 800 in and around the community. We left our gates open and threw out our leftover bread and vegetables for the animals. Every evening up to a dozen deer would be wandering about on our property.

The same group of deer came to visit every evening and we began to recognize some of the deer individually. We kept treats of apples and carrots and various fruit and vegetable peelings for Roo and Mama. The doe had a recognizable scar on her ear and her yearling had the face of a kangaroo. Whenever we spotted them in the yard, we would open our door and throw out some treats onto the deck. After a while the brash yearling, Roo, never hesitated to accept our treats; however, Mama, ever so cautious, reluctantly followed to keep a watchful eye on her offspring.

Within a few weeks, Roo and Mama would regularly venture onto our deck and peer into our windows looking for us.

Indspire is an Aboriginal, education-focused organization, and it fits as one of the remaining passions in my life.

I resigned from all my volunteer organizations, but maintained my directorship with Indspire. Today, Indspire is the only commitment I have outside of my private life.

Lack of education is a major issue within our community, and contributes to a number of shortfalls, including our lack of capacity for management, which, as a businessman, always concerned me. Significant progress has been made in recent years, but the Aboriginal community still severely lags in education behind the Canadian mainstream, due in part to severe under-funding and historical, social and economic factors.

Founder John Kim Bell invited me to join the board of the Native Arts Foundation in 1990, and it wasn't long thereafter that its name was changed to the National Aboriginal Achievement Foundation. The foundation morphed once again in 2013 to become Indspire.

I chaired the foundation from 1997 to 1999, and once again from 2004 to 2010, when the Board of Directors requested I re-assume the position of the Chair to help steer the Foundation through a difficult change in management. In 2010 I stepped down from the chair because in retirement your influence naturally begins to wane. David Tuccaro, whose business star was on the rise, was the natural choice to succeed me.

Roberta Jamieson, a Mohawk woman from Six Nations, was recruited in late 2004 as President and CEO. Under her leadership (and with some encouragement and guidance on my part) the scope of the Foundation expanded its mandate to include crucial assistance to the K-12 Aboriginal educational system.

Indspire's core mandate is to raise and leverage funds for the provision of financial assistance to Aboriginal post-secondary students through disbursements of scholarships and bursaries. To date, the foundation has disbursed over $65 million to over 20,000 First Nations, Métis and Inuit students in need of assistance. With financial assistance from our foundation, many Aboriginal students have gone on to become doctors, nurses, lawyers, teachers, social workers, engineers, and business people to name just a few career choices.

The K-12 Educational component of the foundation was recently included to confront the issue of our problematic drop-out rate of Aboriginal students from high school. The mandate includes organizing educational conferences for teachers and acting as a central location for the dissemination of information and best practices for Aboriginal education.

In 2014, the *Financial Post* named Indspire as one of the top 25 charities in Canada, based on principles of accountability, transparency, and efficiency.

Musings of an Elder

Several years ago, when I turned 70 years of age, I started to second-guess myself about whether I had retired too early, as I was still in good health mentally and physically.

Many people my age were still in the workforce or self-employed, and there were times when I envied them. Knowing what I now know about myself, I am appreciative of the decision I had made to fully retire, devote myself to family, to travel and enjoy the company of friends, to carve out leisure time for myself and Marguerite, and to learn music, play an acoustic guitar, read, and most importantly, to take the time to write.

We enjoyed a number of years of swimming, boating, canoeing, and kayaking with friends and our grandchildren. When winters began to set in, Marguerite and I would leave for Sarasota, Florida to live with our daughter Harmony and her husband Matt.

In recent winters we have been spending our time in Mazatlán, Mexico, with hometown Killarney friends, Brian and Helena Wong, Beaconia friends, Frank and Gail Sabatini, and Minnesota friends Dennis and Shelley Lindbergh, where we have developed a community for swimming, dining, dancing and golf. The Wongs, Sabatinis and Lindberghs, aware of my condition, ensure Marguerite and I are never without assistance when needed and they constantly check on how I am holding up.

In 2013, I had been diagnosed with Idiopathic Pulmonary Fibrosis, a chronic and ultimately fatal disease. The doctor said, "Maybe three years." Another doctor, consulted for a second opinion, said, because my plane of lung-function decline was proving to be less steep than normal, "Maybe five years from the date of diagnosis." There it was. The cold fact hit me like a bucket of ice water in my face. I can prepare for my funeral to take place somewhere between 2016 and 2018.

Recognizing that I did live somewhat an extraordinary life, but no more so than many First Nations, Métis and Inuit activists who strive for social justice, I had always intended on writing about my life experiences. I maintained a private library of notes, articles, copies of my speeches, paper clippings, and books and magazines of interest. I also come from a large family. With eight brothers and four sisters, our family stories are kept alive whenever we visit each other. Family gatherings are occasions for remembrance and laughter. I also intentionally name many people in this book—people that have crossed my path, touched and become part of my life story. My life has been enriched by many people I have met, so much so that it is an impossibility to name them all.

My beautiful wife Marguerite is an early riser. For the past 25 years, when she hears me finally arise, she runs to meet me in the hallway where we tenderly embrace for several moments. Then she brings my first cup of coffee to me in the washroom as I am shaving. That act of love never fails to start my day on a positive note.

I turn to the task of shaving and while shaving, I often look at myself in the mirror and wonder why I have to shave in the first place. Indigenous people of the New World were smooth-skinned, with never more than a few wisps of long hair on the faces of older men that could simply be plucked.

I am amused by the thought of seeing my daughters examining the hair on their arms and legs, and sarcastically turning to me, and saying, "Thanks, Dad." Their beautiful Cree mother, a victim of breast cancer, was smooth-skinned.

I smile as I acknowledge to myself that this, the act of shaving, is the last remaining visible vestige of my Scottish background passed down to me by my great-grandfather, James Flett, from the Orkney Islands. The total and complete assimilation of the Scots by my First Nations family is now almost complete.

I often wonder why I do not think more often about my Scottish heritage. I realize that our society has not really given me the opportunity to acknowledge that aspect of my heritage. My colour has always been an instant identifier. And as long as the social injustice toward Indigenous people continues, I will continue to think of myself foremost as a First Nations person. I had hoped that at some point, I could, with great pride, call myself a Canadian first; however, that time has not yet arrived. And, unfortunately it may never come for me. But it will eventually arrive, and that is the confidence I have for this country, and the hope I hold out for my children and grandchildren.

A number of years ago, as a matter of personal principle, I even gave some thought to returning my Order of Canada, in protest of the social conditions of Aboriginal people in Canada. The Latin motto of the Order of Canada is "Desiderantes Meliorem Patriam." The translation into English of the motto means "They desire a better country." This defines the core of who I have been the past 40 years; therefore to this day, after some consideration, I wear my snowflake pin with pride.

The year after I was diagnosed with my fatal disease was the most difficult. There were often times when the weight of terminal illness draped over me like a wet blanket; heavy, damp and cold. The morbidity would at times be smothering, but short lived, lasting usually for just a few minutes, a few hours; never for more than a day.

It was quickly lifted by a phone call, text message, email or visit from family or friends, loving attention from my wife, or the voice of a child calling me "Grandpa."

Today, I am much more at ease with my condition. I have come to terms somewhat with my lot in life. However, I am not fully accepting, without indignation, that my life is being cut short. And I do not look forward to suffering the indignities of old age and failing health, exacerbated by this relentless disease. I follow developments on euthanasia in Canada with great interest.

When I do feel overwhelmed and my heart grows unbearably heavy, the cloud can be dispelled by a connection to the natural world. I am always delighted by the heart-lifting sight of a chipmunk scampering across our deck. White tail deer browsing in the nearby woods of our property never fails to fill my heart with admiration. In summer, I am entertained by the cacophony of geese on our lake and by the lilting songs of robins welcoming the sun at daybreak. American finches, chickadees, sparrows, and cedar waxed-wings hop from branch to branch as I walk my property, and the sight of turtles basking on the rocks lining the shores of the lake in the early warming rays of the sun calms any anxiety I may be feel.

I love the outdoors. I take deep breaths to appreciate the air, to savour the exquisite scents of nature, and to listen carefully for the rustle of leaves and the chirps of birds and insects.

There is nothing grander in this world than the changing colours and moods of a Canadian sunrise or sunset. Nor the enchanting and colourful dance of our northern lights—the awesomely named "Aurora Borealis." Even the sight of the moon, glistening ghost-like in the dark of night, conveys a sense of quiet awe.

While our natural world fills me with joy, I find that I am most at peace with my condition in the presence of my 18-month-old great-granddaughter, Kayleen. I gently pick her up and carry her in my arms, and as she curiously and solemnly examines me, I look into her charcoal-dark eyes, and I am suddenly startled by a vision of Paquetna gazing back at me. I give my head a gentle shake, and Kayleen smiles at me. My heart melts.

Four generations separate us, yet Kayleen is physical and tangible evidence to me that life does, indeed, carry on. Another great-granddaughter, Astrid, has recently arrived. And Nichole will, in a few months, present me with a third great-grandchild. They affirm the life cycle of which we are all a part.

Kayleen, Astrid and Nichole's baby are miracles of life, much the same as mine. They carry my DNA, and deep down within my spirit, I find this comforting: tiny bits of my life are thus being carried forward in time.

EPILOGUE

As I come to the conclusion of this book, I have reflected on some key points and issues that have always been close to the surface of my mind. I have spent the better part of my life struggling to balance the relationship between our people and Canada. There is a desperate need to figure out our relationship for our long-term mutual benefit as a country. I cannot say that I have the answers. I hope, at the very least, that my story has provided a better understanding of our people and our situation. I also hope that my opinions will initiate thought, dialogue and debate. I have always enjoyed reading and listening to debate and quite often found that the more an issue is debated, the less murky the issue becomes. And while the situation of our Aboriginal people may appear to be completely hopeless at times, it doesn't have to be so. Maybe there are ways, viable options, to resolve our many issues. We just need to keep in mind that the Aboriginal issues of today were many years in the making; therefore it could be many years before positive and constructive change can be realized.

Racism

We simply do not know or understand each other. We can project ourselves back to 1492 and immediately point to the obvious fact that two very different cultures came face to face. The next 500 years saw the gradual domination of one culture over the other creating a mire of issues and problems. A clearer path to a better future requires that we examine our past, recognize and acknowledge where we went wrong, and move forward with a better understanding.

The strikingly beautiful Canadian Museum for Human Rights (CMHR) has, on a very timely basis, just opened its doors in Winnipeg this year.

Its Mission: To promote the idea that all human beings are born free and equal in dignity and rights.

Upon reflection about the present state of the First Nations, I have to remind Canada that there is a constant, ongoing struggle for dignity in the Aboriginal world. And racism is the antithesis of dignity. We have a dire need to develop and encourage respect for each other.

The ugly head of bigotry and racism has and continues to rise most alarmingly within the educational system. As part of the Aboriginal community, we do our best to shield and protect our children and grandchildren, who have integrated into the city's schools, and who are most vulnerable to racism.

The best place to begin the battle against racism is in our schools and with our teachers. It needs to start with grasping the true history of Aboriginal peoples and gaining an understanding of their underlying issues today, and most importantly, acknowledging their many contributions to our country.

Racism makes its obnoxious presence known in many locales and under many different circumstances. Racism is found in areas of housing, education, health, employment and the workplace, justice and policing and right down to playground and street insults and racist jokes in bars and at parties.

Racism in sports and entertainment is particularly irritating. Sports teams with names appropriated from our culture like "Blackhawks" with its offensive caricature, "Braves," "Sioux" or condescending names like "Redskins" tagged by early settlers, are offensive because of their use in competitive sports which pits teams against one another in win or lose situations. In game situations it means half the fans are rooting for you to lose and in many unfortunate cases, it invokes crude tomahawk gestures, war whoops, drumming, and in some instances the wearing of feathered bonnets, paint, beads and buckskins in disrespectful parody of our culture.

I have no idea why people think it is cool and sexy to wear feathered bonnets to rock and folk concerts. It is an insult to those of us who associate the bonnets with leadership and honour.

As a visible minority, I have been subjected to racism in all its forms—insidious or overt—and most painfully, I am aware that my family and relatives at some point have been victimized by it. A simple Facebook posting by Bodiene, a niece—"Too brown for this town"—ripped at my heart because I understood what and how she was feeling. Over the years I have become somewhat immune to the stupidity of some people; however, my concern remains for my young family and relatives who face bigotry and discrimination simply because of the colour of their skin.

The biggest fear, by far, is the thought, never far from mind, that one of my own daughters or granddaughters, or any of my many nieces and grandnieces, would be subject to violence motivated by hatred that is driven by racism, or family violence driven by years of hopelessness and frustration. The missing and murdered Aboriginal women in Canada, numbering over a thousand in recent years, makes this a very valid, very cold fear.

Racism unfortunately has become a commonplace occurrence, so much so that at times it becomes all-numbing. Dwell on it and it becomes emotionally draining. Succumb to the denigration and you become angry, despondent, spiteful and vengeful and, at worst, filled with hatred and hostility.

At this stage in my life, I feel hopeful and optimistic that positive change is in the air. I have always surrounded myself selectively with open-minded people, and in addition, there are many better-educated and sensitive young people striving to make this world a better place in which to live. Our world is becoming more global in nature, and there is less room for racism. For every vitriolic "letter to the editor" from a redneck that I read, there is an immediate positive rebuttal from someone who recognizes injustice and courageously articulates it. That type of response from a member of the majority society never fails to warm my heart and restore my faith in decent mankind.

Enemies of the State

The Indian Act continues to be a blot upon our country's history and greatly impedes us from moving forward in a new relationship with Canada.

It was enacted in 1876 for the purpose of administrating and implementing the terms of the Treaties, however, it did not take long for the Indian Act to usurp the powers of the Treaties. The Indian Act gradually became the main body of law from which the legal rights of Indians flowed, rather than from the treaty themselves.

What is the difference you may ask?

The difference is that the Treaties, as flawed and one-sided as they are, are agreements of the First Nations with Canada.

The Indian Act, on the other hand, is a piece of draconian legislation to which the First Nation had no input. It became the main instrument used by Canada to completely subjugate the First Nations, treating them not as partners to the development of our country, but, upon close examination, as enemies of the state.

I have been asked many times why Aboriginal people look at the Canadian justice system with distrust. The Indian Act is very much a part of the Canadian justice system, and throughout my story I have cited many, many examples of amendments arbitrarily passed as legislation when it so suited Canada, and used for the purpose of oppression and assimilation.

Between 1876 and 1951, whenever it suited Canada to make an amendment to the Indian Act for purposes of depriving the First Nations of their rights, lands, and freedom, Canada simply did so. Numerous oppressive amendments were made in those intervening years. The following is a partial list of these changes:

1884: The Indian Act was amended to prohibit traditional Indian ceremonies, such as the Potlatch, Sun Dance, Sweat Lodge, and Powwows. This was mainly at the behest of the churches. A serious consequence to this piece of legislation was that it prevented the passing down of oral histories and values, much of it Native Spirituality, which governed and shaped First Nation life.

1886 : Indian Act policy was instituted that confined Indians to their reserves. They were required to obtain passes from their Indian Agent before they could leave their reserves for short periods. This policy of apartheid never passed legislation. Nevertheless, it was enforced as if it were, and persisted well into the 1940s.

1906 : The Indian Act was amended, making it possible to remove Indians from reserves near towns with populations over 8000.

1914 : The Indian Act was amended banning Indians from wearing traditional and ceremonial dress in public.

1920 : Duncan Campbell Scott, Deputy Superintendent of Indian Affairs, and known for his views of Indians as "savages" and "pagans," introduced a bill and policy making Residential Schools compulsory for children between the ages of seven and 15 years. This effectively removed the right of First Nation people to raise their own children. This policy wreaked havoc on the First Nation family structure with long-term and tragic consequences.

1920 : The Indian Act was amended by adding Section 141, which made it an offence for Indians to hire lawyers and seek legal counsel.

Department of Indian Affairs Pass

This section was later expanded to prohibit organizing and gathering.

1927 : The Indian Act was amended, making it illegal for Indians to solicit or raise funds for the purpose of filing land claims.

One now naturally asks, "Why is the Indian Act simply not repealed and done away with once and for all?"

The fact is, that with the amendments of 1951, most of the repressive clauses of the Indian Act that I outlined in the previous two pages had been repealed. First Nations were also given the right to vote and to consume alcohol in 1960. What remains of the Indian Act is still very suffocating with its paternalistic treatment of First Nation people. Until something better comes along, we, the First Nations, continue to be recognized and to live, in a somewhat masochistic manner by our own choice, under its legislation.

The White Paper of 1969, Introduced by Prime Minister Pierre Trudeau through his Minister of Indian Affairs, Jean Chrétien, proposed to dismantle the Indian Act and forever end the special relationship First Nations had with Canada. The intent was to swallow up the First Nations and make them no different from the rest of Canadians who had immigrated into our country.

This was viewed by our First Nation elders as cultural genocide—the end of a people as a distinct nation. This was in other words, simply the extermination of a people through assimilation, and we deserved better than this.

Chief Sitting Bull famously said, "If the Great Spirit had desired me to be a white man, he would have made me so in the first place."

Section 35 of the 1982 amendment to our present Constitution merely recognizes and affirms the "existing" Aboriginal and treaty rights in Canada. It does not define the rights. This has been left to the courts to debate and define. Since 1982, there have been a number of cases that collectively have developed into a fragile framework of legal precedence that defines our rights.

The process is excruciatingly slow and extremely expensive. Lawsuits have to be filed and lawyers and consultants hired. In fact, an entire industry has arisen out of this process. There is a desperate need to simplify this process and map out clear and concise procedures in the best interest of our people and Canada.

Our elders have taken a stand and correctly determined that the Indian Act will remain in place until such time something, like an amendment to our Constitution, strengthens, guarantees, and fully articulates the role of Aboriginal people in Canada. Only then would it make sense for our people to agree to abolish, once and for all, the embarrassing Indian Act.

We are a Treaty Nation

Phil Fontaine, then National Chief of the Assembly of First Nations, stated, "We have a past in this country, rooted in the Treaties and in our Aboriginal rights, which are at the core of our existence."

Canada committed a terrible injustice on First Nation people in satisfying its insatiable hunger for land. Canada used the Treaties as legal instruments to separate the Indigenous people from, not just their lands, but the rights to their lands, excluding them from the richness of our natural resources.

The crux of the problem and one of our deeper issues today, is the perspective taken by the government, and subsequently its citizens, about the original ownership of our lands when the Treaties were entered into between Canada and the First Nations. The Treaty making process was marred by the furtive undertones of Terra Nullius and Manifest Destiny which made the colonizing peoples think they were entitled to the lands regardless.

Eastern Canada and the original peoples were simply overwhelmed by immigration. The Oxford dictionary defines "colonialism" as the policy of acquiring full or partial control over another country, occupying it with settlers, and exploiting it economically. There was no reversing the dynamics of the floodtide of migrants arriving from the Old World in search of land and new opportunities. The full story here still needs to be told.

The numbered Treaties of the west, requiring the First Nations to surrender their Aboriginal title to the lands referred to by the Hudson's

Bay Company and the fledgling government of Canada as Rupert's Land is another story. Even the name itself is galling—this land in our view never, at any time, belonged to Prince Rupert. However, the Treaties were negotiated by Canada only after they had purchased Rupert's Land from the Hudson's Bay Company. The issue is the manner in which these transactions were carried out by our fathers of confederation and by the early shareholders of the Hudson's Bay Company in 1870. Clearly they did not hold the concept that First Nations owned these lands in the first place. Or, if there was any doubt in their minds, they simply reverted to subterfuge.

The HBC's Deed of Surrender transferring Rupert's Land to Canada contains a disclaimer under Section 14 which states:

"Any claims of Indians to compensation for lands required for purposes of settlement shall be disposed by the Canadian Government in communication with the Imperial Government; and the Company shall be relieved of all responsibility in respect of them."

In other words, the Hudson's Bay Company said to Canada:

"We are selling this land to you, and as a condition of the sale, you now accept responsibility for any future land claims to be laid by the Indians, and we, the Hudson's Bay Company shall not be held responsible in any way."

The Hudson's Bay Company, fully aware of their part in the duplicity of stripping the lands from the Indians, protected themselves with their disclaimer clause.

The new government of Canada realized they also needed to protect themselves from future litigation. This was accomplished through the Treaties. It was at best, dismissing, and at worst, contemptuous of the Indigenous people of the day. Either way, there is no denying the lack of respect and the dishonesty that under-laid the treaty making process and subsequently permeated the Canadian culture that followed.

Perhaps Canada should have entered into the Treaties, not with the First Nations, but with the Hudson's Bay Company.

Much has been made of the need for the renewal of relations between Canada and our people. It is time for Canada to examine and evaluate its moral and legal position in regard to its social contract with its indigenous population. The disregard for its fiduciary responsible has gone on far too long. It is time to stop wondering about why Aboriginal people are where they are in today's Canadian society. It is time to start implementing policy and programs with long range goals that directly affect our people in a positive manner.

The need to correct the foundation upon which the Treaties were entered into and the need to correct and properly adjust the terms of the Treaties, is one way that Canada, in the long term, can begin to resolve its issues and obligations to its First Nation people. It would be a giant step toward restoring pride in our people and instilling a sense of honour in the minds of all Canadians.

The Treaties are terribly flawed agreements. There is much to clarify and renegotiate to align the terms of the Treaties to our Constitution. To ensure equality, it should start with the premise that all Canadians pay income tax, including First Nations people on reserves. The levying of other taxes, sales tax for goods and services, for example, can and should remain at the discretion of the First Nation governing councils.

Some First Nation leadership may and will claim that personal income tax-free status on reserves is an inalienable right. To kick a sacred cow, that is simply nonsense because in the end, everything is subject to interpretation and is negotiable when both parties agree to negotiate. Convoluted interpretations of laws by all our politicians, including Aboriginal, have been the source of disagreements for far too long. Peace, order and prosperity only can come from mutually agreed interpretations of the laws governing our relationships. To achieve the best negotiating results our Aboriginal political organizations need to be funded independently of the federal government. It is difficult to negotiate on a nation to nation basis that many First Nations insist upon when one is so completely dependent upon the other.

Most First Nation people, in positions to do so, by far already do pay income taxes. In the wider context, our people have not benefitted from this aberration in tax laws. The majority of our people are still mired in poverty, and on top of this, are discriminated against and resented by the general taxpaying population because a few of our population are in fortunate positions, occupying well-paid jobs, and not paying income taxes. Our overall social progress is severely hindered by the interpretation of this peculiar piece of tax legislation.

The blanket accusation very often tossed about that "Indians do not pay taxes" is often rationalized by First Nation leadership that only a small percentage of our Indigenous people do not pay income tax, therefore don't sweat this issue. However, we as First Nation people simply cannot afford to continue to support the very small percentage of our non-income tax paying population that is one of the main sources of contempt and disrespect for the rest of our people.

There is a need to renegotiate and clarify other terms which would provide real and true value for our people, and the proposed change to the interpretation of our existing tax laws could well serve as the opening gambit in a set of negotiations to set our country on a more level keel. There is a dire need, not simply for more money to be thrown at the problem, but most importantly, to create an environment in which our people can develop and eventually prosper on their own. In other words, we need to be provided with the "bootstraps," denied us in the past by the legislative oppression of the Indian Act, so that we can pull ourselves out of the mire in which we presently find ourselves.

Aboriginal people desire and need a fair share of what is due our people—adequate land and resources. The reserve lands allotted to the First Nations were adequate for the purpose of situating their abodes but not for deriving a means of livelihood. It is the understanding of the First Nation people that the Treaties never ceded the right to the use of their traditional lands and waters for fishing, hunting and gathering rights. It is common sense that the First Nation people needed far more than their miserly-allotted reserves in order to survive.

The use of traditional land extends beyond harvesting moose, deer, beaver, and muskrats and the gathering of mushrooms and berries. It includes extracting and benefitting from the resources contained therein, especially for jobs. It also includes the harnessing of the waters in our territories for hydroelectric development. The First Nations want, need and deserve a share of the resources exploited from traditional lands.

Our Treaties and possibly our Constitution itself, relative to Section 35 dealing with Aboriginal people, must be clarified. To do otherwise would be to continue being mired in the painfully slow machinations of our courts, attempting to disentangle ourselves from the legal mess in which we presently find ourselves.

And our people will continued to be mired in poverty and all the issues that come with it, at great cost to Canada—poor health, poor housing, poor education, addictions, suicide, and growing levels of incarceration. Canada cannot afford to continue to maintain its casual attitude toward Indigenous poverty.

Commissions, Committees and Reports

The Royal Commission on Aboriginal People tabled its report in 1996 after 50 million dollars and five years in the making.

It was a huge undertaking, involving seven commissioners, 178 days of public hearings, travel to almost 100 communities, dozens of consultants, and scores of researched studies.

The commissioners eventually made over 400 recommendations, many of them based around the principle first established in 1969, after the release of the infamous "White Paper," that our treaties must be respected.

The Royal Commission on Aboriginal People urged that a "renewed relationship between Aboriginal and non-Aboriginal people in Canada be established on the basis of justice and fairness."

The final report of the Truth and Reconciliation Committee will be released in the fall of 2015. The year 2016 will mark the 20th anniversary of the release of the Royal Commission on Aboriginal People. And the following year, 2017, will be the 150th anniversary of the Confederation of Canada. It would be a shame to let this opportunity for a renewal of relations to slip by again with inaction. The cost of doing nothing simply keeps accumulating on a year-to-year basis. There is also an unnecessary risk to ignoring a discontented minority within our populace.

During my career with The North West Company, I visited many reserves across Canada. There were a few communities that I saw with high standards of development. Many others were very modest, bordering on poverty. However, the shocking and heart-wrenching reality was that I saw far too many impoverished communities, and I could only wonder at the disastrous decisions made by our governments, past and present (including our own Department of Indian Affairs-instituted Chiefs and Councils) for our people to end up in such a downtrodden state.

The report issued in 2014 by James Anaya, former United Nations Special Rapporteur on the Rights of Indigenous Peoples confirmed my personal observations on the state of many of our Aboriginal communities. In his report on Canada, Mr. Anaya pointed out the "distressing socio-economic condition of Indigenous peoples in a highly developed country."

The most shocking statement, even for me, was that "of the bottom 100 Canadian communities on the Community Well-being Index, 96 are First Nation communities." How can the government and citizenship of Canada continue to shrug their shoulders and ignore this fact?

Canada needs to be reminded that many of our reserves are isolated and are in the peculiar position of being "out of sight—out of mind." Perhaps that is why our general population continues to be surprised whenever they are rudely reminded of the woeful economic and social conditions of First Nation people.

Recently, I drove by a church in Winnipeg one early morning, and I noticed a lineup of mostly Aboriginal people waiting for the institution to open its doors and dispense its daily charity of clothes and meals. I was struck with personal grief at how unprepared and naive our people are when migrating from reserves to seek better lives in urban areas. A life in isolation does little to prepare one for life in a city.

Canada needs to ensure that our people have the resources to make their communities livable and desirable for all. The most important requirement for our people is the provision of jobs. Many of our people live on isolated reserves where jobs are scarce; however, Saskatchewan has done a fairly good job of commuting their labour requirements to and from similar communities to job sites, often mines and hydro stations in the isolated north.

There are trucking, road construction and maintenance, logging, general construction, infrastructure like water and sewage, electricity, and environmental reclamation that require heavy equipment operators and specialized trade workers. There are needs for carpenters, plumbers, electricians in addition to administrators trained in business and accounting. Our communities, those destined to survive, are in absolute need of more professional teachers, social workers, police, conservation officers, doctors and nurses.

Many Canadians are of the opinion that our people should be moved into, or at least closer to, urban areas where more opportunities exist.

This presents a dichotomy for our people, born and raised on the isolated but traditional lands of their ancestors. One of the most impressive monuments of our time under construction is the Crazy Horse monument, being carved into the mountains of the Black Hills in South Dakota. When completed, the monument will dwarf Mount Rushmore. Crazy Horse, the great Oglala Sioux warrior chief is depicted with his arm outstretched, pointing westward, emphasizing his accompanying statement, "My lands are where my people are buried."

Crazy Horse's sentiments are the sentiments of most First Nation people where they concern their traditional homelands.

It does not mean that relocation is an impossibility. Perhaps there are instances where this is possible and desirable and a number of communities immediately come to my mind. The key word is desirable and needs the full participation of the community to avoid the past disasters of forced relocations.

However, in today's world, our people in many communities that once depended upon the fur trade, commercial fishing, and tourism already are aware that their futures are bleak and dismal. Our upcoming youth will determine the futures of our communities. A number of our communities are struggling along, caught in a flux of swirling change, as our people begin to adjust to a modern economy. Where it is not possible to develop communities of independent sustainability, our people must ensure we have access to options such as commutable employment—employment provided by mines, forestry, construction, etc., for example where employees are flown in and out on weekly or biweekly bases. Seasonal employment must be carved out and planned for our people. Finally, whether other options exist or not, education and training must be available to assist our people in transitioning for relocation to other centres for employment.

In the meanwhile, they cannot and must not resign themselves to lives as is in those overcrowded, poverty-stricken communities that are dependent upon a welfare economy and that are awash with alcohol and drug abuse.

Approximately 60% of the Aboriginal population now live off-reserve and this figure continues to grow. The youth sector, the future of our people, all under the age of thirty, comprise about half of the Aboriginal population. While some current progress is being made, long term stability depends upon our youth reaching ever-increasing heights of academic achievement. This can only be accomplished, or at least encouraged, by overcoming the current high levels and rates of drop-outs.

A stronger and prouder sense of cultural identity is required in many of our youth. This need to strengthen the inner spirit within our children and youth can be achieved through our institutions implementing Indigenous-focused academic curricula in history, science, language, art, music, drama, dance, philosophy. Every effort needs to be made to teach and keep our Aboriginal languages alive. In short, we need to reverse recent history and re-instill and strengthen the "Indian" in the child.

Wab Kinew and Niigaanwewidam James Sinclair of Winnipeg, University of Manitoba academics; Derek Nepinak, Grand Chief of the Assembly of Manitoba Chiefs; Dr. Pamela Palmater, a strong First Nations spokesperson; and Chelsea Vowel, teacher, activist and "blogger extraordinaire;" and my own nephew Derek Fox who, armed with a law degree, is now flexing his leadership wings with a political position within Nishnawbe Aski Nation, are prime examples of how education, language, and a strong cultural identity can develop and set young people onto roads of accomplishment and leadership.

The Royal Commission on Aboriginal People said, "Aboriginal children are entitled to learn and achieve in an environment that supports their development as whole individuals." We need to do a better job of providing education and training at the community level so that when the people do migrate to urban areas to fill the demands of employers for skilled labour, they are better prepared.

This means investing in community colleges and universities, along with improved elementary and high schools on our homelands. Every community should of course be served by an elementary and high school. Every community should be serviced by high speed internet to make available distant education. In addition, every region should be served by a community college offering skills training, and every province should provide a university located in a central location within our homelands, easily accessed by all indigenous communities. Why can't we foster university communities on some of our reserves? There is also a dire need for books in our communities so that even adults can be encouraged to continue their lifelong learning experiences. So few of our reserves have libraries. This also means ensuring our people are not under-funded in educational matters and that they are provided opportunities to share in resource developments and jobs to help meet and share those costs. It is now very common knowledge that our people have been underfunded in education for far too long. This issue is much too important to continue pushing into the background.

It is also common sense to ensure any funding is transparent and accountable; however, why does our government continue to insist that it has complete control over all expenditures and curricula? The Harper government trashed the Kelowna Accord once they came into power simply because it was a program negotiated by the previous government. They decided they wanted to negotiate their own agreement. The result was a draconian agreement ham-handedly negotiated with the AFN that bypassed all consultations with First Nations. Governments need to function for the benefit of its people—not for the benefit of its political party. The agreement, even though it promised more funding for education, was rightly rejected by our people. It is not a matter of simply more dollars. Honour, integrity and respect must also be included.

Make no mistake about it. The First Nation people will continue to migrate to our major centres in search of better opportunities, whether trained and educated or not. Surely, we can better prepare ourselves for the future. It can be as simple as ensuring that our Indigenous people are provided with the resources and, most importantly, an environment in which they can develop and prosper along with the rest of Canada. And then patience, lots of patience. Nothing will change overnight.

The deliberate destruction of a people was many years in the making: the process of rebuilding a shattered culture and a disintegrated community could similarly involve many years. But the changes need to start now.

APPENDIX

JAMES' AND MARY'S CHILDREN

(referenced on page 37)

James and Mary's firstborn was John, born December 31, 1859 in Norway House. He died at the age of 26 on October 15, 1885 in Berens River.

William Flett was born September 29, 1861 in Norway House and died at age 72 on April 28, 1933. He married Philomene Chartrand in 1883 at Duck Bay, Manitoba and they had 12 children, all raised in the Duck Bay and Winnipegosis area.

Jane Flett was born about July 17, 1864 and died around 1870.

Christiana Flett was born about 1865

Margaret Flett was born July 9, 1867 in Nelson River, Manitoba, the same year the Dominion of Canada came into being.

Francis Flett was born December 31, 1868 in Nelson River and she married Duncan McIvor who was also born around 1868. They are the parents of Donald and Albert "Toots" McIvor. Dad often spoke of his cousin Toots as he was also employed by the Company. When they were younger and unmarried they occasionally went south to Winnipeg together for vacations. "Toots" retired from Fort Hope, Ontario in 1962, just a few years before I arrived there in 1967. He was well known in Fort Hope as the man who could lift a full 45-gallon

318 From the Barren Lands · Flett

drum of fuel, which would weigh close to 500 pounds.

Alexander Flett, my grandfather, was born in Norway House on August 21, 1870, the same year Manitoba became a province.

Elizabeth Flett was born February 15,1872 in Berens River.

Donald Flett was born January 24, 1874 in Berens River. He became a boat pilot who plied Lake Winnipeg between Norway House and Selkirk and several stops between hauling freight and passengers. He retired in Norway House and most of the Fletts there are his descendents.

George Richard Flett was born September 24, 1875 in Berens River and died March 27, 1940. He married Mary Sabel who was from St. Peters around 1904.

Alice Louisa Flett was born May 25,1877 in Berens River and she married Alfred James Monkman who was born in Selkirk June 23, 1876.

A baby who died the same day was born October 5, 1878.

Catherine Flett was born January 25, 1880 in Berens River.

Caroline Flett, a twin, was born September 4, 1881 in Berens River.

James Flett, a twin, was born September 4, 1881 and died February 28, 1882 in Berens River.

Edith Flett was born about 1883.

Ellen Elizabeth Flett was born about 1885.

Mary Flett was born about 1887.

LINGUISTIC TABLE

(Referenced on page 203)

Linguistic Group	Nation	Sub-tribe
Algonkian	Cree	Woodland Cree
		Swampy Cree
		Plains Cree
	Naskapi	
	Montagnais (Innu)	
	Algonquin	
	Ojibwe	Mississauga
		Ottawa
		Nipissing
		Potawatomi
		Saulteaux
	Abenaki	
	Mi'kmaq/Mi'kmaw	
	Malecite	
	Passamaquoddy	
Athapaskans (Dene)	Sekani / Tsek'ene	Chilcotin / Tsilhgot'in
		Carrier
		Tahltan
	Beaver	
	Chipewyan	
	Yellowknife	
	Slavey	
	Dogrib	

Linguistic Group	Nation	Sub-tribe
	Hare	
	Nahanni	Kaska
		Tsuu T'ina
	Gwich'in / Loucheaux	
Haidan	Haida	
Iroquoian	Huron / Wyandot	Erie
	Petun	
	Neutral / Attawadaron	
	Iroquois League (Haudenosaunee)	Mohawk
		Oneida
		Onondaga
		Cayuga
		Seneca
		Tuscarora
Siouan	Sioux	Lakota
		Dakota
		Nakota
	Assiniboine	
	Blackfoot	Blackfoot
		Blood
		Piegan
	Sarcee	
	Gros Venture	
	Crow	
	Stoney	
Tlinkit	Tagish	
	Tlinkit	
Tsimshian	Tsimshian	
	Gitksan	
	Niska	

Linguistic Group	Nation	Sub-tribe
Salishan	Bella Coola	
	Nootka	
	Coast Salish	
	Lilloet	
	Thompson	
	Okanagan	
Kootenayan	Leak	
	Shuswap	Kootenay
		Interior Salish
Wakashan	Haisla	
	Heiltsuk	
	Kwakiutl	
Beothukan	Beothuk (Now extinct)	

INDEX

This Agreement made in triplicate this _Seventh_ day of _July_ 19 36.

BETWEEN

The Governor and Company of Adventurers of England Trading into Hudson's Bay

_F 7_

herein called "The Company,"

AND

OF THE FIRST PART,

H. Flett

herein called "The Employee,"

OF THE SECOND PART.

WITNESSETH that in consideration of the mutual agreements herein the parties agree as follows:

1. The Employee will serve the Company in its Fur Trade Department at such place as the Company or

its officers shall direct from the _First_ day of _June_ 19 36.

until this agreement is terminated, in the capacity of _Outpost Manager_
and in such other capacity as the Company or its Officers shall from time to time direct, and will diligently, honestly and faithfully perform all such work and services as he shall be required or directed to perform by its Officers, and will obey all rules and regulations now or hereafter made by the Company applicable to his employment, and will not during his period of employment engage or be concerned directly or indirectly in any trade or employment whatsoever except for the benefit of the Company and according to its orders.

2. The Employee's remuneration shall be _----------------------------------_

--------Five Hundred and Forty ---------------------- Dollars per _annum._

to be computed from the _First_ day of _June_ 19 36.

2b. It is further agreed that the Company will provide the said employee with

such board and lodging, or, at the option of the Company, an allowance in lieu of same,

as may be decided upon from time to time by the Company.

3. The Employee does not come within the Company's Pension Scheme.

4. This agreement may be terminated at any time by either party giving to the other _one_
month's notice in writing to that effect, or by the Company at its option paying to the Employee salary for a like period in lieu of such notice. Such notice shall be given by the Employee to the officer in charge of his Post, District or Department.

For the HUDSON'S BAY COMPANY

Witness _Jo Kimpton_

Witness _E. Little_

H. G. Flett
Employee

Registered_____

N.B.—This form will be filled out and signed in triplicate, one copy for the Employee, one for the office where the Employee is engaged, and one forwarded to the Fur Trade Commissioner for registration.
When an agreement is terminated or cancelled, the circumstances are to be given below and the office copy returned to the Fur Trade Commissioner's Office.